GW00601616

Contents

INDEX ON CENSORSHIP
VOLUME 43 NUMBER 04
WINTER 2014

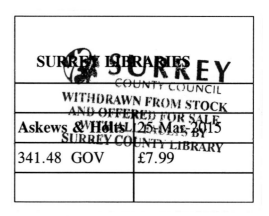

index on censorship

92-94 TOOLEY STREET, LONDON SE1 2TH

EDITOR
RACHAEL JOLLEY
DEPUTY EDITOR
VICKY BAKER
SUB EDITOR
SALLY GIMSON, PAUL ANDERSON
CONTRIBUTING EDITORS:
KAYA GENC (TURKEY), NATASHA JOSEPH
(SOUTH AFRICA), JEMIMAH STEINFELD

EDITORIAL ASSISTANT:
Aimée Hamilton

THANKS TO: Jodie Ginsberg, Sean Gallagher,
Milana Knezevic, Matthew Hasteley, Brett
Biedscheid, Jennifer Janiak, David Coscia

Supported by
**ARTS COUNCIL
ENGLAND**

Out of the shadows

by **Rachael Jolley**

EDITORIAL

43(4): 3/5 | DOI: 10.1177/0306422014563014

"**WE HAD TONGUES,** but could not speak. We had feet but could not walk. Now that we have land, we have the strength to speak and walk," said a group of women quoted in Ritu Menon's article discussing why ownership of land has started to shift the power balance in India.

When England's barons forced their King to sign the Magna Carta in 1215, it was an attempt to wrest absolute power from the monarch by his wealthiest subjects, those who already held position and fortune. It was by no means an equality drive, intended to spread rights to the common folk, but every journey begins with a single step, and every action has unintended consequences.

Notably, those who won some power from King John were those who already held land themselves. Menon's article for this magazine explores, as does the story by Sue Branford, whether land and freedom are connected, and whether with that freedom comes increased power. While Menon explores the rights and roles of women in India, Branford looks at the South American context.

Back in 2012 British Prime Minister David Cameron was quizzed by US chat show host David Letterman about the Magna Carta. While Americans were astounded that Cameron didn't know more about the historic document, what they didn't recognise was that Americans have a much closer and special relationship with the Magna Carta than Brits do. The influence of the Magna Carta on the US Bill of Rights is well known, and taught in US schools, while in the UK the document is not often referenced in schools, or elsewhere.

In fact, the Magna Carta is widely recognised outside the UK, some Mexicans refer to the "Mexican Magna Carta", as Duncan Tucker mentions in his article on the current state of justice, impunity and crackdowns on both the right to protest and the right to report on national scandals. While the world's eyes are fixed firmly on the Middle East, in Mexico in the past few months, journalists are being threatened, while 42 student protesters who had the temerity to question authorities have disappeared. Burnt bodies of 17 appear to have been found buried in a mass grave nearby.

Twelve months ago, this magazine covered a story about the photojournalists in Azerbaijan being attacked for covering stories, illustrated by horrifying photography. A year on, we return to the story, with one of the co-authors Rebecca Vincent, who discusses how the situation has become even worse. Her co-writer, lawyer Rasul Jafarov, is now being held in prison, while other writers and activists are coming under enormous pressure, aimed at both themselves and their families, to stop writing and speaking critically of the government, or face similar consequences. Others also face charges or jail. International attention can be distracted and inconsistent; while the world's news cameras and web searches are focused on ISIS or the Ukraine, developments in Azerbaijan and Uzbekistan catch far less page views. That means that those authoritarian governments have a chance to operate out of the headlights →

ABOVE: Tintoretto's image of justice

→ and are less concerned about international public opinion. And in another part of the former Soviet Union, Russia and Ukraine continue to go eyeball to eyeball. Andrei Aliaksandrau has spent much of the past six months in Ukraine, where he reports for Index on the new propaganda war, and how new and old tools are being deployed to rally public support to fever pitch.

Index has, from its very first days in 1972, cast a watchful eye on what was then the Soviet Union, and we continue to do so. We intend to keep on telling stories, and to do our best to remind the world of what is going on, sometimes where others fail to do so, or where we feel important news is being ignored. ☒

© Rachael Jolley
www.indexoncensorship.org

Rachael Jolley is editor of Index on Censorship. Follow the magazine @index_magazine

SPECIAL REPORT

In this section

Magna Carta and the cause of freedom

43(4): 7/50 | DOI: 10.1177/0306422014563902

On its 800th anniversary RACHAEL JOLLEY explains why the Magna Carta has inspired this issue's special report

*I*N 1215, *a group of barons came together in England to limit the powers of their king and to establish certain rules as a reasonable basis of a relationship between the state and the people. The people, in this case, were a small group of influential individuals, not the wider populace, but the intention of this early document was ultimately to create some kind of balance of power between the ruler and his citizens. To read it is to be surprised at its breadth. It deals with debts, marriage, bridges, military conscription, the forest and, perhaps most importantly, the idea of a fair system of justice. The document they drew up was the Magna Carta, and on this anniversary of its creation we discuss its relevance today. It came to have resonance far outside the borders of ancient England, and to inspire systems of justice and freedom in many corners of the world.*

Making a 21st-century Magna Carta?

43(4): 8/16 | DOI: 10.1177/0306422014563902

To kick off this special report, **Index** asked writers from around the world to propose ideas for a modern-day Magna Carta

THE LANGUAGE AND ideas within the Magna Carta may surprise many in the modernity of their outlook, in places anyway. For instance, on scale of punishment: "for a trivial offence a free man should be fined only in proportion to the degree of the offence" and "for a serious offence ... not so heavily as to deprive him of his livelihood". On giving evidence: "In future no official shall place a man on trial upon his own unsupported statement, without producing credible witnesses to the truth of it." And on the right to justice: "To no one will we sell, to no one deny or delay right or justice". These ideas are still at the core of battles for fair justice systems. While the Magna Carta is centuries old, and other sections of this document reflect that, its influence is clearly traceable to the modern day, and it is in parts, still cited, by people desiring a fair and transparent

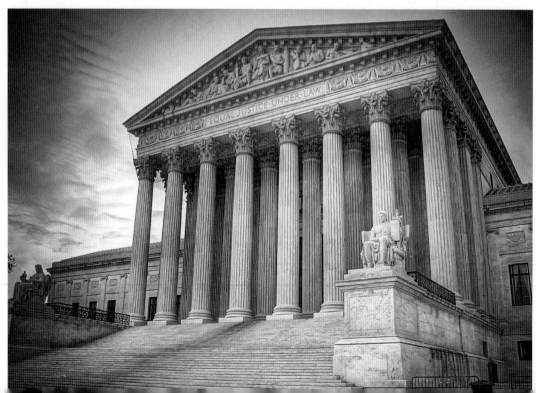

RIGHT: The US Supreme Court: Americans recognise the influence of the Magna Carta on the constitution

LEFT: King John and
the Magna Carta at
Runnymede

system of government and justice. In the following section we ask writers from around the world to contribute their ideas for a 21st-century version of the Magna Carta.

In the following special report, we also consider the ideas and expectations at the heart of this document; justice, freedom, liberty, and a balance of powers between those who rule and those who are ruled. We consider the global consequence of such ideas, and their relevance throughout history and today for those who struggle for individual freedoms. We consider whether land ownership still confers greater freedoms and rights of freedom of expression. And we look at countries where public trust in their justice system is waning, or being destroyed by the way the state operates. When the Magna Carta was drawn up, it gave certain powers to a small number of English people. Throughout the centuries though it has been used as a basis, or inspiration, for laws around the world, from the US Constitution to the UN Declaration of Human Rights that give power and rights, and freedom of ex-

pression, to an ever wider group of citizens.

A few months ago, Syrian activist Mazen Darwish was awarded the PEN/Pinter International Writer of Courage award, in his acceptance speech he said: "For a long time I've wished that one day I might set foot in London, so that I'd perhaps be able to touch

While the Magna Carta is centuries old, its influence is clearly traceable to the modern day, and still cited

the soul of that great city, and discover the traces left by John Locke, Shakespeare, and the men who drafted the Magna Carta". The heritage of the ideas behind the Magna Carta lives on, and inspires those who seek freedom to think, live, speak and act. ▨

Rachael Jolley
Editor, Index on Censorship

Abolish the death penalty

Robert McCrum

On this 800th anniversary, it's probably worth remembering that the Magna Carta, so often revered, in the words of William Pitt, as "the Bible of the English Constitution" is really no such thing. A classic English fudge, with some very eccentric clauses that have nothing to do with English freedom, it began as a response to overseas military disaster (the loss of Normandy in 1214), and the celebrated "charter of liberties" was mainly a shopping list of barons' grievances against a capricious king (for instance, the sovereign's power to force a baronial widow to remarry so that the crown could collect a stiff remarriage fee).

Nevertheless, these caveats aside, the Magna Carta did contain language that would become an important touchstone of individual liberties, and established the vital principal of Habeas Corpus. As Index itself reported, when the House of Lords considered the use of torture in the Iraq war, the law lords framed their judgement with explicit reference to the Magna Carta. In hindsight, broadly, the king promised to restore the practice of government by law. Who really knows if John intended to comply with this charter? Two years later he was dead, from dysentery. The iconic status of this document is one of English history's richest unintended consequences.

Nonetheless, in the 21st century, the Magna Carta is an important totem. The arenas of Western, civil society that I'd be most interested to see regulated by a new "charter of liberties" include: the so-called "dark web" as well as the more accessible parts of the internet; "big pharma"; international copyright; refugees' rights; and the responsibilities of corporate banks.

Further afield, and with correspondingly less chance

of success, a Magna Carta might be negotiated to curb the unfettered power of despotic regimes in Africa and the Middle East. Such a document should also enshrine principles of human rights unknown either in sub-equatorial Africa or in many parts of the Arabian peninsula.

Closest to home, and most uncomfortable of all, a Magna Carta Redux should be swiftly introduced in the USA, independent of either congress or the US Supreme Court, to achieve the following: 1. abolish the death penalty; 2. fully enfranchise immigrants with no criminal records; and 3. outlaw semi-automatic and automatic firearms.

Another thing: unlike the sacred original, the new Magna Carta should be written in English. ☒

© Robert McCrum
www.indexoncensorship.org

Robert McCrum is the associate editor of The Observer newspaper in the UK

Education for girls and boys must be a fundamental right

Hans-Joachim Neubauer

John F. Kennedy believed: "A child miseducated is a child lost." He was right. No money, no job, no future: those deprived of an education are sentenced to a life without social or personal prospects. The more inadequate the education, the greater the likelihood of marginalisation. Those who know nothing will be excluded. This is just as true in the rich, industrialised countries of the north as it is in emerging countries and the countries of the so-called third world. Education is the answer to the three fundamental issues that we face today. Education alone can help fight against the earth's destruction, the unfair distribution of wealth and resources, and religious fundamentalism.

There are too many people on our planet. In the rich countries of the north there are too few young people, in the poorer countries children are the only thing in abundance. A worldwide education campaign could curtail overpopulation. The educated are capable of providing for themselves and their families. Only those who appreciate that local action has global consequences can understand the necessity of protecting their surroundings. Education can save the environment.

In industrialised countries the gap between rich and poor is forever widening. Fewer and fewer people have more and more control over capital, influence and power. A similar gap between the top and bottom exists between the north and south. This has to change. For individuals, particularly for girls and women, the way out of poverty begins with a good education. Only education delivers justice. The right to an education for girls and boys must be a fundamental right.

Religious fundamentalism is a form of barbarism. Preachers of hate offer young jihadists a simple world view: one-sided, authoritarian, anti-intellectual. They find their followers among men without education or prospects. Religious radicals fear nothing more than education. That is because those who look beyond the ideologue can free themselves from their constraints. Education creates humanity. "A child miseducated is a child lost." Those who want a future, must first obtain an education.

© Hans-Joachim Neubauer
www.indexoncensorship.org

Translated by Rachel Hansed

Hans-Joachim Neubauer is a journalist and literary scholar. He is an editor of the Christ & Welt (Christ and the World) supplement of the weekly German newspaper Die Zeit

|||||||||||||||||||||||||||||||||||||||||||||||||||||

We need a powerful clause to tackle climate change
....
Danny Sriskandarajah

In 2015, just as the Magna Carta marks its 800th anniversary, world leaders will agree a set of new universal goals aimed at sustainable and equitable development that will succeed the Millennium Development Goals.

Although next year's agreement will be an intergovernmental settlement – and not a national settlement as in the Magna Carta – its impact in the years to come could be just as powerful. Faced with heinous levels of inequality and potentially disastrous climate change impacts, we need a powerful document that binds not just leaders and citizens together, but also nations together in a new progressive settlement.

One can already see the transformative potential of what is being discussed at the United Nations in the lead up to 2015: from a commitment to accountable governance institutions to access to justice even for the very poorest to sustainable consumption limits on the very richest. If our leaders can agree a set of ambitious binding goals, that requires concerted action on all their parts, we could go beyond the warm words embodied in multilateral agreements of the past.

The true impact of the original Magna Carta was the unexpected nature of the settlement and the fact that several elements of it remain at the heart of today's laws. If we are looking for a contemporary equivalent of the Magna Carta, we need a new binding agreement between the world's leaders and the world's citizens on achieving sustainable development underpinned by effective and accountable institutions. 🗙

© Danny Sriskandarajah
www.indexoncensorship.org

Danny Sriskandarajah is based in Johannesburg, where he is secretary general of Civicus

|||||||||||||||||||||||||||||||||||||||||||||||||||||

Women should have full equality with men
....
Rita El Khayat

I desire a world in which women have the full equality with men that I have not experienced in my lifetime. I think my life has been made very hard and very painful by the social, legal and psychological pressures that exist in Morocco, and have barely softened. It is for this reason that a new Magna Carta must be written for all of humanity. Every life is unique and must be lived to its full possibilities. This is where my fight and struggle always leads. 🗙

© Rita El Khayat
www.indexoncensorship.org

Rita El Khayat was nominated for the Nobel Prize for Peace in 2008. She is an author and a Moroccan psychiatrist and anthropologist

The right to freedom of speech and imagination

Elif Shafak

One day in spring 2012, Turkey's Prime Minister Recep Tayyip Erdogan announced, completely out of the blue, that every abortion was an *Uludere*, the term for the tragic massacre of 33 Kurdish smugglers killed by Turkish military pilots who took them for terrorists. Erdogan further added that "abortion was an insidious plan to eliminate the Turkish nation from the world stage".

For those of us who believe in women's rights and full gender equality, it is deeply disturbing to observe the ease with which male politicians in Turkey can take decisions about women's personal lives and women's bodies. What is even more alarming, however, is the sense that rights we take for granted can someday be taken back.

It's a valuable lesson for us all around the world. The basic human rights that we are used to thinking of as "natural" and "indispensable" are endangered by the whimsical arbitrariness of politics and power. We might not suspect that we could lose our individual rights, but it can happen. And for it not to happen, we, women and men of all backgrounds, ought to understand, appreciate and expand democratic constitutions that limit the power of rulers and protect the rights of the ruled. In the 21st century, we need to remember and revive the Magna Carta.

A vital principle that needs to be incorporated into modern Magna Carta is freedom of speech and freedom of imagination. Without the freedom to criticise, question and challenge the dominant narrative, societies cannot make progress. This requires a plurality of voices and discourses, where not only those at the centre, but those on the periphery can be heard equally. It is not how content the majority is, but how free minorities are that shows us the depth of democracy in a particular country.

In developed democracies individuals and minorities are protected against the excessive power of the state.

In countries, such as Turkey or Russia, it's usually the other way round: the state is protected from the criticism of the individuals and the state takes priority over everything.

Limiting, controlling and diffusing political power is one of the prerequisites of a true, working democracy. Nobody, no political power or economic lobby or ideological group, should possess absolute power at the expense of other voices in civil society.

On the 800th anniversary of the Magna Carta, it is this spirit and awareness that we need to remember. The Magna Carta has an enormous importance not only for the citizens of Britain, where it was initiated historically, but for people all over the world, especially in places where democracy still remains an unfulfilled dream. ☒

© Elif Shafak
www.indexoncensorship.org

Elif Shafak is an award-winning Turkish novelist. She has published 13 books, nine of which are novels, including: The Bastard of Istanbul, The Forty Rules of Love, Honour. Her latest novel The Architect's Apprentice (Penguin) was published in November

Preserve the neutrality of the net

Renata Avila

A new Magna Carta should ensure that fundamental human rights apply regardless of the medium or technology we use. This is hugely important for the next 100 years. And we should not only be thinking about the web that we know and use today, but also the way we communicate and connect to others might be very different in the next decades.

A Magna Carta for our century should also preserve the neutrality of the net, requiring that the internet is maintained as an open platform, on which network providers treat all content, applications and services equally, without discrimination of content or users.

Anonymity and the right to communicate in private shall be expressly mentioned, preserved and defended. In a world under almost total surveillance, the right to preserve private spaces – protected from the technologies used by governments, corporations and even individuals – needs urgent attention.

The right to participate in culture and the right to access to knowledge and education should be given the place they deserve in our time. Current legislation is even criminalising new forms of speech and young people are under particular threat because they are experimenting with new modes of expression and action.

Increasingly, unbalanced, outdated copyright laws all over the world are harming freedom of speech and limiting the possibilities to create and share, innovate and find new business models and mechanisms to benefit both authors and the general public. We are blocking the possibility of a very different future by applying laws from the 19th century to a more versatile and fluid system that is just starting to unleash its potential. ▣

© Renata Avila
www.indexoncensorship.org

Renata Avila is a human rights lawyer from Guatemala, currently living in Berlin. She is global manager for the Web We Want campaign (webwewant. org), and a board member for Creative Commons and the Courage Foundation

All global transactions must be open to the scrutiny of civil society

Ferial Haffajee

Sitting where I do on the bottom tip of Africa in a newly democratic country, it was not long before the men bearing arms and alms arrived.

The new state wanted to refresh its stock of arms (heaven knows why given our other challenges) and the German men of defence were soon in town. Then the French, the Italians and the British followed.

The corrupting effect was quick. And cheap. A discount on a Mercedes Benz. A holiday in Mauritius. An emolument of R500,000 ($42,500) a year to pay to a politician with responsibilities deeper than his salary.

And so we were corrupted.

Henceforth, all global transactions from the first to the third world will be open to the scrutiny of civil society from the start to the end. Each meeting, each contract, each deal will be open to all.

Extreme transparency will have a disinfecting effect.

As Africa rises to take her place in the assembly of nations, not as a beggar, but as an equal, access to information is essential to make sure that growth and development are spread for the greater good.

We can imagine it now. When a tender is issued, it will be made public. All expressions of interest will be placed on the internet and where there is no internet, it will be placed in public halls for scrutiny.

All officials charged with the procurement will hold public meetings with interested parties and the terms

of trade will be transparent. All gifts, from a pen to a pin, will be declared and discouraged.

All this will be done as a matter of course and where it does not happen, then international access to information laws, which are cheap and easy to manage will be used to gain access to clarifying information. ⊠

© Ferial Haffajee
www.indexoncensorship.org

Ferial Haffajee is the editor of the weekly City Press newspaper in Johannesburg

The right to trigger a constitutional convention

Stuart White

In the USA, commentators such as Lawrence Lessig (@lessig) have argued that in congressional politics, money speaks to a degree that drowns out the voices of most citizens on most issues. Colin Crouch has termed politics in the US and EU "post-democracy": a system that combines free speech and competitive elections with a systematic gearing of influence to corporations and the very wealthy.

Lessig has called for a popular, constitutional convention to address the problem of money in politics, a possibility set out in Article V of the US constitution. The convention would have the power to develop a proposal which then has to be ratified by three quarters of the states. Constitutional conventions, organised in different ways, have recently been held in Iceland and Ireland, and there have been calls for a constitutional convention in the UK, following the independence referendum in Scotland.

One feature of a new Magna Carta should be an effective right to a constitutional convention. Imagine, for example, that a convention is triggered whenever a large enough proportion of the electorate (20%? 30%? 50%?) sign a petition calling for one. Or a convention could be triggered, perhaps, when a supermajority of parliamentarians call for one. The members of this convention will be drawn largely at random from the population (as in the recent Irish convention). Its agenda will be determined in part by the public or

parliament that triggers it, but it might be given some room to develop its own program. Its proposals will go to a referendum.

Against the background of the oligarchic shift described by Lessig and Crouch, an effective right to a constitutional convention is one way to empower citizens to better address sources of arbitrary, unaccountable power, giving a new significance to rights of free speech and assembly. X

© Stuart White
www.indexoncensorship.org

Stuart White is director of the public policy unit, Jesus College, Oxford

Credit: Image bymatchefoto/iStock

1215 and all that

43(4): 18/23 | DOI: 10.1177/0306422014560980

In his distinct digested style, **John Crace** takes a tongue-in-cheek trip throughout the history of the Magna Carta and its manifestations

CALL IT A free-for-all. Call it an innate sense of fair play. Call it what you will, but the English had always had a way of making their feelings known to a monarch who got a bit above himself by hitting the country for too much money in taxes or losing overseas military campaigns or both. They rebelled. Sometimes it worked, sometimes it didn't but it was the closest medieval England had to due process. Then came John, a king every bit as unloved – if not more so – as any of his predecessors; a ruler who had gone back on many of his promises and was doing his best to lose all England's French possessions and all of a sudden the barons had a problem. There wasn't any obvious candidate to replace him. So instead of deposing him, they took him on by limiting his powers.

Kings never have much liked being told what to do and John was no exception. If he could have got out of cutting a deal with the barons he would have done. But even he understood that impoverishing the people he relied on to keep him in power hadn't been the cleverest of moves, and so he reluctantly agreed to take part in the negotiations that led to the sealing of the Articles of the Barons – later known as the Magna Carta – at Runnymede on 15 June 1215. Which isn't to say he didn't kick and scream his way through them before agreeing to the 61 demands, which were the bare minimum for his remaining in power. He did, though, keep his fingers cunningly crossed when the seal was being applied. As soon as the barons had left London, King John announced – with the Pope's blessing – that he was having no more to do with it. The barons were outraged and went into open rebellion, though dysentery got to King John before they did and he died the following year. Don't shit with the people, or the people shit with you. Or something like that.

With the original Magna Carta having lasted barely three months, there were some who reckoned they could have saved themselves a lot of time and effort by topping King John rather than negotiating with him. But wiser – or perhaps, more peaceful – counsel prevailed and its spirit has endured through various subsequent mutations – most notably the 1216 Charter, the Great Charter of 1225 and the Confirmation of Charters of 1297 – and has widely come to be seen as the foundation stone of constitutional law, both in England and many countries around the world. It was the first time limitations had been formally placed on a monarch's power as the rights of citizens to the due process of law and trial by jury had been affirmed. Well, not quite all citizens. When the various charters talked of the rights of Freemen, it didn't mean everyone; far from it. Freemen just meant that small class of people, below the barons, who weren't tied to land as serfs. The Brits have never liked to rush things. They like their revolutions to be orderly. The underclass would just have to wait.

The Magna Carta and its derivative charters were never quite the symbols of enlightened noblesse oblige they are often held to be. The noblemen didn't sit around earnestly thinking about how they could turn England into a communal paradise. What was the point of having fought and back-stabbed your way to the top only to give power away to the undeserving? The charters were matters of political expedience. The nobles needed the Freemen on their side in their face-off with the king and an extension of their rights was the bargaining chip to secure it. Benevolence never really entered the equation. Nor was the Magna Carta ever really a legal constitutional framework. Even if King John hadn't decided to ignore it within months, it would still have been virtually unenforceable as it had no statutory authority. It was more wish-list than law.

Ironically, though, it is the Magna Carta's weaknesses that have turned out to have guaranteed its survival. Over the centuries, the Magna Carta has become the symbol of freedom rather than its guarantor as different generations have cherry-picked its clauses and interpreted them in their own way. While wars and poverty might have been the prime catalyst for the Peasant's Revolt against King Richard II in 1381, it was the Magna Carta to which the rebellion looked for its intellectual legitimacy. The Freemen were now seen to be free men; constitutional rights were no longer seen as residing in the few. The king and his court were outraged that the peasants had made such an elementary mistake as to mistake the implied capital F in Freemen for a small f and the leaders were executed for their illiteracy as much as their impudence.

Bit by bit, starting in 1829 with the section dealing with offences against a person, the clauses of the Magna Carta were repealed such that by 1960 only three still survived. Some, such as those concerning "scutage"

– a tax that allowed knights to buy out of military service – and fish weirs, had become outdated; others had already been superseded by later statutes. Two of those that remained related to the privileges of both the Church of England and the City of London – a telling insight into the priorities of the establishment. Those who still wonder, following the global financial collapse of 2008, why the bankers were allowed to get away with making up the rules to suit themselves need look no further than the Magna Carta. The bankers had been used to getting away with it for the best of 800 years. You win some, you lose some.

The survival of clause 39 of the original Magna Carta has been rather more significant for the rest of us. "No Freeman shall be taken or imprisoned, or be disseised of his Freehold, or Liberties, or free Customs, or

Don't shit with the people, or the people shit with you. Or something like that

be outlawed, or exiled, or any other wise destroyed; nor will We not pass upon him, nor condemn him, but by lawful judgment of his Peers, or by the Law of the Land. We will sell to no man, we will not deny or defer to any man either Justice or Right." Or in layman's terms, due process: the legal requirement of the state to recognise and respect all the legal rights of the individual. The guarantee of justice, fairness and liberty that not only underpins – well, most of the time – the UK's constitutional framework, but those of many other countries as well.

Britain has no written constitution. Not because parliament has been too lazy to get round to drawing one up, but because one is already assumed to be in the lifeblood of everyone living in Britain. Queen Mary may have had "Calais" written on her heart, but the rest of us all have "Magna Carta" →

→ inscribed there. It can be found on the inside of the left ventricle, for those of you who are interested in detail. Other countries haven't been so trusting in the genetic inheritance of feudal England and have insisted on getting their constitutions down in non-fugitive ink.

That Magna Carta has also been the lodestone for the constitutions of so many other countries, most notably the USA, is less a sign of the global reach of democratic principles – much as that might resonate with romantic ideals of justice – than of the spread of British people and British imperial power. After the Mayflower arrived in what became the USA from Plymouth in 1620, the first settlers' only reference point for the establishment of civil society was

In the USA, they settled for an off-the-peg version. And some poor spelling

the Magna Carta. The settlers had a lot of other things on their minds in the early years – most notably their own survival and the share price of British American Tobacco – and they hadn't got time to dream up their own bespoke constitution. If they had, they might have come up with something that abolished slavery and gave equal rights to black people sometime before the 1960s. So they settled for an off-the-peg version of the Magna Carta, with various US amendments. And some poor spelling. In 1687 William Penn published the first version of the Magna Carta to be printed in America. By the time the fifth amendment – part of the Bill of Rights – was ratified four years after the original US Constitution in 1791, the Magna Carta had been enshrined in American law with "No person shall be deprived of life, liberty or property without due process of law."

The fact that the American idea of the Magna Carta was not one that would necessarily have been recognised in Britain was neither here nor there. For the Americans, the notion of the rights of a people to govern themselves was more than something that had been fought for over many centuries – a gradual taking back of power from an absolute ruler – that had been ratified on paper. They were fundamental rights that pre-existed any country and transcended national borders. And even if there was no one left alive on Earth, these rights would remain. They might as well have been handed down by God, though it's probably just as well Adam hadn't read the sections on the right to defend himself and bear arms. If he had shot the serpent, the whole history of the world might have been very different. As it is, when the Americans took on the British in the War of Independence, they weren't fighting against a colonial overlord so much as for their basic rights to freedom.

The distinction is a subtle but important one. For though the more recent constitutions of former British colonies, such as Australia, India, Canada and New Zealand, more closely reflected the way the Magna Carta was understood back in the mothership, those interpretations of it were still very much a product of their time. As a historical document, the Magna Carta remains fixed in the 13th century: a practical solution to the problem of an iffy king. But as a concept it is a shifting, timeless expression of the democratic ideal. It can mean and explain anything. Up to and including that Britain always knows best.

Yet the appeal of the Magna Carta endures and it remains the gold standard for democracy in any debate. Whatever side of it you happen to be on. British eurosceptics argue that the UK's continuing membership of the European Union threatens the very parchment on which it was written; that Britain is being turned into a serf by a European despot. Pro-Europeans argue that the

EU does more than just enshrine the ideals of the Magna Carta, it turns the most threatened elements of it into law.

Eight hundred years on, Magna Carta remains a moving target. Something to be aspired to but never truly attained. A highly combustible compound of idealism and pragmatism. Somehow, though, you can't help feeling that King John and the feudal barons would have understood that. And approved. ☒

© John Crace
www.indexoncensorship.org

John Crace is The Guardian's parliamentary sketch writer and the author of the Digested Read column. He has written 12 books including Baby Alarm: A Neurotic's Guide to Fatherhood, Brideshead Abbreviated, Vertigo: Spurs, Bale and One Fan's Fear of Success, and the Digested 21st century. His most recent book, I Never Promised You a Rose Garden: A Short Guide to Modern Politics, the Coalition and the General Election, was published in November 2014

Battle royal

43(4): 24/27 | DOI: 10.1177/0306422014560514

As Thailand's King Bhumibol Adulyadej - the world's longest reigning monarch - celebrates his 87th birthday, any comment about his country, its future or the royal family can result in a lengthy jail term. **Mark Fenn** reports

A **PROMINENT THAI HISTORIAN,** Sulak Sivaraksa, faces up to 15 years in jail. His crime? In a speech at a Bangkok university in October, the avowed royalist questioned traditional accounts of an elephant battle featuring King Naresuan, who ruled a Thai kingdom in the late 16th century. Two retired army officers filed complaints against 81-year-old Sulak, claiming he had dishonoured the former king, who died in 1605.

Such is the air of hysteria in modern Thailand – a country under martial law and gripped by anxiety as the current monarch nears the end of his reign – that any discussion of the royal family is taboo. The generals who seized power in a military coup last May have vowed to crack down on anti-monarchists, heightening the climate of fear in the so-called "land of smiles".

As Index went to press, millions of people across Thailand were preparing to celebrate the 87th birthday of King Bhumibol Adulyadej on 5 December. He is the world's longest reigning monarch, crowned in 1946, and revered by many as a semi-divine ruler.

But Bhumibol is now frail and ailing, leading to acute end-of-reign anxiety among his subjects. The political turmoil that has racked Thailand for the past decade is closely linked to the battle over the forthcoming royal succession – yet honest discussion of these issues is impossible without risking a lengthy jail sentence.

Lèse-majesté, or defaming the monarchy, has been prohibited by Thai law since 1908, when the country was ruled by an absolute monarch. Article 112 of the criminal code specifies that "whoever defames, insults or threatens the king, queen, the heir-apparent or the regent, shall be punished with imprisonment of three to 15 years".

Pavin Chachavalpongpun of Kyoto University's Centre for South-East Asian Studies is an outspoken democracy activist who was stripped of his Thai passport following the coup and is currently applying for asylum in Japan. "The anxiety over the new reign has driven some royalists to use the draconian law to punish those thinking differently about the monarchy," he told Index. "Sadly, there has been no attempt on the part of the Thai elite to address this problem seriously."

Trials are held in secret, with offenders deemed a threat to national security, and information is often difficult to come by. However, the number of cases has escalated dramatically since 2005, coinciding with Thailand's political turmoil and following a speech by the king in which he indicated that he could be criticised.

US historian David Streckfuss, author of Truth on Trial in Thailand: Defamation,

ABOVE: With Thailand's King Bhumibol (pictured centre with other members of the royal family) elderly and frail, a battle over his succession includes the ruling generals seeking extradition of critics of the monarchy, and court cases against those who criticise the state

Treason and Lèse-majesté, published in 2011, said 1,237 cases were sent to trial from 2005 to 2013 – an average of 137 charges per year – and 455 judgments were handed down in the same period.

"There is hard information on only a handful of cases," he said. "It has been assumed by observers that most lèse-majesté cases are not even officially 'cases' yet, as officials in the police or prosecution departments decide how to proceed further."

The promotion of the monarchy as a central component of national identity began under military governments in the 1950s, aided by the US Central Intelligence Agency, which saw Thailand as a useful ally in the fight against communism in south-east Asia. Officials, military men, businessmen and others have long sought to win prestige by associating themselves with the palace, engaging in what some scholars have called "flattery inflation".

Since the 22 May coup, the ruling junta has cracked down on debate and dissent, including perceived threats to the monarchy, with an iron fist. In recent years, tens of thousands of websites have been blocked, according to human rights groups. The junta has announced that it is actively monitoring social media for signs of lèse-majesté.

Any citizen can file a lèse-majesté complaint – although no member of the royal family ever has – and the police are obliged to investigate. The law has often been misused for political purposes, according to

A taxi driver was sentenced to 30 months in jail after a passenger recorded their conversation about social inequality on his mobile phone

Human Rights Watch (HRW), which says it has a "devastating impact on freedom of expression in Thailand". HRW says that the "police, public prosecutors, courts, and other state authorities appear to be afraid to reject any allegations of lèse-majesté out of concern they might be accused of disloyalty to the monarchy".

→ Last year, a man was jailed on an unprecedented charge of attempted lèse-majesté, and the supreme court ruled that the term "king" also applied to previous monarchs.

In August, two activists were charged for staging a performance of a play, The Wolf Bride, which the junta deemed "insulting to the monarchy". The same month, a taxi driver was sentenced to 30 months in jail after a passenger recorded their conversation about social inequality on his mobile phone. The junta also banned a computer game, Tropico 5, because it allows players to name a country and its king or leader as they please. This was deemed offensive to the monarchy and might affect the country's dignity, the head of the Cultural Promotion Department said.

Trials are held in secret, with offenders deemed a threat to national security, and information is often difficult to come by

The ruling generals also announced in June that they would seek the extradition of critics of the Thai monarchy who are based abroad, such as the London hairdresser Chatwadee "Rose" Amornphat, who now has British citizenship. Her own parents had earlier filed a lèse-majesté complaint against her.

Yet some citizens believe that not enough is being done to protect the monarchy's reputation. A doctor and hospital director, Reinthong Nannah, earlier this year formed the Rubbish Collection Organisation – a vigilante group aimed at hunting down people it believes have insulted the king.

Reinthong, whose group claims more than 200,000 followers, has referred to lèse-majesté offenders as "garbage" and says they must be "eliminated". He reportedly

refers to himself as Van Helsing, after Bram Stoker's fictional vampire hunter in Dracula.

Through most of Thailand's recent history there were only a few lèse-majesté convictions per year, and the law was enforced arbitrarily rather than focusing on obvious targets. This was a deliberate strategy designed to "inculcate fear and obedience by making an example of the unlucky few and destroying their lives", writes British journalist Andrew MacGregor Marshall in his book A Kingdom in Crisis: Thailand's Struggle for Democracy in the Twenty-First Century, which was published in October and is banned in Thailand.

Among these unlucky few was a student sentenced to six years in jail in 1983 after writing to the king, whom she revered, asking him to abdicate and enter politics. Another was a grandfather known to supporters as "Uncle SMS", who died in jail in 2012, after he was found guilty of sending four text messages insulting the queen to a government official. He had denied the charges, saying he did not even know how to send a text message, but was sentenced to 20 years.

Foreigners are not exempt. In 2009, an Australian, Harry Nicolaides, was jailed for six months over a passage in his self-published novel – which sold just seven copies – dealing with the romantic entanglements of a fictional crown prince. A Thai-born American, Joe Gordon, was also jailed after reportedly posting passages he had translated from a banned English-language biography of Bhumibol, The King Never Smiles, on his blog.

In July, a leaked document apparently showed that the junta considers a British comedian, John Oliver, a threat to the monarchy after he mocked the crown prince on his US television show Last Week Tonight.

Thailand's political scene has been bitterly divided for the past decade between supporters and opponents of the former prime minister, Thaksin Shinawatra, who was deposed in a 2006 coup and is seen as close to the king's presumed heir, Crown Prince Vajiralongkorn. Both sides have used the lèse-majesté law to try to discredit their opponents, although the pro-Thaksin "red shirts" – a broadly progressive movement that draws its strength from rural areas – have been targeted more often.

Last year, Somyot Prueksakasemsuk, editor of a red-shirt magazine, was sentenced to 11 years in jail for insulting the monarchy.

"The courts seem to have adopted the role of chief protector of the monarchy at the expense of free expression rights," a Human Rights Watch spokesman said at the time. "The court's ruling appears to be more about Somyot's strong support for amending the lèse-majesté law than about any harm incurred by the monarchy."

The harsh sentencing, and the presence of online spies and police informers, has had a chilling effect on the media in Thailand. Journalists – including this one – routinely practice self-censorship and reports of lèse-majesté cases are kept deliberately vague to avoid repeating the offending words.

"Thailand's use of the lèse-majesté law has become unique in the world and its elaboration and justifications have become an art," said Streckfuss. "The law's defenders claim that Thailand's love and reverence for its king is incomparable. Its critics say the law has become the foremost threat to freedom of expression." ☒

© Mark Fenn
www.indexoncensorship.org

Mark Fenn is a journalist based in Thailand

Land and freedom?

43(4): 28/30 | DOI: 10.1177/0306422014561169

The Magna Carta gave specific rights to those who owned land. **Ritu Menon** reports on how Indian women find property ownership gives them more power to be heard

"WE WANT LAND, all the rest is humbug," women in a South Indian village told feminist researchers Maria Mies and Lalita Kumari when asked whether they wanted better houses. The village women said they wanted land that they could till and preferably own, so they could make a modest profit from the crops they grew and have access to agricultural credit and subsidies.

Not only is land a highly emotive issue, it's a hugely complicated one, with ownership being governed by a plethora of laws and customary practice. In India, legislation relating to land, especially agricultural land, is a state subject. This means that each of the country's 28 states can enact its own laws regarding, for example, forest cover, the state's right to appropriate land under the law of eminent domain, and the alienation of land held by a community or tribe.

There are increasing numbers of women engaged in agricultural work as men migrate to urban areas in search of paid jobs. Although rural women are responsible for 60 to 80 per cent of India's food production, only nine per cent own the land they till, according to government figures.

The depth of these women's importance is illustrated by agriculture's place in India's economy. Six out of 10 people are still engaged in farming. That is roughly 600 million, of whom the vast majority – 80 per cent

– are women. Most are not recognised as farmers, either legally or socially.

Then there are laws governing inheritance and succession, depending on which religion you belong to. As of 2005, Hindu women can now inherit all property equally, and sons and daughters have equal co-parcenary rights: that is they can be joint heirs to an undivided property. Non-Hindu women on the other do not enjoy such rights. This is because they are governed by the inheritance and succession provisions of their religious laws, Christian, Muslim or Parsi. Yet even when the law grants women equal rights, patriarchal attitudes and a strong bias in favour of men mean the possibility of them becoming landowners is reduced.

Extensive land reform in India began soon after the country's independence in 1947. Huge feudal landholdings were taken over by the state and redistributed. The princely states, which collected agricultural revenue and even had their own militia, were no longer recognised. Their lands, which had covered significant parts of the country, came under state control.

States with more socialist governments, particularly the southern state of Kerala, and West Bengal in the east, went in for extensive redistribution of agricultural land, and as early as the 1970s, movements for making over land to women had begun to emerge. The Bodh Gaya movement in Bihar, one of

ABOVE: Only nine per cent of Indian women own the land they till. Here, women pick leaves from tea plants in Vandiperiyar, Kerala

India's poorest states, managed for the first time in the country's history to wrest land titles for women. In Bina Agarwal's article Why Property Rights for Women Matter she quotes women who spoke powerfully about the importance of land ownership. They said: "We had tongues, but could not speak. We had feet but could not walk. Now that we have land. We have the strength to speak and walk."

Landesa Rural Development Institute is an international NGO that partners with state governments in four states in India, to develop policies that allow poor women to lease farmland and to ensure that their names are included in land titles. One of these states is Orissa, on the east coast of the country, where less than three per cent of agricultural land is owned by women.

In 2005-2006, the state announced an innovative government scheme, Vasundhara, by which all poor, landless families in rural areas are eligible for land allotment, whether they are male or female-headed.

Budhi Pradhan, a 62-year-old woman of Chilipoi village in Orissa, is one of the beneficiaries of this scheme. She, along with 19 other families, received joint titles to small homestead plots in 2010, which increased farmland to one acre each, in 2011. →

→ According to Rakhi Ghosh, a journalist with the independent Women's Feature Service, who visited Chilipoi, the women have proved to be excellent landowners, and their influence in the village has grown. She reports: "Once the women had their plots they decided to look beyond their family's needs and play a bigger role in the development of their village."

In 2011 they took over the management of the common resource of the village, a four-acre cashew plantation. Ghosh quotes Hatu Pradhan, a member of the women's self-help group: "We got the plantation on lease and worked day and night to ensure a return on our investment. That year itself we earned INR25,000 ($407) and, after paying back all expenses and the cost of leasing, we were left with a surplus income of INR15,900 ($258)."

Now that we have land, we have the strength to speak and walk

An additional INR2,000 ($32) was made from the sale of jackfruit from another community plantation they had acquired on lease at around the same time. Pradhan said: "We collected all this money to start fish farming in a pond that was provided by the block development office as a water harvesting structure." Now, even the men in their families seek the women's opinion on what to cultivate, how to sell their crops and how to invest the money earned. Laxmi, another member, said: "Land ownership has changed our lives. We now have a voice and our own standing in society."

Today, a mere three years later, the women are focusing on issues such as education and electricity.

Owning land can afford safeguards that go beyond the economic ones of income. Feminist economist Bina Agarwal studied 502 married women between the ages of 15 and 49 in the rural and urban areas of Thiruvananthapuram district in Kerala. She found that spousal violence against women was at 49 per cent for those women who neither owned land nor a house, but dropped to seven per cent among those who owned both. For those who owned only a house or land, it was 10 per cent and 18 per cent respectively.

Other studies, however, have pointed out that owning land can be a mixed blessing: husbands, brothers, uncles and sons may resort to physical violence in order to gain control of property owned by women in their families. Intimidation can be an effective deterrent for a woman who insists on claiming her rights, and since 86 per cent of arable land in India is still privately owned, the scope for coercion and retaining patriarchal control is considerable.

Any attempt to break free of oppression is a two steps forward, one-step-back exercise, so too with women's access to land, and power. But, as the women of Chilipoi say: "It took 40 years for the government to understand the need to give women titles to land, it is good to see that those who once could not even speak to the men in their village are now taking the lead in rural development." ⊠

© Ritu Menon
www.indexoncensorship.org

Additional reporting by the Women's Feature Service

Ritu Menon is the co-founder of the feminist publisher Kali for Women, and founder of its partner organisation, Women Unlimited. She is the author of Borders & Boundaries: Women in India's Partition. Her most recent book is Out of Line: A Literary and Political Biography of Nayantara Sahgal

Give me liberty

43(4): 31/34 | DOI: 10.1177/0306422014561398

Author **Peter Kellner** takes the long view of parliamentary democracy and freedom, and its debt to the Magna Carta

BY COMMON CONSENT, the Magna Carta is the most important source of the liberties we enjoy today; so the coming 800th anniversary celebrations mark a vital moment in our island story. And, in an important sense, that is true. It asserted: "No free men shall be seized or imprisoned, or stripped of his rights or possessions, or outlawed or exiled, or deprived of his standing in any other way... except by the lawful judgement of his equals or by the law of the land." Those twin pillars of a decent society – human rights and the rule of law – have seldom been articulated more clearly.

And yet, for the vast majority of men and women living in England at the time, the Magna Carta was supremely irrelevant, and would remain so for at least four, and arguably six, of the eight centuries that have elapsed since King John signed it. A clue to the reason lies in the content. Yes, it mentions "rights"; but most of it is concerned with less elevated issues: bridge-building, corn, carts and horses, "merchandise", wood, land, castles – and "money [borrowed] from Jews".

The prosaic truth is that the Magna Carta was, at its heart, a financial deal that was forced on the king. He was running out of money to fight the French; and the barons decided to impose seriously tough conditions in return for giving him some more. Running through the Magna Carta is their demand that the king should stop pushing them around and confiscating their assets. They wanted him to obey some basic rules. If there was a dispute, they wanted these to be resolved by an independent judicial process, not the king's cronies. Don't be fooled by the reference to "free men". The barons meant rich people like them, not the ordinary folk that they oppressed rather more completely than the king oppressed his landowning critics.

So what happened to transform the Magna Carta from a fix, protecting the wealth of the rich, to the defining event in our journey towards democracy? The answer is essentially simple. The term "free men" was gradually expanded to include all adults, poor as well as rich, male as well as female. Rights that were originally designed for very few people came eventually to apply to everybody.

In other words, in as far as the Magna Carta came eventually to symbolise our basic freedoms, it did so as a by-product of a struggle about something completely different. Normally, we talk about "the law of unintended consequences" to mean something designed to do good that ends up having bad side-effects. The story of British liberty supplies us with examples of the opposite: often self-serving and sometimes grubby arrangements leading to an expansion of liberty.

Consider the career of Sir Edward Coke. He was no bleeding-heart liberal. As chief justice he prosecuted Sir Walter Raleigh for treason and presided over the trial of Guy Fawkes following the Gunpowder Plot. It was Coke who designed Fawkes' punishment: "He is to →

ABOVE: History shows the Magna Carta is one of the influences on extending liberty including suffrage for women. Here, performers from the 2012 Olympics form part of a protest for women's rights

be cut down alive, and to have his Privy Parts cut off and burnt before his face". Coke ended up as one of Britain's wealthiest men; few have accused him of a generous spirit or a commitment to financial integrity.

Yet, in the power struggles of the early decades of the 17th century, it was Coke who killed off the divine right of kings by telling James I that the law should apply to monarchs as much as anyone else – and some years later, persuaded parliament to adopt the Petition of Right, which made more universal the Magna Carta principles that people should not be taxed or imprisoned except by due process of law and according to Acts of Parliament. Had Coke decided that it was in his best interest to side with James I and Charles I, instead of opposing them, these reforms might not have taken place. Or, at least, Coke would not now be the man remembered for securing them.

Then there is the way censorship ended in 1695. Until then, any publication had to be approved by the Stationers' Company. The original intention, more than a century earlier, had been to ensure that the advent of printing did not lead to an avalanche of seditious literature. But by the final decade of the 17th century, the company was accused of using the Licencing Act to make excessive monopoly profits. It came into conflict with publishers, printers and booksellers who felt the company was inhibiting their trade. Had the Stationers been less greedy and more far-sighted, it might have headed off such conflicts. Instead, parliament responded to these commercial battles by repealing the Licencing Act.

Within 10 years, a range of newspapers started publication across the country. Books and pamphlets containing literature, dissent and satire flourished, subject only to the laws of sedition (though these could sometimes be applied harshly). The open contest of ideas transformed Britain. It helped to propel the Age of Enlightenment and the Industrial Revolution. More than 100 years later, the great historian, Thomas Macaulay, described that parliament's decision to repeal the Licencing Act as "a vote which has done more than liberty and for civilisation than the Magna Carta or the Bill of Rights".

These episodes support what has been called the Whig view of history: that, slowly and with interruptions, but inevitably, the story of human history is one of eventual social progress. Our freedoms have been a long time in coming, and forward lurches have sometimes been by-products of other battles, but in the end they could not be stopped.

One of our more dramatic contests between progress and caution was the struggle for votes for women. Until the second half of the 19th century, the campaigns to extend the franchise were almost exclusively about

Books and pamphlets containing literature, dissent and satire flourished, transforming Britain

extending it towards more men. True, Mary Wollstonecraft had put the case for gender equality as early as 1792, in A Vindication of the Rights of Women; but for some decades, most progressive men in a position to make a difference either ignored or opposed her arguments. Here is what John Bright, one of the most reform-minded Liberal MPs of his time, wrote in 1882:

I act from a belief that to introduce women into the strife of political life would be a great evil to them, and that to our sex no possible good could arrive ... As civilisation founded upon Christian principle advances, women will gain all that is right for them, although they are not seen contending in the strife of political parties. In my experience I have observed evil results to many women who have entered hotly into political conflict and discussion. I would save them from it. If all the men in a nation →

→ do not and cannot adequately express its will and defend its interests, to add all the women will not better the result, and the representative system is a mistake.

Fortunately his views did not prevail – although it took another 46 years before women enjoyed the vote on the same terms as men. Even then, women were excluded from the House of Lords. This did not change until 1958 when life peerages were introduced and women could then be appointed to the Lords. But even then the idea of gender equality met resistance. One hereditary peer, Earl Ferrers, said this in one of the Lords debates on the bill:

It's worth remembering that Britain took 713 years to progress from Magna Carta to universal suffrage for all adult men and women

I hope very strongly that this provision will not become law because, in my humble opinion, I think it would be an unmitigated disaster to have women in this House ... Frankly, I find women in politics highly distasteful. In general, they are organising, they are pushing and they are commanding. Some of them do not even know where their loyalty to their country lies ... It is generally accepted, for better or worse, that a man's judgment is generally more logical and less tempestuous than that of a woman. Why then should we encourage women to eat their way, like acid into metal, into positions of trust and responsibility which previously men have held?

The ludicrous thoughts of an old man brought up in the Victorian era? Not a bit of it. Ferrers was only 28 when he made that speech – he had inherited his title when he was 25 – and he died as recently as 2012. In due course he changed his mind; or at least we should assume so, for in the 1980s he was happy to serve as a junior minister under Margaret Thatcher.

Taking the long view, it's worth remembering that Britain took 713 years to progress from Magna Carta to universal suffrage for all adult men and women. Rightly we support far faster progress towards freedom, equality and the rule of law in countries with more recent experience of tyrannies. But when we seek to accelerate their journey, we should recall with some humility how slow ours has been – and how fragile and imperfect our liberties continue to be.

On the other hand, we can take pride in the way Britain blazed a trail for other countries. The Habeas Corpus Act was passed in 1679, and has since been adopted by much of the world. And the United States Bill of Rights, approved by Congress in 1789, lifts much of its language from the British version exactly 100 years earlier – for example, the ban on "cruel and unusual punishment".

Perhaps the US would have done better to have copied our Bill of Rights on another contentious matter. Our Bill of Rights allowed people to bear arms "suitable to their conditions and as allowed by law". That vital qualification, which would allow for sensible gun control laws, was omitted in the American version.

Nevertheless, the larger truth remains. The struggle to secure freedom in Britain was long; the struggle to defend freedom everywhere, including in our own country, will never end. ⊠

© Peter Kellner
www.indexoncensorship.org

Peter Kellner is author of Democracy, 1,000 Years in Pursuit of British Liberty, published by Mainstream, and is president of pollsters YouGov

Constitutionally challenged

43(4): 35/38 | DOI: 10.1177/0306422014561166

Mexico's constitution was modified 45 times in the first half of 2014. **Duncan Tucker** reports from Guadalajara on the "Mexican Magna Carta" and the population's struggle with state power

IN SEVERAL COMMUNIQUÉS issued from his remote jungle hideaway, Subcomandante Marcos, the iconic, pipe-smoking spokesperson of the Zapatista rebel movement, has invoked the Mexican Magna Carta – as the nation's constitution is often informally referred to – to assert the indigenous population's right to common resources and protection from state power.

Yet the Zapatistas say their demands for work, land, housing, food, healthcare, education, independence, freedom, democracy, justice and peace have forever been ignored.

Meanwhile, Mexico's constitution is being stripped of its relevance with every passing year: basic rights including freedom of expression are being threatened by an avalanche of constitutional amendments and even existing rights are being eroded by the government's failure to enforce the rule of law.

After independence in 1810, Mexico adopted several constitutions before settling on the current version which was enacted in 1917 during the ongoing Mexican revolution. Each constitution was derived from the last, but all drew some influence from the United States constitution of 1789, which in turn was partly based on England's original Magna Carta of 1215.

The Mexican constitution has never been quite as venerated as its US equivalent but throughout the 20th century it remained an important touchstone to which elements of society would cling.

The Mexican left was once "obsessed by invoking elements of the constitution, whether it's about the freedom of the press, land rights, workers' rights or the secularisation of education", said Benjamin Smith, a professor of Mexican history at the University of Warwick.

"People did believe in it for quite a long period of the 20th century. I would say it's only been the last 20 years since President Carlos Salinas de Gortari got rid of all the socially distributive parts of the constitution that people have really ceased to believe in it," Dr Smith added.

There have been over 600 amendments to the constitution since 1917. Salinas, who modified the constitution 55 times in six years in order to pass a range of neo-liberal reforms, including the controversial land reform that sparked the Zapatista uprising in 1994, looks, in retrospect, like someone who held the constitution in high regard.

Compare him to the last president, Felipe Calderón, who made 110 changes, and his successor, President Enrique Peña Nieto, who is already well on course to surpass →

ABOVE: Members of the indigenous Zapatista National Liberation Army hold a march in Ocosingo, Chiapas

→ that figure. He made 45 modifications in the first half of 2014 alone, more than in any other year in Mexican history.

Most Mexicans are not even aware of many of these changes, much less consulted about them. Recent amendments range from minor alterations to major reforms of the education and energy sectors, aimed at modernising Mexican society and galvanising the underperforming economy.

One of the most controversial recent amendments to Mexico's constitution, which did provoke public outcry, was that which paved the way for a telecommunications bill passed in July 2014. Although primarily aimed at creating greater competition in this heavily monopolised sector, the legislation provoked major demonstrations with thousands of protesters claiming it infringed the public's rights to privacy and freedom of expression.

When the new law was proposed, a group of digital rights activists known as ContigenteMX (the Mexican Contingent) and another 13 international organisations wrote an open letter to congress warning of the bill's implications. The legislation undermined constitutional changes made just a year earlier that were "based on input from unprecedented social and political participation" and promised to "bring Mexico's digital human rights up to international standards", the activists claimed.

The activists said the telecom bill "threatens freedom of expression, net neutrality, as well as the right to access opportune and plural information through the internet. It imposes real-time surveillance of people's communications and movements. It also authorises the state to censor the internet by restricting both publication and access without even a court order."

The legislation also allowed the government to block mobile phone signals during protests and keep a record of all communications for a period of two years. The bill was passed without public consultation, in spite of the Mexican Senate receiving a petition with over 200,000 signatures in favour of increasing public access to the internet and emphasising the right to public information.

Nevertheless, Mexico's constitution has never offered quite the robust and clear cut protection of freedom of expression which its defenders claim. Freedom of the press was first established in the constitution of 1824 and it was enshrined again alongside freedom of speech in the 1857 and 1917 versions of the constitution. Articles 6 and 7 of the two most recent editions respectively guarantee freedom of expression and prohibit state censorship.

However, Smith points out a major caveat. "Articles 6 and 7 establish complete freedom of speech and freedom of the press, unless you infringe the law of the press, which is a federal law that curtails journalists' rights. Many state governments have also passed their own press laws which curtail journalists' rights even further," he explained. "So in the 1920s and 1930s loads of journalists were imprisoned, but at the same time the Mexican government was very keen to persuade the outside world – like it is today – that there was freedom of the press, which is central tenet of being a democracy."

The western state of Sinaloa, for instance, which is notorious for drug-related violence, passed a law in July 2014 which prohibited local journalists from reporting "information related to public safety or law enforcement", accessing crime scenes or photographing, filming or recording audio of anyone involved in a crime. Under the new law, the media would have been limited to publishing information from official press releases issued by the Sinaloa Attorney General's office. The law caused such an uproar across Mexico that it was hastily repealed.

The story of the constitution and press freedom in Mexico has not all been about the state restricting the activities of journalists. In fact there have been attempts by

Basic rights like freedom of expression are being threatened by an avalanche of constitutional amendments

the government, through amendments to the constitution in 2012 and 2013, to ensure greater legal protection for journalists, demonstrators and anyone else targeted for exercising their freedom of expression, by allowing the federal authorities to step in when crimes against them are committed. Previously the responsibility for investigating such crimes came under state law but many cases, particularly of murdered journalists, went unsolved.

"Until now, the federal authorities, claiming lack of competence over these crimes, have exacerbated impunity," reported the press freedom watchdog Article 19 at the time. Article 19 said it hoped the reform would "be a step towards combating the environment of impunity for crimes against freedom of expression", but there has been little evidence of this and none of the murder cases have been solved. →

→   This reflects a much wider problem across Mexico. According to the latest government statistics, only 6.2 per cent of the 33.1 million crimes committed in Mexico last year were investigated, while even fewer of these crimes were ever solved or punished. As recently as October a blogger, who regularly wrote about violent crime and corruption, María del Rosario Fuentes Rubio, known by the pseudonym "Felina", was kidnapped by armed men, and killed in the Mexican state of Tamaulipas. The following day a photograph of her body was posted to her Twitter account with messages warning others to be silent.

Also in October, news started to come out about a group of 43 student protesters who had gone missing, presumed kidnapped. After bodies were found in a mass grave in Guerrevo state, accusations circulated of police involvement, and nationwide protests ensued.

In this context of absolute impunity, Mexico's biggest problem is not the content of its constitution but the government's complete inability to enforce its existing laws. ☒

© Duncan Tucker
www.indexoncensorship.org

Duncan Tucker is a freelance journalist based in Guadalajara, Mexico. He is the author of www.thetequilafiles.com

Courting disapproval

43(4): 39/42 | DOI: 10.1177/0306422014561584

As Egypt approaches the fourth anniversary of the 2011 uprising that deposed President Hosni Mubarak, **Shahira Amin** looks at how the brutal suppression of dissent, supported by the judiciary and some media, has left newly won freedoms hanging in the balance

THE SPACE FOR free expression has shrunk dramatically in Egypt since a military takeover of the country 18 months ago. The authorities, who came to power in July 2013 after army-backed mass protests against the Islamist regime, are engaged in a crackdown of dissenters. They have not spared secular pro-democracy activists who initially supported the military either.

Justice is elusive. In early 2014 more than 1,200 people were sentenced to death in two mass trials denounced by rights groups as contrary to the rule of law. The defendants were accused of launching attacks on police stations and churches in Egypt's southern province of Minya that resulted in the death of a police officer and a civilian. The unrest had followed the forced dispersal by security forces of two Muslim Brotherhood sit-ins in Cairo that left up to 1,000 supporters of deposed President Mohamed Morsi dead and thousands more injured. Despite international condemnation, of what human rights groups have described as sham trials, the mass death sentences were upheld for 183 Muslim Brotherhood leaders, including the group's spiritual leader Mohamed Badie.

Not all those imprisoned since the military takeover are linked to the outlawed Muslim Brotherhood, the Islamist group designated by Egypt as a terrorist organisation in December 2013. An estimated 9,000 are secular activists or bystanders who have been arrested for being at, or near, protest sites during the violence. Among the jailed activists are several iconic symbols of the 2011 uprising including: Ahmed Maher, the leader and co-founder of the pro-democracy 6 April Youth Movement which helped topple Mubarak; Mohamed Adel; and Ahmed Douma. They were all jailed for demonstrating against a controversial law banning protests without prior permission from the authorities.

A number of other prominent activists have also been arrested or imprisoned for breaching the new protest law, including Alaa Abdel Fattah, the nephew of novelist and political commentator Ahdaf Soueif. He was detained in October, a day after his younger sister Sanaa Seif was sentenced to three years in prison along with 23 others.

Dozens of detainees have gone on hunger strike as a protest against their detentions and what they say are the inhumane conditions under which they are being held. Some detainees claim they have been tortured and abused inside prisons. Others complain of being denied access to justice. Scores have been kept in prison for weeks, and in some cases, months, without charges being brought against them. Many complain they are being denied visits from family or lawyers.

Last January, 26-year-old Egyptian-American activist Mohamed Soltan →

ABOVE: Riot police during clashes with student supporters of the Muslim Brotherhood and ousted President Mohamed Morsi outside the Al Azhar University campus, in Cairo, May 2014

Credit: Amr Dalsh/Reuters

began a hunger strike in prison to protest against his lengthy detention without charge. No evidence had even been laid against him and Soltan told the judge presiding over his case that his hunger strike was "the only peaceful means left to me to resist injustice and oppression". He was hospitalised in early November after he went into a coma and was fighting for his life at the time this article went to print.

By the end of September this year, a total of 143 people were on hunger strike in the country, according to a report from the Arabic Network for Human Rights Information, with dozens of activists outside prison joining the strike to express their solidarity with those detained. In an article for The Guardian newspaper, Egyptian author Ahdaf Soueif described the response of the authorities to the hunger strikes as "bordering on criminal irresponsibility".

Criticism of the judiciary is a red line in the new Egypt. Those criticising judges or their verdicts risk arrest and prosecution as was demonstrated when prominent liberal intellectual Amr Hamzawy used Twitter to criticise an "unjust verdict" against foreign non-governmental organisations. He faced criminal charges of insulting the judiciary, after a lawyer filed a legal complaint against him. However, not all those in the judiciary are resistant to reform. A judge at a public prosecutor's office, who wished to remain anonymous, acknowledged the need for change. He told Index: "The problem lies with senior judges who do not understand the concept of human rights. We need to modernise the judicial system and educate judges who fail to comprehend the rapid changes taking place around the world – changes that have come about as a result of new methods of communication, particularly social media."

The lack of effective justice in Egypt has been highlighted internationally by the case involving three journalists working for the news network Al Jazeera. The evidence incriminating the defendants included private home videos, family vacation photos, a music video and a press conference by a Kenyan official that had nothing to do with the case. The journalists were nevertheless sentenced to between seven and 10 years in prison on charges of aiding a terrorist group and fabricating false news, charges described by Al Jazeera and human rights groups as politically motivated.

The three Al Jazeera journalists are among 125 detained in Egypt since July 2013, according to Reporters without Borders, making Egypt among the top 10 jailers of journalists in the world. No fewer than five journalists reporting on the clashes between protesters and the military/police have been shot and killed by security forces during the past year. In the current atmosphere of fear

The problem lies with senior judges who do not understand the concept of human rights

and intimidation, several journalists have reported verbal harassment and physical assaults by mobs on the streets who accuse them of being pro-Muslim Brotherhood and of fabricating news. Foreign journalists are particularly at risk as xenophobia in Egypt rises, fuelled by a media narrative that depicts foreigners as spies.

Journalists are not the only groups at risk. Violence has continued unabated at state universities since the start of the new academic year in October, with near daily clashes between security forces and students protesting the arrests and detention of their colleagues. There have been restrictions placed on activities at universities, including the stationing of police forces on campus and a ban imposed on students' partisan and religious groups. Tear gas and live ammunition has been used to quell protests, which have sparked fatalities, including that of Omar Sherif, a second-year engineering →

→ student at Alexandria University, who died of wounds sustained in clashes with security forces.

In a bid to curb protests, the authorities have issued stern warnings to students that they would adopt a zero-tolerance approach towards dissent, including military trials for students. "Resentment is spreading," Wesam Atta, a student at Al Azhar University, where some of the worst violence has occurred, told state-sponsored Al Ahram. "The rights to free expression, to organise politically and for universities to be administratively independent, which were gained after the 2011 uprising, are being eaten away."

Violence is also having a chilling effect on the media. In the wake of two attacks on the Sinai Peninsula on 24 October that killed at least 33 soldiers and wounded dozens more, editors of 17 private and state-owned newspapers and publications pledged to support of the government. In an unprecedented move they vowed to "refrain from criticising state institutions." In a statement published in the privately owned Al Wafd newspaper, the editors reiterated their "rejection of any attempts to challenge state institutions and insult the military, the police or the judiciary as such insults may negatively affect the performance of these institutions".

Hundreds of journalists opposed the editors' declaration. They argued that the move was designed to create "a one-voice media". In a statement of their own posted on 2 November on social media networks, the journalists said: "Fighting terrorism has nothing to do with the 'voluntary surrender' of the freedom of expression as outlined in the editors' 26 October declaration."

For the young revolutionaries who mobilised the public for the 2011 mass protests, the rapid about-turn in attitudes towards new found freedoms like that of public assembly and free expression has been devastating. Asmaa Mahfouz, a member of the 6 April Youth Movement now been banned by

a Cairo court, told Index: "Losing the gains made by our revolution has caused many of us to despair." Mahfouz, who recently found out that she was barred by the authorities from leaving the country, added: "Despite the failures, we will not give up. We have made many sacrifices and paid a high price. Our revolution will continue." X

© Shahira Amin
www.indexoncensorship.org

Shahira Amin is a journalist based in Cairo, Egypt. She tweets @sherryamin13

Digging in to the power system

43(4): 43/46 | DOI: 10.1177/0306422014561650

Indigenous movements have increased power and won land reform in Bolivia and Ecuador, but not without obstacles, reports **Sue Branford**

EVO MORALES, THE first democratically elected Bolivian president to come from an indigenous family, will begin his third term of office in January. His next will take place in a country that has embraced its roots and made the recognition of indigenous rights a cornerstone of reforms.

"We have done a lot for the 26 indigenous people in the country since we came to office in 2006," said Celima Torrico, a Quechua Indian who became the country's first indigenous minister of justice under Morales, in an interview in October with the Inter Press Service. Torrico said the country's new constitution, approved during Morales's first term, made the power of indigenous groups much stronger, giving them the right to vote for seven special deputies to represent their interests.

The indigenous population voted for these deputies for the first time in October's elections. Indigenous leader Rodolfo Machaca told the independent Global Research organisation at the time: "Bolivia is one of the few places in the world where indigenous people are taken into account and are given responsibility and influence in the political sphere of administrating the state ... In our country we are experiencing a high-intensity democracy."

Álvaro García Linera, Morales' chief aide, told me a couple of years ago that while there has been "a major popular, indigenous awakening" in much of Latin America, it is only in Bolivia that the state itself has become "plurinational". In a recent interview with IPS, he explained more fully: "While in other countries, there is social and cultural diversity, a strong social presence of indigenous peoples to a greater or lesser extent. But the state remains monocultural, and to a certain point ethnocidal, because it kills the diversity of cultures. So Bolivia has been a pioneer in showing the need for plurinational states." In other words, Bolivia now recognises that all the country's diverse cultures and ethnic groups must be represented in the state itself.

Along with other forms of participatory democracy, Bolivia has 15,000 territorially based organisations that allow local people to take part in the planning process. It is this greater participation, not only in government but in the state itself, that is leading to real, structural change. More than a million people, many of them indigenous, have been given land. Almost one quarter of the land titles have been given to women, and another third to men and women jointly. This has given a much greater voice and power to women, who have historically been excluded from land ownership. In this, and other ways, Morales is moving towards a form of democracy that is far more inclusive. →

ABOVE: The growing power of indigenous groups in Bolivia was believed to be a factor in the recent re-election of President Evo Morales. Here, people wait to vote in presidential elections in Achacachi, La Paz, October 2014

→ But some indigenous leaders are dissatisfied. They believe that, in Morales' desire to generate funds to pay for his so-

As well as providing land titles to more than a million people, Morales has succeeded in creating a form of participatory democracy

cial welfare programmes, he has followed traditional forms of economic development, giving business too much power. There have

been protests against the government's pro-business legislation, including a new mining law that, they claim, will contaminate drinking water and agriculture. One indigenous critic, Fernando Vargas, who led the successful campaign to stop the construction of a road across the indigenous territory of Isiboro-Sécure (TIPNIS), has repeatedly criticised Morales for his decisions.

Ecuador is another South American country where the indigenous population is finally gaining a voice in the running of the country. During his brief stint as finance minister in 2006, Rafael Correa became critical of the country's subordination to the IMF and the

World Bank. He resigned as minister and began to travel the country. In an interview with New Left Review in October 2012, he explained why he took this step: "Faced with the delegitimisation of the political class, which no longer represented anyone but itself, we said to ourselves that it was we citizens who had to reveal its inadequacies. So we decided to call it a citizens' revolution, a revolt of indignant citizens. In that sense, we anticipated the *indignado* movement in Europe by five or six years." Correa's message was enthusiastically received, and he was elected president at the end of the year.

One of Correa's first steps was to draw up a new constitution. It proposes an alternative model of development based on a new concept – *sumak kawsay*. If it is ever fully implemented, *sumak kawsay*, which is generally translated as "good living", is an idea that is interpreted as putting a much greater emphasis on collective rights, reciprocity, solidarity and participation, values that do not coexist easily with the western emphasis on individual rights.

However, since his election Correa has concentrated on generating wealth to fund social welfare programmes. He has redistributed income and created what is widely seen as a more egalitarian society, achieving all this without antagonising the rich. He was re-elected president for his third term in February 2013.

But, just as in Bolivia, some indigenous leaders feel betrayed. One of Correa's most vociferous critics is Carlos Pérez Guartambel, the leader of Ecuarunari (Ecuador Runacunapak Rikcharimui, Confederation of the Kichwa peoples of Ecuador), the historically powerful indigenous organisation in the Ecuadorian highlands. He said recently in an interview with a local newspaper: "I think the next decade is going to be the decade of social conflict because of mega-mining, mega-projects in the fields of oil, monoculture for biofuels, sugar cane, maize, soya – we are going to experience more or less what has happened in Brazil and Paraguay where millions of hectares are dedicated to the cultivation of soya which is just going to feed the stomachs of cars to the detriment of stomachs of people. This will lead to resistance from the original inhabitants who don't want to be divorced from nature … And they will clash with the extractivist model proposed by Correa."

Indeed, what is currently happening in Brazil is a warning that advances can be reversed. In Brazil, the giant of South America, the indigenous population is much smaller, some 800,000 people, less than 0.5 per cent of the total population. Even so, in the wave of democratic enthusiasm that swept over the country after the return to civilian rule after 21 years of military dictatorship,

This has given a much greater voice and power to women, who have historically been excluded from land ownership

article 231 of the new constitution, passed in 1988, gave the indigenous population "inalienable" rights to their land. Today the Indians occupy about 115 million hectares of land, or about 13 per cent of Brazilian territory. Much of it is in the Amazon basin and the indigenous communities are widely considered as playing an important role in environmental conservation.

However, the agribusiness lobby, which has long campaigned against the "excessive" amount of land given to the Indians, is growing in strength. Mauricio Guetta, a lawyer working for a large Brazilian non-governmental organisation, the ISA (Instituto Socioambiental or Social-Environmental Institute), finds this very worrying. He wrote in a recent blog: "The big centres of economic power (banking, arms industry, mining, pharmaceutical companies, engineering, agro-business) have →

→ found ways of managing the democratic system established by the 1988 constitution, and distorting the pillars of our democratic republic. In this way, they are appropriating political power, in violation of the constitutional principle that 'all power emanates from the people'."

It is for this reason that, despite having won their land rights, some indigenous Brazilians feel that their voices are being increasingly ignored. In September 2014, Davi Kapenawa, the leader of the Yanomami indigenous people in Brazil, told me: "The federal government will not listen to us. It is becoming harder and harder to talk to them. They listen only to the powerful landowners and business people. They do not value our culture or our profound knowledge pf the forest. I am fearful for the future." Brazil is fast becoming a modern, sophisticated economy. Indigenous leaders in Bolivia and Ecuador may well fear that a similar fate awaits them, as their economies develop. ☒

© Sue Branford
www.indexoncensorship.org

Sue Branford lived in Brazil for more than a decade, working as a foreign correspondent for the Financial Times and The Economist. She then returned to the UK where she was worked for the BBC World Service as a Latin America specialist

Critical role

43(4): 47/50 | DOI: 10.1177/0306422014560494

Twenty years after becoming a democracy, South Africa still has two parallel systems of justice. Even so, accusations of witchcraft have led some to take matters into their own hands, reports **Natasha Joseph**

WHEN SOUTH AFRICA'S police commissioner General Riah Phiyega visited Thomo village in the country's Limpopo province last August, she set herself two aims. She was there to catch two kinds of criminals: those who kill for body parts that are used ritualistically and those who kill "witches".

Two months earlier, a 52-year-old woman named Catherine Nkovani-Chauke was murdered by a mob that declared her a witch. Phiyega's visit was billed as part of an outreach programme. Her officers had visited police stations in Thomo and its surrounding area to gather information about recent witchcraft-linked cases, both those in which a suspect "witch" was attacked and those in which elements of witchcraft were part of a crime's modus operandi.

She addressed hundreds of people at the Thomo Sports Grounds, urging them not to take the law into their own hands. Instead, she said, residents should work with the police to keep their villages safe. The commissioner's visit, 20 years after South Africa became a democracy, did not highlight a new problem in Limpopo.

In the politically turbulent decade between 1985 and 1996, as South Africa made the transition from apartheid to democracy, killings and "witch purging" were very common in the province. The violence reached such a scale that a Commission of Inquiry into Witchcraft, Violence and Ritual Murder in the Northern Province was set up. It was chaired by Professor Victor Ralushai, an eminent scholar of African knowledge systems and became known as the Ralushai Commission.

Katherine Howe, editor of the recently published Penguin Book of Witches, writes of the Puritans who settled North America in the 1600s: "Witches served as both literal and figurative scapegoats for frontier communities under profound economic, religious, and political pressure."

Centuries and continents away, consider this extract from the Ralushai Commission's report in 1995: "All kinds of misfortune, including matters as varied as financial problems, illness, drought or lightening [sic] strikes, are blamed on witchcraft."

The commission recommended police-led interventions to teach communities about the dangers of false allegations and witch hunts. For the past two decades, these killings have been rare, or rarely reported. But last August Phiyega stood before the residents of Thomo, listing recent examples of suspected witches who had been driven out of their homes, attacked by mobs and stoned to death.

"South Africa is a country emerging from a past characterised by horrific scenes of violence. As we approach our maturity →

ABOVE: Police Commissioner General Riah Phiyega (left) has been investigating "witch killings" in South Africa

→ as a democracy, we continue to witness extreme violence perpetrated against women and children. We are seeing acts of gross violation of basic human rights. Vigilantism, ritual killings and mob justice have no place under our constitutional democratic dispensation. These so-called *muti* (traditional medicine) killings are serious crimes against humanity and need a collaborative approach to combat," Phiyega said.

"A study prepared for the United Nations' special rapporteur on extrajudicial summary or arbitrary executions in 2011 documented that witchcraft had been widely practised in African societies since before the colonial time. Belief in how witchcraft is practised varies from state to state, but the practice of witchcraft is often to give a justification for why bad things happen to certain people ... Accusations of witchcraft can lead to violations of a wide range of human rights, including the right to life."

Politically South Africa is far more stable than it was 20 years ago. Economically, it remains one of the world's most unequal societies. In under-developed rural areas where residents remain largely unemployed and under-educated, where job opportunities are rare and resources are scarce, the conditions are ripe for scapegoating.

Credit: Gallo Images/ City Press /Leon Sadiki/Alamy Live News

Ranson Mashile is one such scapegoat. As a headman, he is the first port of call for people who want help and guidance in Ga-Boelang village in the north of Mpumalanga province. As chief headman, Mashile and others in the area's Sehlare Tribal Authority are responsible for resolving disputes between neighbours. They must adjudicate in cases of theft or disagreements about property boundaries. Headmen are also called to intervene when a resident is accused of witchcraft. There are no reliable statistics for how many people are falsely accused of witchcraft in South Africa each year. Old, single women in rural villages are particularly vulnerable to allegations.

Mashile's standing in his community did not help him when, in August 2012, his home was razed by a group of people who accused him of bewitching and killing one of his closest friends. He knew what was coming: by the time the torch-wielding mob arrived, the 67-year-old was hiding at the local Acornhoek police station. He was never formally tried for his alleged crimes, neither before a traditional court convened by his fellow headmen in the tribal authority, nor in one of South Africa's regional or magistrates' courts. Instead, he arrived at a community meeting one Sunday morning in Ga-Boelang and found a local politician, Delta Mokoena, accusing him of murder.

Mashile told South Africa's City Press in late 2013 in an interview in the police station that is now his home: "I run an initiation [circumcision] school and my late friend, Pebane, used to have his own. He was sick and eventually died, but [Mokoena] said I bewitched him. When I arrived [at the meeting], Mokoena said I had killed Pebane ... I left my house the same day in fear. A week later, it was burnt."

Mokoena leads the Bushbuckridge Residents' Association or BRA. It splintered from the powerful governing party, the African National Congress, in 2010 and has repeatedly been implicated in arson attacks and assaults. Mokoena has two criminal convictions: one, for accusing Mashile of practising witchcraft and for arson, and the other for intimidation. He unlawfully evicted a man from his Ga-Boelang home in 2010 after accusing the man's son of theft and threatening to burn the family's house down while they were inside.

In the three years from 2010 to 2013, at least 20 families were thrown out of their homes in Ga-Boelang and surrounding villages in this rural corner of Mpumalanga. Houses were looted and torched. City Press reported alongside its interview with Mashile that "schools [were] shut down for weeks after teachers were accused of dabbling in the dark arts and the children of 'witches' and 'satanists' were forced to drop out of school".

All kinds of misfortune, including financial problems, drought or lightning strikes, are blamed on witchcraft

These allegations were not placed before the area's traditional courts where the accused might have been given a chance to defend themselves. The courts, most common in South Africa's sprawling rural areas in the provinces of KwaZulu-Natal, the Eastern Cape, North West, Limpopo and Mpumalanga, largely use mediation to ensure that custom and tradition are honoured. Here, there are no lawyers. You may call witnesses to defend your version of events. Ultimately, traditional courts are a space in which respected, often conservative, and almost always male leaders assert their power in a bid to keep their constituencies harmonious.

A review of traditional leadership and courts conducted by the country's government in 2008 describes their ideal role in rural communities: "They were seen as →

→ having a unique role in jurisprudence – one that 'tries people' not to punish them but to repair relationships between them. The manner in which negotiations are facilitated in courts was cited as an example of how traditional courts are not about analysis of the sum total of fact to reach a verdict but about ensuring that the accused and the aggrieved come to terms with the ills of their relationship."

The courts' detractors say this ideal could not be further from the truth. The Traditional Courts Bill, first tabled for discussion in South Africa's Parliament in 2008, sparked a vicious six-year battle between traditional leaders and those opposed to handing them more power. Women's rights activists were particularly engaged. In

I don't have 10 fingers because the traditional leader stood by and did nothing to protect me because I am a woman

September 2012, a woman named Stombi Hlombe told parliament: "I was born with 10 fingers. Now I don't have 10 fingers because the traditional leader stood by and did nothing to protect me because I am a woman."

Hlombe's "crime"? She was a woman in authority – voted on to her area's Amahlubi Traditional Council alongside male leaders. A legislative change in 2007 meant that women could finally be represented in traditional leadership structures, including hearing evidence and mediating disputes in traditional courts. Hlombe lodged a complaint against another councillor, a man who swore at her when she spoke at meetings.

"Nobody, not even the chief Mzuwenkosi Hadebe, protected me. So I made a case against him with that very traditional council, and he lost the case and was ordered to pay a fine of R5,000", she testified

in parliament. "He told the chief and the traditional council that he would not pay anything. They all kept quiet."

Weeks later, another council member attacked her in a taxi and bit her finger so badly that it had to be amputated.

This is the dark side of traditional justice. Those who opposed the bill said it would do nothing to protect South Africa's rural citizens, particularly women.

"It's oppressive to women and discriminatory ... We don't think traditional courts should be allowed to impose forced labour [one of the "sentences" that can be passed by the courts]. Why are we taking our people to the dark ages?" South Africa's then-minister of women, children and people with disabilities, Lulu Xingwana, asked parliament in September 2012.

"The department of justice admitted that the bill was drafted on the basis of talking to the houses of traditional leaders who are mostly male," she said, adding that women are usually those on the receiving end of decisions of traditional courts. "On ... witchcraft killings the bill is also quiet."

The controversial bill was ultimately scrapped at the beginning of 2014, months before Phiyega went to Thomo to plead for the killings to stop. There have been no high-profile cases in Limpopo since her visit, and in neighbouring Mpumalanga, Ranson Mashile has finally been able to leave the Acornhoek police station. But with South Africa's local government elections set for 2016 and inequality deepening each year, it seems unlikely the search for scapegoats is over. X

© Natasha Joseph
www.indexoncensorship.org

Additional reporting by Sizwe sama Yende

Natasha Joseph is news editor at City Press in Johannesburg. She tweets @tashjoeza

Global view

43(4): 51/52 | DOI: 10.1177/0306422014561178

As we approach the 25th anniversary of the first free elections after the fall of communism in many countries across eastern Europe, **Jodie Ginsberg** examines people power and the power of noise

IN AN ERA of clicktivism – where it is possible to make a "stand" about something simply by ticking a box online with little or no understanding of the cause – it is easy to dismiss the power that collective action can have. But making a noise, whether it be a petition, a letter-writing campaign, or even a handful of placard-waving protestors outside an embassy, can force even the most brutal of regimes to think twice before punishing those it seeks to repress. As poetry publisher and Russian dissident Alexander Ginzburg recalled following his arrest by Soviet authorities in 1977: "At least I knew they would not kill me before the trial. This was because I was a defended person, someone whom the West knew about and was likely to make a fuss about. Without this form of defence, political prisoners just die."

I have written about Ginzburg elsewhere, but was reminded again of the importance of making a fuss when Bahraini activist Maryam Al Khawaja was detained earlier this year as she arrived in Bahrain from her home in Denmark to visit her father, who is serving a life sentence for his part in the 2011 pro-democracy protests in Bahrain, and who was on hunger strike.

Assaulted by police, Maryam was held by the authorities for nearly three weeks before being released on bail. Her release came after a high-profile international campaign led by Nabeel Rajab, co-founder with Maryam's father of the Bahrain Centre for Human Rights, winner of the 2012 Index on Censorship Freedom of Expression Advocacy award. Rajab spearheaded a campaign that focused on persuading international governments to put pressure on Bahrain to free Al Khawaja. Together with a number of human rights organisations, including Index on Censorship, he petitioned members of parliament from a host of European countries including the UK and Denmark, as well as members of the US Congress and Senate, to speak out publicly in support of Al Khawaja.

"My release from prison was the result of international pressure," Al Khawaja wrote after her release. "I have been working in the field of human rights since 2010. What has become increasingly clear to me is that international pressure on the United Kingdom and the United States, the closest allies to Bahrain, is how we can have an influence.'

Once she was freed, Al Khawaja found herself having to do the same for Rajab, who was arrested a day after he returned to Bahrain for a tweet in which he suggested that the country's security institutions were a breeding ground for terrorists. Bahrain's defence and interior ministries accused him of "denigrating government institutions", →

→ and Rajab now faces three years in prison for his 140-character comment. Al Khawaja urged governments and parliamentary members to protest his arrest and demand his release. Again, the noise created appears to have worked. As I finished this column, the news came through that Rajab had also been released on bail, although – like Al Khawaja – he still faces a trial in which he could face three years in jail for simply exercising his right to free expression.

Noise can bring a greater degree of protection but it does not guarantee it – nor does it assure justice, as the prison sentences handed down to three Al Jazeera journalists by an Egyptian court earlier this year demonstrated. Detained and jailed simply for doing their jobs as reporters, the men could spend the next seven to 10 years behind bars. The international noise about their case has, so far, not led to their freedom.

We have been reflecting on the power that international recognition can have on individuals and organisations as we head towards the next Index on Censorship Freedom of Expression Awards, now entering their 15th year. International awards are not just recognition that these people and groups are doing vital work. Nor does their value lie in them sitting, shiny and prominent, on a mantelpiece. Rather, their power lies in the same power harnessed by Rajab and Al Khawaja and countless others like them, in creating noise that, in some cases, can offer a degree of protection for winners and nominees alike. Rommy Mom, a 2014 nominee in the advocacy category of Index awards, tells how shortly after the international and local media covered his work exposing corruption in his home state, a state from which he was forced to flee because of that work, the governor of that state contacted him to discuss the possibility of Mom returning. A previous journalism award winner, Azerbaijani reporter Idrak Abbasov, has said "Maybe the...award kept me from getting killed." In each case, it is not the award itself that is the

crucial element, but the knowledge it gives to authoritarian regimes that someone is watching them – and watching out for those they target. ⊠

© Jodie Ginsberg
www.indexoncensorship.org

Jodie Ginsberg is the CEO of Index on Censorship

ABOVE: Nationalism has become a key factor in the propaganda war between Russi and Ukraine. Here, soldiers commemorate Victory Day – the anniversary of capitulation of Nazi Germany to the Soviet Union in 1945 – at the war memorial monument, Donetsk, Ukraine

IN FOCUS

In this section

Brave new war

43(4): 56/60 | DOI: 10.1177/0306422014560963

Andrei Aliaksandrau investigates the new information war as he travels across Ukraine, and **Helen Womack** reports from Moscow

"**THERE IS NO** civil war in Ukraine. It is a war between Russia and Ukraine, and it is inspired by heavy Russian propaganda," says Volodymyr Parasyuk as we sit in a café on the main square of the regional capital Lviv in western Ukraine.

This year Parasyuk became a national hero in his country. Some say he changed history when he made a passionate speech on Maidan Nezalezhnosti in Kiev on 21 February 2014, after the police killed about 100 protesters. Parasyuk, head of a *sotnia*, a unit of 100 men, and part of the protesters' defence force, demanded President Yanukovich resign and said otherwise protesters would launch an armed attack. The next day the head of state fled the country, and there was a new government formed in Ukraine.

Parasyuk knows what he is saying about war. He joined a voluntary battalion of Ukrainian forces and fought separatists in the east of his country during the summer and autumn. He was wounded and spent a couple of days in detention, but managed to escape.

"This is direct aggression by the Kremlin against my country. This war is completely directed from Russia. We do not have internal reasons to fight each other, the conflict is provoked by lies and propaganda that come from the east," says Parasyuk.

Antonina Cherevko, a Kiev-based lawyer, was born in Dnipropetrovsk, in eastern Ukraine, almost a 1,000 kilometres away from Lviv. She agrees the conflict in her country has to do with lies and propaganda coming from Russia.

"What has been going on in Ukraine since November 2013 is not a revolution, and not a civil war, it is a classic anti-colonial war. Ukraine was in fact a colony of Russia in different forms for three centuries. Once we decided we were ready to make our own decisions, the empire got hysterical and they use lies to make the point we are not a 'valid' nation," Cherevko says.

The Ukrainian authorities refuse to call the bloody events in the east of the country a war. According to them this is an "anti-terrorist operation". But the death toll in Donetsk and Lugansk regions runs into thousands. And there is a different war that is definitely going on in Ukraine and around it – an information war. Its battles might seem less bloody, but it causes many more casualties.

The information war is nothing new. Homer wrote about the role of poets mobilising the Greeks to a war against Troy. The great Prussian statesman Otto von Bismarck is known for saying his wars were not won on the battlefield but by local Prussian teachers. During World War II, propaganda leaflets were dropped over enemy lines. But today the information wars are different.

Information wars used to be a necessary component that accompanied "real" wars, the ones with shootings, bombings, explosions and killing. Today it is the opposite

ABOVE: As eastern Ukraine seethes, Kiev speaks of anti-terrorist actions and Russia warns of fascism. Here, soldiers mark the 70th anniversary of the country's liberation from Nazi occupation at the tomb of the unknown soldier in the capital

– shootings and bombings now accompany information wars. The more you lie, the less you need to shoot. And if you are very good at propaganda, you don't need to shoot at all to win a war.

The principles of an information war remain unchanged: you need to de-humanise the enemy. You inspire yourself, your troops and your supporters with a general appeal which says: "We are fighting for the right cause – that is why we have the right to kill someone who is evil." What has changed is the scale of propaganda and the number of different platforms used to distribute it. In a time of social networks and with the whole world online, there is no need to throw leaflets over enemy lines, instead you hire 1,000 internet trolls. The ways people pro-

The same woman was found "starring" in different TV clips on different channels, first as a soldier's mother, then a refugee

duce and consume information have changed dramatically over the last few decades, and these changes affect the methods information warriors use as well.

→ Several new interesting media projects appeared in Ukraine last spring. Online publications, including Stopfake.com, were launched in order to expose the false stories, photographs and general lies which they claimed were being told about events in Ukraine and that circulated on internet as well as being disseminated through the Russian media.

Examples cited by online publications are numerous and horrible. Pictures of dead bodies, burnt-down towns and murdered children with captions such as: "Look what Ukrainian fascists do in Donetsk", or "Here is how the Ukrainian junta deals with east of the country", were exposed as being photos taken not in today's Ukraine, but years ago in different places, including Syria, Chechnya or Bosnia, during different armed conflicts, accidents or natural disasters.

Ukrainian bloggers, social media activists and journalists are educating their audiences on how to identify fakes. You can google pictures. You can find sources. You can pay attention to dates of publication of videos on YouTube. Attentive viewers revealed another technique used by Russian TV channels: "travelling actors" who feature in interviews in different roles in different places. The same woman was found "starring" in different TV clips on different channels – first, as a mother of a soldier, then as an inhabitant of Odessa who called on Russia for help, and finally as a refugee from Donetsk who allegedly barely managed to escape the horrors of Ukrainian bombings.

Traditional media have lost their monopoly on content creation and distribution, but are still important, because they reach large audiences, and are still used as the "regular army" in the information wars. But ordinary people, activists and bloggers have also become the foot soldiers of these new wars and sometimes they are no less effective than journalists.

"Every Ukrainian can also find a way to contribute to this information war. Do not

Propaganda war obscures Russian soldiers' deaths

Helen Womack *writes about reports of secret burials of Russian soldiers killed in action in eastern Ukraine*

In the information war with Ukraine, Russian media have made heroes of the separatist fighters and demonised Kiev government forces while trying to maintain a news blackout on what should be of greatest concern to the Russian public – Russia's own involvement in the conflict and the fate of her serving sons.

The Kremlin continues to deny it deployed troops to Ukraine, but Russian newspapers and human rights activists, including the Committee of Soldiers' Mothers, say discreet funerals held in far-flung Russian provinces indicate Russian soldiers were not only on the ground there this summer but in some cases lost their lives.

Bereaved families have been discouraged from talking to the media but an independent newspaper Novaya Gazeta, for which assassinated journalist Anna Politkovskaya used to work, has argued it was obvious Russians had been killed in the war in Ukraine. "We as a society should find a dignified way of bidding farewell to those slain," it said.

The business daily RBK has named a dozen Russian soldiers it said had died in Ukraine. It carried photographs of their graves (see right). It quoted cemetery officials in the Volga city of Kostroma as saying three fresh graves had appeared in the "Afghan alley" of their graveyard, dedicated to those who died in war zones. The men, who died in late August and early September, were named as Sergei Gerasimov, 26, Alexei Kasyanov, 32, and Yevgeny Kamenev, 27. Those who have tried to find out about this so-called Cargo 200, the military jargon for returning soldiers' remains, which come home in sealed zinc coffins, have been intimidated.

Back in August, Lev Shlosberg, a newspaper publisher and opposition politician in the regional assembly in the north-western city of Pskov, was beaten up and hospitalised after looking into the funerals of two Pskov-based paratroopers thought to have died in Ukraine.

The arrest in October of Soldiers' Mothers activist Lyudmila Bogatenkova, a 73-year-old grandmother from Budyonnovsk, near Chechnya, caused an outcry among her colleagues. She was charged with fraud, an offence carrying a possible six-year jail sentence, in what appeared to be retribution for her having drawn up lists of Russian military casualties in Ukraine. After an intervention from the head of the Kremlin's own human rights council, Mikhail Fedotov, she was released from custody. It remains to be seen whether the charges will be pursued against her. The Russian daily Vedomosti commented that Bogatenkova had been a target because, like Shlosberg, she demanded the truth. "A fallen soldier must remain unknown: the state insists," Vedomosti said. "Since war has not been declared, the state's answer to society's questions about dead servicemen is unofficial – in the form of arrests and beatings."

Yevgeny Kiselyov, who was a well-known face on Russian TV in the Yeltsin era but now writes for Russia's New Times from Kiev said: "There is a need to nip in the bud murmurs spreading all over the country about Cargo 200 arriving from abroad." On 12 October, President Vladimir Putin ordered nearly 18,000 Russian troops who he said had been exercising near the border with Ukraine to pull back to their bases inside Russia. Western sanctions, or possibly Russian deaths and casualties, might have been factors in his thinking. ☒

© Helen Womack
www.indexoncensorship.org

Helen Womack is a journalist in Moscow, where she has been based since 1985. She writes regularly for Index on Censorship

ABOVE: Business daily newspaper RBK named Sergei Gerasimov as one of the dozen Russian soldiers said to have been killed in Ukraine

→ consume propaganda. Think critically. Speak up. Or do what the Israeli government asked students to do in 2013: add comments to material written about Israel. When war is here, all ideas are priceless," Yevhen Fedchenko, a director of the Mohyla School of Journalism and co-founder of StopFake.org, wrote in the Kiev Post, a leading English-language newspaper in Ukraine.

When the war is on and stakes are high, anything goes. The question is whether a war like this can be decisively won by any side. The impact propaganda has had on societies in the whole post-Soviet region is tremendous. Russians support President Putin and think Ukrainians are fascists. As a response there is a huge growth of anti-Russian attitudes in Ukraine, where people are sure Russia is the aggressor. This alienation between neighbouring nations, which have centuries of history in common – sometimes tragically in common, will take decades to fade away.

People in countries that are not directly involved in the conflict become victims of the information war as well. In neighbouring Belarus people keep arguing whether Ukraine is going the right way after its revolution of 2013-2014. These arguments fall far beyond the virtual world of social networks and affect real life. Mova ci Kava, a popular Belarusian language course held in Minsk, stopped in October 2014, because the organisers had different positions on the events in Ukraine, and could not reconcile their differences to offer a coherent syllabus.

One of the problems with the information war today is that the amount of content produced and the speed the content can be disseminated makes it hard to track all lies and expose all fakes. There is probably no need to, says Uladzimir Matskevich, a philosopher and a public figure from Belarus.

"The content transmitted in an information war is not facts, but ready-made schemes of their interpretation. One example of such a scheme is: 'a normal person would never join an armed revolution' or 'you can go out in a street to protest only if you are paid for it'. A person who becomes a 'victim' of an information war gets this scheme installed in his or her mind. Once it happens, all facts that you try to provide this person with get filtered by them, and only those that match the ready-made scheme are perceived," says Matskevich.

In other words, people like thinking they are right. Critical thinking and readiness to consider a different point of view can theoretically be a remedy. Otherwise, the truth becomes the main casualty of an information war. X

© Andrei Aliaksandrau
www.indexoncensorship.org

Andrei Aliaksandrau is a Belarusian journalist who reports from Ukraine

FRONTLINE CLUB *London*

"Frontline will be remembered as one of the high peaks of journalism. Martha Gellhorn certainly thought so, and she was a pretty good judge."
— John Simpson

Through its extensive programme of debates, screenings and workshops, the Frontline Club promotes engagement and dialogue on international affairs, champions independent journalism and provides a diverse range of training for journalists and other media workers. While the restaurant serves classic, elegant British food.

The Frontline Club
13 Norfolk Place, Paddington, London W2 1QJ
www.frontlineclub.com

Frontline Club Events and Workshops
+44 (0)20 7479 8940

Frontline Restaurant
+44 (0)20 7479 8960

Azeri attack

43(4): 62/67 | DOI: 10.1177/0306422014563901

Twelve months ago **Rebecca Vincent** and Rasul Jafarov wrote for this magazine on a crackdown on photojournalists in Azerbaijan. A year later Jafarov is in jail. Here, Vincent writes about Jafarov's imprisonment, and the events of 2014

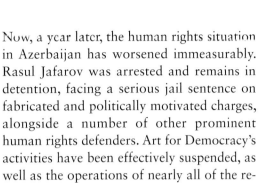

Now, a year later, the human rights situation in Azerbaijan has worsened immeasurably. Rasul Jafarov was arrested and remains in detention, facing a serious jail sentence on fabricated and politically motivated charges, alongside a number of other prominent human rights defenders. Art for Democracy's activities have been effectively suspended, as well as the operations of nearly all of the remaining human rights NGOs in the country.

The authorities work aggressively to silence the country's few remaining voices

Indeed, the past year has seen the most unprecedented of all human rights crackdowns to date in Azerbaijan, as the authorities work aggressively to silence the country's few remaining voices. As a result, there are currently more than 90 reported political prisoners in Azerbaijan, including some of the country's leading human rights defenders, lawyers, journalists, and bloggers.

Rasul Jafarov's case bears all the hallmarks of the pressure exerted on human rights defenders in Azerbaijan. He had been on the authorities' radar for years, with his earlier work for the Institute for Reporters' Freedom and Safety and, since December 2010, in his role as the founder and Chairman of the Human Rights Club. Perhaps most notably, Jafarov co-ordinated the Sing for Democracy campaign, which used the May 2012 Eurovision Song Contest, held in the capital Baku, as a platform to expose ongoing human rights violations in the country and promote democratic change. He was the driving force behind the creation of the Art for Democracy campaign.

Alongside Art for Democracy's activities, Jafarov worked to expose the situation of political prisoners. On the eve of the →

NEARLY A YEAR ago, Azerbaijani human rights defender Rasul Jafarov and I co-authored a piece for Index on Censorship on behalf of the Art for Democracy campaign, focusing on the pressure faced by Azerbaijani photographers who covered risky topics, such as corruption and human rights abuses. The piece ran alongside a photo story by some of the country's most talented independent photographers.

That piece was typical of the work of the Art for Democracy campaign, which used all forms of artistic expression to promote democracy and human rights in Azerbaijan.

MAIN: One of the photojournalists featured in the article 12 months ago, Jahangir Yusif, took the pictures for this year's update. Above, police and activists clash during the run-up to the presidential election

→ October 2013 presidential election, the Human Rights Club released a list Jafarov had compiled of political prisoners, revealing a shocking 144 cases. The election itself was marred by widespread electoral fraud and saw incumbent President Ilham Aliyev re-elected for a third term in office.

In 2014, Jafarov continued working on the list and co-ordinating efforts among

After having his bank account frozen and being prevented from travelling outside of the country, Jafarov was arrested

NGOs to achieve consensus and develop a joint version of the list, which would prove crucial to international advocacy efforts. Along with some of the other human rights defenders who have since been targeted, Jafarov repeatedly raised the issue at the Council of Europe, and advocated the appointment of a new special rapporteur to take up the work of a previous rapporteur whose efforts were defeated by lobbying from the Azerbaijani government. Jafarov also announced plans to launch a new campaign, Sports for Rights, ahead of the first European Games, which are due to be held in Baku in June 2015.

As a result of these activities, Jafarov faced a number of pressures from the authorities, but he persevered. He was aware of the risks, but also remained hopeful that the situation in his country would improve. He was dedicated to his work defending the rights of others and attempting to hold his government to account. Indeed he remains passionately committed to these aims even now, in detention.

After having his bank account frozen and being prevented from travelling outside of the country, Jafarov was arrested on 2 August and charged with illegal →

The political is personal
....
Azerbaijan's crackdown on dissenting voices is causing fear, frustration and family rifts. Azerbaijani journalist **Arzu Geybullayeva**, *reflects on the risks of being outspoken*

For the first time in many years, I am having difficulty in writing. It is taking me more time and effort. It is hard to recap everything that happened in the past year and I admit, there are things and moments, I would rather not remember. It certainly has been a challenging year. I cannot seem to remember moments of true joy, with few exceptions. Most of 2014 is covered with a thick cloud of frustration, sadness and void.

I remember meeting friends was something you did at school, parties and various gatherings. But this past year, I have made friends with people standing in front of the court rooms, waiting for news on their loved ones, with advocates and rights defenders and, most recently, with children of those unjustly thrown behind bars.

Wishes of "get better soon" were replaced with "I hope they are released soon". It seems I have wished a lot more of these this past year. And not just to friends but strangers, with whom our paths have crossed because of injustice, blindness and corruption. Texting a family member became a stressful ordeal – the uncertainty of whether that person still loves you despite the work you do, whether that person still has not disowned you.

A particular memory on this topic comes to mind. It was just few months back, in May, just after eight activists from N!DA [a young Azerbaijani civil movement] were sentenced, I received a phone call. On the other end of the line was my brother, busting his vocal chords. For a few days now he was calling, distressed, telling me he had been questioned about my work by the relevant authorities in Azerbaijan.

"You and your work," he shouted, "will cost me my job!" I was worried. The last thing I wanted was to cost my brother anything, let alone his job. I tried my best to calm him down. He refused. "You ought to go public and tell everyone that you are stepping down from whatever it is you are doing," he said. "Enough is enough!" I took a deep breath and said I would do it. I was broken down to tiny little pieces. It was his job on the line. On the other hand, it was my work too. After all, everything I have done so far, be it in writing, statements, conference talks – all of it has been for the sake of pushing for a change back home. I couldn't give up just like that.

The next thing I remember was telling my brother to disown me. He didn't do it, although I am sure he did give it a long thought or two. At the end he decided not to. A decision he regrets often. And this is what Azerbaijani government does to its people. It imprisons people's perceptions of a family; it scares people and creates an environment where even your family could turn on you. But silence and fear isn't a way forward.

This is how the past year felt mostly.

From January to the end of October 2014, a total of 13 people were arrested because of their pro-democracy work. While the charges vary from drug possession, hooliganism and espionage to name a few, these people are all known for their critical writing, outspokenness and their overall perception of the deteriorating situation in the country.

Among these are rights defenders, journalists and social media activists. In the same period, a total of 15 people, including youth activists, were sentenced. Several journalists and civil society activists fled the country. One person remains in hiding. One journalist was brutally beaten and is currently facing with a possibility of blindness.

Despite the international attention, the calls and demands of immediate release, the possibility of anything changing in Azerbaijan is as dim as ever. There are fewer voices to speak to and more people behind bars.

It is hard to write about future of a country where most of its independent minds are being silenced.

To me, my home was always about our colourful carpets, our rich culture, the laughter of our jokes and the spirit of our people. I am afraid our carpets are fading, our culture is dying, and there is little place for laughter. Azerbaijani government has slowly broken the spirit of its own people. They are nothing more but grey matters, shuffling hopelessly, aimlessly in what is no doubt, a frightening end. X

© Arzu Geybullayeva
www.indexoncensorship.org

Arzu Geybullayeva is an Azerbaijani blogger and journalist. She is currently based in Istanbul

During 2014 …

A list of 13 people arrested in Azerbaijan between January and October 2014, on various charges, but allegedly because of their pro-democracy work.

Arrested:
• Khalid Garayev, anchor of internet TV show Azerbaijan Hour
• Seymur Hazi, anchor of Azerbaijan Hour, hooliganism charges
• Murad Adilov, member of opposition, charged with drug possession
• Rauf Mirgadirov, charged with espionage
• Khagani Mammad, hooliganism charges
• Leyla Yunus, charged with economic crimes and treason
• Arif Yunus, charged with economic crimes and treason

• Intigam Aliyev, accused of tax evasion
• Rasul Jafarov, charges of tax evasion, operating an illegal enterprise and abuse of official power
• Hasan Huseynli, hooliganism charges (recently pardoned)
• Orkhan Ayyubzade, resisting police
• Faraj Karimov, drug possession charges
• Ilham Muradov, drug possession charges

Sentenced:
• Parviz Hashimli
• Ilgar Mammadov
• Tofig Yagublu
• Yadigar Sadigov
• Anar Mammadli
• 7 members of NIDA
• Abdul Adilov
• Omar Mammadov
• Ilgar Nasibov, beaten
• Emin Huysenov, hiding

This is a list of names reported to Index and may not be fully comprehensive.

A year ago:

In Index 42, 03, Rasul Jafarov and Rebecca Vincent wrote on the increasing dangers facing human rights protesters and photographers in Azerbaijan. The selected images showed various unsanctioned political protests, and the chaotic attempts by authorities to shut them down. Photographing these clashes is a high-risk pursuit, with photojournalists then facing the problem of finding somewhere to publish or display their work. The brave few that persevere capture a very different side of the country to the glossy image the government likes to present.

→ entrepreneurship, abuse of office, and tax evasion. The fabricated and politically motivated charges were similar to those used against other prominent human rights defenders. Some of the charges were linked to the fact that the Human Rights Club remained unregistered, despite the fact that Jafarov had been attempting to register the NGO with the state for more than three years, an issue pending consideration by the European Court of Human Rights. Jafarov remains held at the Kurdekhani detention centre, awaiting trial.

Jafarov is only one of many prominent human rights defenders to have been targeted in Azerbaijan in recent months. On 26 May, the chairman of the Election Monitoring and Democracy Studies Centre Anar Mammadli, was sentenced to five and a half years in jail, and his colleague Bashir Suleymanli to three and a half years on charges including illegal entrepreneurship, abuse of office, and tax evasion. Elnur Mammadov of the Volunteers International Cooperation Public Union was also sentenced to three and a half years in prison with two years on probation.

On 30 July, the head of the Institute for Peace and Democracy, Leyla Yunus, was arrested on politically motivated charges of treason, fraud, forgery, tax evasion, and abuse of office. Her husband, an activist in his own right, Arif Yunus, was arrested on 5 August on charges of treason and fraud. On 8 August, the head of the Legal Education Society Intigam Aliyev was arrested on similar politically motivated charges: illegal entrepreneurship, abuse of office, and tax evasion. There are now a total of nine human rights defenders behind bars in Azerbaijan. In addition, the whereabouts of the director of the Institute for Reporters' Freedom and Safety Emin Huseynov have been unknown since 8 August, the day his organisation's office was searched and sealed shut by police.

Parallel to these arrests, the authorities have stepped up other forms of pressure against both local and foreign NGOs, making it nearly impossible for organisations working on issues related to human rights and democracy to continue operating in the country. This has resulted in the closure or suspension of activities of many of the remaining human rights NGOs in the country. Parliament continues to tighten legislation related to the operations and financing of NGOs, cutting off vital sources of funding for independent groups and making it difficult to carry out even routine activities.

At the same time, other violations continue, such as pressure against the few remaining opposition and independent media outlets in the country. Prominent investigative journalist Khadija Ismayilova continues to face serious pressure and possible arrest, as government officials and their supporters employ new tactics in their relentless attempts to silence her. Journalists Seymur Khaziyev and Khalid Garayev, both presenters of the Azerbaijan Hour programme, were arrested on 29 August and 29 October respectively, bringing the current total of journalists and bloggers behind bars to 14. The Azadliq newspaper, the country's main opposition daily newspaper, teeters on the brink of closure, facing serious financial hardship because of excessive fines from civil

defamation lawsuits and a number of other pressures from the authorities.

In an ironic twist of fate, in the midst of this unprecedented crackdown, Azerbaijan in May 2014 assumed the chairmanship of Council of Europe, a body whose very purpose is to safeguard human rights and democratic values. Sadly, during Azerbaijan's chairmanship, the Council of Europe, and, the broader international community, has done little to hold the government to account for its human rights obligations.

Now, with Jafarov and so many of his colleagues behind bars and the organisations they represent effectively paralysed, concrete international support is needed more than ever. Azerbaijan's few remaining independent voices are under siege and will not be able to hold out much longer.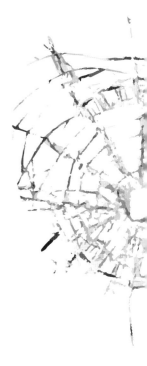

© Rebecca Vincent
www.indexoncensorship.org

Rebecca Vincent is a human rights activist and former diplomat who writes regularly on human rights issues in Azerbaijan. She served as advocacy director of the Art for Democracy campaign until April 2014

BELOW: Protesters campaign for the release of imprisoned activists

LEFT-HAND PAGE: Campaigners outside the Baku court where members of N!DA were being sentenced

Really good omens

43(4): 68/72 | DOI: 10.1177/0306422014560518

Fantasy writer Neil Gaiman speaks to political cartoonist **Martin Rowson** about horror, censorship, art and being mainstream

THE SCIENCE FICTION, horror and fantasy writer Neil Gaiman and I have never met. But when he spoke to me via Skype from his home in Boston, Massachusetts, one warm afternoon early this autumn, we bonded instantly. As a writer of scripts for graphic novels, such as his groundbreaking Sandman series for DC Comics, Gaiman shares my interest in both the power of the visual and its role in cartoons and comics. But far more important than that, as English men of a certain age, we are inescapably joined at the hip by Doctor Who, the BBC science fiction series that's now been airing for more than 50 years. (For the record, he also wrote the script of The Doctor's Wife, one of the very best Doctor Who episodes of recent years.)

After we'd chatted for a while about the latest doctor, Peter Capaldi, and the show as a political allegory for post-war Britain, Gaiman observed that in our brutal yet over-sensitive world there's something else about the series: "When I was being interviewed in America about Coraline the movie [Gaiman's 2003 children's horror novel] they would say: 'You've made something scary for children.' As if I'd done something terrible that nobody else had done before. And all I could try and explain to them was the joy of watching Doctor Who from behind the sofa, the joy of climbing into your dad's or your mum's lap and being scared and being safe at the same time."

We had, eventually, to move on from Doctor Who and its comforting and redemptive power to scare small children witless. Instead, I asked Gaiman if he'd caught up with recent news reports about the response to Hilary Mantel's short story The Assassination of Margaret Thatcher, including the demand by former UK Prime Minister Margaret Thatcher's former adman Tim Bell that Mantel be investigated by the police under terrorism laws.

"As long as people are getting upset, then a medium is not dead. And as long as Tim Bell can call for the arrest of Hilary Mantel for writing a short story, then the short story is not dead," he said.

But while I agreed that it was heartening that Bell had shown himself to be so indestructibly stupid, he'd actually called out loud for a writer to be investigated by the police because of something they'd made up in their head, which hadn't happened and which wasn't real. I suggested to Gaiman there was an ever present danger here, and quoted his own words: "A nice easy place for freedom of speech to be eroded is comics because comics are a natural target whenever an election comes up."

We're both of an age where we can remember the authorities impounding the works of the American underground comic artist Robert Crumb to stop them coming into Britain in the late 1970s. Gaiman said: "The last Robert Crumb thing that I

ABOVE: Inside the mind of Neil Gaiman

remember was about 1987 or 1988 and it was particularly notable because customs were impounding Crumb and it was stuff being imported to tie-in with a BBC2 Arena special on Robert Crumb."

It was a nice irony, but as a practitioner myself (I've written and drawn comic book adaptations of Eliot's The Waste Land, Sterne's Tristram Shandy and Swift's Gulliver's Travels), I'm conscious of deeper ironies, particularly in genres like comics and cartoons. I suggested to Gaiman that when there are BBC Arena specials about Robert Crumb, that's the moment the medium

starts dying. Didn't he feel that he should being doing something sufficiently vile and

People would say, 'You've made something scary for children'. I'd try to explain to them the joy of watching Doctor Who from behind the sofa

Crumbian to get his own books burnt in the high streets of the United States and, for →

→ that matter, Britain too? He recognised the dilemma at the heart of my question. He said: "On the one hand, I love that comics get power from being a gutter medium. But on the other hand, I spent 12 years on the board of the Comic Book Legal Defense Fund, having to oversee legal cases where the whole point was proving that comics were literature and art, and were worthy of a first amendment defence and not just trash."

He then referred to a notorious case when the state of California surreptitiously tried to reclassify the art of the Furry Freak Brothers artist Paul Mavrides as sign painting which, unlike art or literature, is subject in California to sales tax. The message the state was sending was clear: comics are so trashy you should pay tax on them.

I think that comics, because of the capacity of offence that an image can give, will always have one foot in the gutter

"It was their way of trying to tax the ["Peanuts" creator] Charles Schulz's of the world. And suddenly here's the Comic Book Legal Defense Fund having to get out and muster our experts to say: 'No, this is art, this is absolutely art.' [In 1997 a California State Board of Equalization ruling found in Malrides' favour.] So you've always got those tensions, but I think that comics, because of the capacity of offence that an image can give, will always have one foot in the gutter. You know it may be walking wobbly because it's got one foot on the pavement, but it really will be walking wobbly because it has one foot in the gutter."

Gaiman writes stuff, others draw. I wondered how this worked, and how well, so I asked him if he'd ever been offended himself by something someone had produced to illustrate his words.

He said one of his very first comics was for Knockabout's Outrageous Tales From The Old Testament, a 1987 portmanteau comic book published by Knockabout Books illustrating biblical stories and produced in ironic response to the latest calls from MPs and religious groups for comic books to be banned. "I was fascinated by the Book of Judges, mostly because it was these monstrous immoral stories where God keeps telling people to commit genocide and they're never quite doing it the way he told them.

"I did one story about a man whose wife whores around and he sends her away but then has second thoughts, gets her from her dad's, and on the road to Bethlehem they stop in a little village. A nice stranger takes the guy in and that night a whole bunch of people come out in the street and say: 'That bloke who came to stay with you tonight, we want to have sex with him.' And the host says: 'Good people, you are being evil, what an awful thing you are saying. You cannot rape this nice man, but I'll tell you what, he's got a concubine and I have a virgin daughter who's known no man, you can have them.'

"So he threw them out and, according to the Bible, they used them and abused them till dawn and left them dead on the doorstep. The guy puts his wife on the back of his donkey, takes her home, cuts her up into 12 pieces, and sends one to each of the 12 tribes in Israel to let them know what a terrible thing has happened.

"I had Steve Gibson, who is a fantastic artist, drawing this. When he got to the rape page, I had said this is not a sexy rape: it's awful and monstrous. Steve drew a gang rape so monstrous and terrible that Knockabout and I agreed it should not see print. We had Mark Matthews draw a replacement page."

Even so, he added, the book was not without controversy: a Swedish publisher of Outrageous Tales From The Old Testament was still arrested and threatened with prison for having published images breaking Swedish laws against depictions of violence towards women.

He thinks they saved the publisher from going to jail by playing up the biblical dimension. "I was saying: 'Look, if you're going to go after this, what about that incredibly disturbing image of a guy nailed to a piece of wood hanging there in his death robes? We may want to start removing those because it's pretty harrowing and it seems to be some kind of image of torture crime.'" Nonetheless, remembering Gibson's rape artwork, he reflects: "I think that was the only time I've looked at something and said: 'That's too disturbing.'"

That was nearly 30 years ago, when Gaiman's work was defined by a punkish mission to offend. These days he's rich, very influential and very, very successful. So does he think he's now part of the mainstream or has he sold out?

"You know 30 years ago, I was sushi, in a world in which if you wanted to have sushi in any little town or any big city you had to go and find the one place that sells it and it might be full, but that was the one place because it definitely wasn't mainstream. And now every little town seems to have

sushi and any big city has a lot of places that sell it."

But, maybe in 30 years of post-modernism we have just seen what we used to call the mainstream hit the floodplain and engulf the whole of the culture?

"The key word for the last 20 years, for me, is confluence, and I love the fact that you've said it's become a floodplain because that is a confluence, it's all of the rivers, all of the mainstream and the outlying tributaries, have come together."

Yet, however apparently respectable both Gaiman and the genres he works in may have become, the old threats remain. Book banning is still a problem in the US. When John Green's 2012 novel The Fault In Our

I was saying: 'Look, if you're going to go after this, what about that incredibly disturbing image of a guy nailed to a piece of wood?'

Stars was taken out of a Los Angeles school system, there was, said Gaiman, "a note saying it could not even be donated, if it was donated it had to be given back or burned".

"This is probably the bestselling book of the last three years. And now a huge movie. I think popularity and mainstream success does not mean that the people who want to save you from the stuff that could contaminate your brain will not save you, they are out there and they are determined to save you from anything, and popularity for them genuinely means nothing."

And, of course, even if Gaiman's not moved an inch while the culture's washed over him, the fault lines of taking offence never rest.

"I was pondering the fact that in 1987, one of the Sandman graphic novels was getting banned and attacked because it →

→ featured the first transsexual character in a mainstream comic, who was transsexual and sympathetic and smart and charming and fucked up like all of the characters in Sandman were and I was getting attacked from conservative elements, from people who thought there should be no transsexuals in comics. The American Family Association put me on their banned list because of that and the Concerned Mothers of America actually boycotted DC Comics and as far as I know, never lifted their boycott because of me writing my transsexual character. And now I get attacked by young transsexuals, young trans activists, going: 'Look at this character, you kill this character and bad things happen to this character which proves you are transphobic and why could you do this?'"

He recalled some of the comments. One person said: "Gaiman's transphobia makes Sandman unreadable for me and this is offensive and this is awful." Gaiman remembered thinking: "And I'm going, you know a part of me just goes: 'I wish you could have been there in 1988 when I was writing it and looked at the world that you're in now.'"

That was good point to end on, though during the previous hour and a half our conversation had ranged across everything, from how cereal crops had domesticated human beings, to the empowering nature of fiction. Gaiman also said something that I thought not only described the power of his chosen genre of fantasy fiction, but also pointed to a more universal truth: "Where there is a monster there is a miracle." Of course this observation applies equally to the unending struggles of the world of politics as to Gaiman's realm of the imagination. ⊠

© Martin Rowson
www.indexoncensorship.org

Martin Rowson is a cartoonist and writer. He tweets @martinrowson

Police in(action)

43(4): 73/75 | DOI: 10.1177/0306422014561580

A new hysteria is creating bullying tactics in the theatre. Police should do more to protect and defend our right to attend controversial plays and works of art, argues award-winning actor **Simon Callow**

ALARMING EVENTS SHOOK the theatre this year: two successful bids, from very different quarters and on very different grounds, to stop legally constituted performances from going ahead.

The theatre and suppression are, of course, old acquaintances. Theatres are by definition public assemblies which always make authority anxious. Ideas, it seems, are a hundred times more volatile when expressed from a stage. The first fully fledged British theatre censor was Sir Edmund Tilney, Elizabeth I's Master of the Revels, whom I had the pleasure of impersonating in the film Shakespeare in Love: not only did he arrange her entertainment, he had wide-ranging powers to scrutinise plays for sedition and possible diplomatic offence. In 1597, he caused Ben Jonson and a group of fellow dramatists to be imprisoned for writing the satirical play The Isle of Dogs. One hundred and fifty years later, Tilney's general remit was formalised into an Act of Parliament: in 1737, goaded by Henry Fielding's vicious onstage lampoons of him, the then Prime Minister Robert Walpole introducing the Licensing Act, giving government ultimate authority over theatres and the work they performed. The act's provisions – which were of enormous scope, covering offence to individuals, to religion, to the monarch – remained in force until 1968, when, under sustained assault from all sides, the Theatres'

Act specifically and formally abolished official censorship in the theatre.

Once the state stepped back, from time to time private individuals and organisations tried to force their views on the public by using existing legislation for purposes for which it had never been intended, most notoriously in 1980, when the public morality campaigner Mary Whitehouse invoked the Sexual Offences Act of 1956 to try to close down the National Theatre's production of Howard Brenton's The Romans in Britain. A scene in the play showed a British druid being raped by a Roman soldier, an almost too obvious metaphor for what Britain was, according to the author, doing to Ireland; Whitehouse and her cohorts (who were evidently oblivious to the political dimension of the play) secured a writ against the play's director Michael Bogdanov alleging that he had procured an act of gross indecency between the two actors; had he been found guilty he would have been liable to up to three years in jail.

In the event the case was abandoned amid widespread derision when the prosecuting counsel withdrew. Various taboos and shibboleths quietly melted away. In the 1990s, also at the National Theatre, the Queen was represented on stage for the first time, in Alan Bennett's Single Spies, which pleasurably ruffled a few feathers but caused no outrage.

ABOVE: Police stand by at a silent outside performance by Incubator Theatre, after their show was cancelled because of anti-Israel protests, at Edinburgh Festival Fringe in 2014

Credit: The List

→ From now on, it was assumed that pretty much anything went, as long as it didn't break the law. Again at the National Theatre, as if to demonstrate the proposition, Nick Hytner chose to open his regime in 2003 with Jerry Springer: The Opera, a veritable carnival of blasphemy and profanity, which played to packed houses despite solid picketing from deeply offended Christians, who nonetheless confined their protest to distributing leaflets and singing hymns.

In Birmingham a year later, the normally low-profile Sikh community showed no such restraint when confronted with the play Behzti, which featured scenes of rape and murder in a Sikh temple. Though the author was a young Sikh woman – perhaps because the author was a young Sikh woman – a huge, noisy and dangerous protest, barely contained by the police, was mounted outside the theatre; on the third performance the demonstration spilled over into an attempted occupation of the theatre, causing the play to be abandoned. The following day, all further performances of the play were cancelled after consultations between the local authorities and the theatre. The author went into hiding; the play was never performed again in this country. An uneasy precedent was set: if you protest violently enough, you will win.

At the 2014 Edinburgh Fringe Festival, a group of demonstrators coming from an entirely different part of the spectrum from the anti-Behzti faction seemed to prove the point when they forced the closure of The City, a non-political play performed by the Jerusalem-based theatre company Incubator, whose programme is avowedly pluralistic, and whose company includes non-Jewish actors. The picketers, who were protesting against the Israeli bombardment of Gaza, had no quarrel with the play: it was the fact that the company was partially state-funded by the Israeli government that condemned it in their eyes. The protesters harassed ticket-holders alarmingly, which prompted the venue and Police Scotland to announce that future performances would be cancelled because "the logistics of policing and stewarding" made it "untenable for the show to continue". What about the logistics of free speech? This is the Police Scotland who steward the famous Rangers/Celtic derbies, keeping the peace among thousands of over-excited fans. A small protest outside a theatre, one might have imagined, would be a stroll in the park for them.

The producers were unable to find another venue in the city; game, set and match to the protesters. Shortly afterwards, the Jewish Film Festival was forced to withdraw from the Tricycle Theatre after a disagreement over funding from the Israeli Embassy. In both cases, the protest was not against the art, but about the funding.

Then in September a work of art itself, produced in London by The Barbican, was attacked head on. An almost universally acclaimed theatre installation called Exhibit B, created by the white South African artist Brett Bailey, in which the humiliations meted out to slaves were reconstructed in order to give the spectator a direct sense of how profoundly demeaning the experience was, was violently picketed by a group of mainly black protesters. Again, after taking police advice about public safety, The Barbican's staff felt they were left with little option but to close the show.

Protests and picketing of theatres will always be with us: they are legal and legitimate, and indeed, in the case of Behzti and Exibit B, they are a testimony to the depth of emotion and public discussion that the theatre can provoke. The new hysteria that is increasingly dominating political discourse has produced a particularly nasty outcrop of bullying tactics in the theatre, sometimes, alas, from theatre practitioners themselves, especially in the area of anything concerning Israel, a country with whom we are not at war and with whom we have full diplomatic relations. But the refusal of the police to accept responsibility for ensuring the safety of theatre goers who want to see plays or events which are perfectly legal is a fundamental threat to freedom. So far they have failed to articulate their position. Do they think this is small beer, compared to a march or a rally or a riot? Or a football match, where they are so much in evidence? Surely it is the primary duty of the police to preserve the citizens' right to pursue their lawful activities unmolested?

This concerns all of us, of whatever persuasion, because let no one imagine that protests of this sort are the exclusive preserve of the left: in the current dodgy climate, we can confidently expect right-wing and religious fundamentalist protests which are likely to be every bit as aggressive, if not more so.

Tense, dangerous times for the theatre. And not just the theatre. It is, as John Osborne so brilliantly remarked, a minority art with a majority influence. Where theatre leads, the rest of the world often follows. So it behooves us to keep a very sharp eye on these developments. ⊠

© Simon Callow
www.indexoncensorship.org

Simon Callow is an actor, writer and director

At The Swarm, we help companies plan for the future of media.

The Swarm is a digital creative agency providing consultancy, production and design services to broadcasters and publishers globally. Founded in 2010, we have worked with a range of media organisations, universities and think tanks to plan the future of media.

With engagements in over twenty countries, we drive content innovation through collaboration with clients, audiences and our world-class experts. To discuss how media in your country is changing and how to stay connected with audiences in a digital age, contact us for an initial discussion about how we can help you.

We can help you solve challenges that relate to:

- *Big/Open Data*
- *Multiplatform Audiences*
- *Digital Distribution*

- *Digital Product Management*
- *Content & Storytelling Strategy*
- *Start-up Advice*

If you'd like us to help you plan your media future, check us out online at **entertherswarm.com**

Drawing fire

43(4): 77/80 | DOI: 10.1177/0306422014560983

Two of South America's leading cartoonists – **Rayma** from Venezuela and **Bonil** from Ecuador – present exclusive new works for Index and speak out about how their work has been targeted by censors

Rayma (aka Rayma Suprani)

Cartoons are a thermometer for a country's freedoms. When a cartoonist is persecuted because of their work, it is a sign of a failed democracy. Cartoons are like mirrors in which governments can see themselves, and that's why authoritarian regimes don't like them.

I lost my job at the Caracas-based El Universal newspaper in September for a cartoon that criticised Venezuela's health system. I had worked for the paper for 19

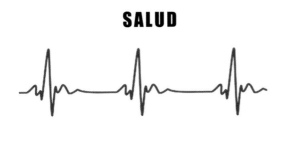

years, but it had been recently taken over by a little-known Spanish company, which some suspect to be a front for pro-government investments. Their aim has been to silence voices like mine.

My offending cartoon (pictured bottom left) showed a normal heart-rate monitor and another, based on the signature of the late president Hugo Chavez, flat-lining to show how the politicisation of hospitals had become a disease.

I have never self-censored my work. My role is to highlight and criticise Venezuela's most acute problems – corruption, economics, power, health and insecurity. This is why up to the point where I lost my job, I received death threats, anonymous insults and government pressure. In August, the newspaper tweeted that I had apologised for a cartoon I drew of Colombia's president Juan Manuel Santos, with a pig's head. I hadn't.

In Venezuela there is hardly any independent media left. The government started by buying radio stations, then failed to renew the licences of those that were about to expire. Next, the government moved on to television stations, and finally it bought newspapers and other publications, which are now being choked by the country's inability to buy newsprint. [See Paper Chase: Overcoming Venezuela's Newsprint Shortage, Index 43, 3/2014.] →

BONIL

→ This all creates a terrible situation for free expression in Venezuela and I have been left with nowhere in the mainstream media that will publish my work. It's hugely important that the foreign media and NGOs write about my case, because we feel we can't. The political situation here is very delicate. Hopefully, it will turn around at some point so we will see more tolerance and freedom, but, for the moment, that seems like it is a long way off.

Bonil (aka Xavier Bonilla)

I believe that humour is the best antidote to fear and the best defence against abuses of power. I have been drawing for 30 years and I am not going to back down, even though things are hard in Ecuador, especially with the new criminal code. The Communication Law, introduced in 2013, now allows a government body to fine and prosecute the media.

One of my cartoons, for the newspaper El Universo, became one of the biggest examples of the reach of the new law and showed its attempts to censor critical voices. It related to a raid in late 2013, by the police and the public prosecutor on the home of Fernando Villavicencio, a journalist and parliamentary adviser for the opposition. They did it without warning, and in response to calls from President Rafael Correa, who accused Villavicencio of hacking presidential emails.

My work showed the officers using heavy-handed tactics when they entered the journalist's house. The president saw the cartoon, insulted me personally, and ordered the communications superintendent to open a case against me. They concluded that I should "rectify" my cartoon, because it was inciting social unrest. They also fined El Universo $92,000 for having published it, saying the newspaper had violated article 25 of the law, prohibiting the media from taking an "institutional position" over the guilt or innocence of people involved in investigations. I maintain that my cartoon remained neutral on Villavicencio's guilt or innocence.

The newspaper paid the fine and also published my "correction", which, with its ironic tone, irritated the president even more. It included an overly polite exchange between Villavicencio and the authorities. "Nice to meet you, Mr Villavicencio. We have come to confiscate your computers and tablets. Why don't you call your lawyer?" "No, no need. I trust you. You're the legitimate authorities. Take everything you need."

Correa said at the time: "The problem is not the cartoon, it is that they are lying and that's very serious." The president's abuse of power brought me great support and the solidarity of many colleagues in Latin America and around the world. Rayma's firing was another case of intolerance and sectarianism in the region, and it is something totally unacceptable, against which we all have to unite. ⌧

© Xavier Bonilla
© Rayma Suprani

www.indexoncensorship.org

Translated by Vicky Baker

Xavier Bonilla – known as Bonil – is an Ecuadorean cartoonist.

Rayma Suprani is a cartoonist from Venezuela.

Thoughts policed

43(4): 81/83 | DOI: 10.1177/0306422014560668

Have we created a media culture where politicians fear voicing an opinion that's not the party line? **Max Wind-Cowie** reports

WE ARE OFTEN, rightly, concerned about our politicians censoring us. The power of the state, combined with the obvious temptation to quiet criticism, is a constant threat to our freedom to speak. It's important we watch our rulers closely and are alert to their machinations when it comes to our right to ridicule, attack and examine them. But here in the West, where, with the best will in the world, our politicians are somewhat lacking in the iron rod of tyranny most of the time, I'm beginning to wonder whether we may not have turned the tables on our politicians to the detriment of public discourse.

Let me give you an example. In the UK, once a year the major political parties pack up sticks and spend a week each in a corner of parochial England, or sometimes Scotland. The party conferences bring activists, ministers, lobbyists and journalists together for discussion and debate, or at least, that's the idea. Inevitably these weird gatherings of Westminster insiders and the party faithful have become more sterilised over the years; the speeches are vetted, the members themselves are discouraged from attending, the husbandly patting of the wife's stomach after the leader's speech is expertly choreographed. But this year, all pretence that these events were a chance for the free expression of ideas and opinions was dropped.

Lord Freud, a charming and thoughtful – if politically naïve – Conservative minister in the UK, was caught committing an appalling crime. Asked a question of theoretical policy by an audience member at a fringe meeting, Freud gave an answer. "Yes," he said, he could understand why enforcing the minimum wage might mean accidentally forcing those with physical and learning difficulties out of the work place. What Freud didn't know was that he was being covertly recorded. Nor that his words would then be released at the moment of most critical, political damage to him and his party. Or, finally, that his attempt to answer the question put to him would result in the kind of social media outrage that is usually reserved for mass murderers and foreign dictators.

Why? He wasn't announcing government policy. He was thinking aloud, throwing ideas around in a forum where political and philosophical debate are the name of the game, not drafting legislation. What's more, the kind of policy upon which he was musing is the kind of policy that just a few short years before disability charities were punting themselves. So why the fuss?

It's not solely an issue for British politics. Consider the case of Donald Rumsfeld. Now, there's plenty about which to potentially disagree with the former US secretary of state for defense – from the principles →

ABOVE: Protesters demand the sacking of UK minister Lord Freud for comments he made at a Conservative Party event in 2014

Credit: Ruth Whitworth/Demotix/Press Association

→   of a just war to the logistics of fighting a successful conflict – but what is he most famous for? Talking about America's ongoing conflicts in the Middle East, he thought aloud, saying "because as we know, there are known knowns; there are things we know we know. We also know there are known unknowns; that is to say we know there are some things we do not know. But there are also unknown unknowns – the ones we don't know we don't know." The response? Derision, accompanied by the sense that in speaking thus Rumsfeld was somehow demonstrating the innate ignorance and stupidity of the administration

he served. Never mind that, to me at least, his taxonomy of doubt makes perfect sense – the point is this: when a politician speaks in anything other than the smooth, scripted pap of the media relations machine they are wont to be crucified on a cross of either outrage, mockery or both. Why? Because we don't allow our politicians to muse any longer. We expect them to present us with well-polished packages of pre-spun, offence-free, fully-formed answers packed with the kind of delusional certainty we now demand of our rulers. Any deviation – be it a "U-turn", an "I don't know" or a "maybe" – is punished mercilessly by the

→ media mob and the social media censors that now drive 24-hour news coverage.

Let me be clear about what I don't mean. I am not upset about "political correctness" – or manners, as those of us with any would call it – and I am not angry that people object to ideas and policies with which they disagree. I am worried that as we close down the avenues for discussion, debate and indeed for dissent if we box our politicians in whenever they try to consider options in public – not by arguing but by howling with outrage and demanding their head – then we will exacerbate two worrying trends in our politics.

First, the consensus will be arrived at in safe spaces, behind closed doors. Politicians will speak only to other politicians until they are certain of themselves and of their "line-to-take". They will present themselves ever more blandly and ever less honestly to the public and the notion that our ruling class is homogenous, boring and cowardly will grow still further.

Which leads us to a second, interrelated consequence – the rise of the taboo-breaker. Men – and it is, for the most part, men – such as Nigel Farage and Russell Brand in the UK, Beppe Grillo in Italy, Jon Gnarr in Iceland, storm to power on their supposed daringness. They say what other politicians will not say and the relief that they supply to that portion of the population who find the tedium of our politics both unbearable and offensive is palpable. It is only a veneer of radicalism, of course – built often from a hodge-podge of fringe beliefs and personal vanity – but the willingness to break the rules captures the imagination and renders scrutiny impotent. Where there are no ideas to be debated the clown is the most interesting man in the room.

They say we get the politicians we deserve. And when it comes to the twin plaques of modern politics you can see what they mean. On the one hand we sit, fingers hovering over keyboards, ready to express our disgust at the latest "gaffe" from a minister trying to think things through. On the other we complain about how boring, monotonous and uninspiring they all are, so vote for a populist to "make a point". Who is to blame? We are. It is time to self-censor, to show some self-restraint, and to stop censoring our politicians into oblivion. ☒

© Max Wind Cowie
www.indexoncensorship.org

Max Wind-Cowie is an associate at the Demos thinktank, and writes a column for the London Evening Standard

Media under siege or a freer press?

43(4): 84/87 | DOI: 10.1177/0306422014560981

Cynthia Ottaviano has her work cut out as Argentina's first public defender for communications. As the country looks ahead to its 2015 general election, **Vicky Baker** speaks to her about audience rights, media monopolies and the controversial communications law

"I'M A VERY intense person," says Cynthia Ottaviano, Argentina's public defender for communications, and laughs down the telephone line. "I'm a workaholic, but even I didn't expect to be working this much." Yet, however big the challenge, her upbeat demeanour implies she is relishing her role as a national ombudsman for the media.

Ottaviano, a former investigative journalist, was appointed in 2012 as the first person to take the newly created post, an outcome of the country's controversial 2009 Audiovisual Media Law. Recently, the law has been making headlines again in Argentina, with the government preparing to impose a plan to dismantle the vast Clarín media group, having rejected the company's own reorganisation plan in October.

The ombudsman is autonomous, with no jurisdiction to impose penalties. Ottaviano was selected as a result of a public nominations process and elected by Congress. Now she and her team of 65 are responsible for dealing with citizens' complaints, helping to resolve issues with various media companies, and making public recommendations. She is, she says, "a bridge" between the audiences and various organisations and institutions.

In its first 10 months, the office received 3,600 queries and complaints. Of them, 75 per cent related to access issues (including problems with signals and interference) and 25 per cent were about representation – including complaints relating to causing offence, discrimination, violence, invasion of privacy, and misuse of personal image. Ottaviano says that 70 per cent of cases have been resolved – sometimes via an apology on air or in print, sometimes by arranging a follow-up piece, or by giving the right to reply. The unresolved 30 per cent of cases remain "in process".

Now that she's halfway through her four-year term, has she noticed a difference between the role she imagined and the reality? "I didn't think this role was going to get such a good reception. You only think of the contentions, which is logical. But when you are looking at ways to repair the violations of rights, there is great predisposition here – across all areas of the media – for dialogue."

This predisposition, as she says, stems from the aftermath of the 1976-1983 military dictatorship – during which an estimated 15,000 to 30,000 people were killed as part of a so-called "national reorganisation process". Dissenting voices were silenced or "disappeared", with journalists among those killed and tortured. Communication is now widely seen as a fundamental human right, and the Audiovisual Media Law was designed to replace the 1980 Radio Broadcasting Law, which had been established by the junta and which accelerated the monopolisation of the country's media.

The military regime had ruled that the media had to be "objective", "truthful" and "opportune". Ottaviano says the new media law steers deliberately clear of the same language. "Usually when you talk about these qualities in other parts of the world – say, in Europe – they have positive associations," she says. "But Argentina's media history is complex. Our current law doesn't use words like 'truth' and 'objectivity', because who determines this? This can't be determined by the state. The role of the state is to safeguard human rights. Communication has to be created collectively, with plurality and diversity."

Plurality is another key part of the wider 2008 media law, and indeed its most contentious aspect. The law has put limits on the market share a media company can hold, up to a maximum of 35 per cent. There has been a move to break up monopolies and redistribute licences. Although some praised this, others deemed it an attack on dissenting voices – an assault against the free press. The biggest media companies are also the government's biggest critics.

At the centre of the story is media giant Grupo Clarín, a very vocal opponent of the current government. The group owns the country's biggest daily newspaper, Clarín, and multiple media licences across the country – more than 200 according to the government's figures. The new law rules that any one company can only have 24 cable licences and 10 free-to-air licences for radio and television.

And the story runs much deeper. Clarín thrived during the time of dictatorship, much

ABOVE: Cynthia Ottaviano, Argentina's first public defender for communications

as the Globo network did during the Brazilian dictatorship and El Mercurio did in Chile's, with both retaining great power to this day. But in Argentina, it's also personal.

Argentina's media law is bigger than the current Fernández government, but the two are very much intertwined

President Cristina Fernández de Kirchner has been warring with Clarín since the beginning of her term of office in 2008, when the newspaper didn't support her in a dispute with farmers. The mutual animosity between the president and the news group has been vicious ever since, with each party claiming →

ABOVE: La Nación, Argentina's leading conservative daily, says it has faced a government advert boycott

→ the other is wholly self-serving and out to ruin the country.

When the media law was first announced, the worldwide press largely latched on to the Clarín viewpoint. This was perhaps a sign of the strength of its voice, or a link to wider concerns over Fernández's government.

Ottaviano sees the situation as far more complicated. "This law has 166 articles; it can't be summed up with the case of one media group," she says. "In the past, you could only have a radio or TV licence if you had money. This law shows communication not as a commodity, but as in the public interest. It should be developed with social responsibility."

Clarín announced Ottaviano's appointment by reminding readers that she was also one "of the founders of the pro-government newspaper Tiempo Argentina". But Ottaviano points out, repeatedly, that she was appointed by parliamentary election in a bicameral system; and the public had 10 days to object to her appointment.

Mostly, she tries to distance herself from political conflict and gets stuck into the day job, dealing with 4,000 media outlets nationwide. "We treat everyone equally," she insists. "There is no bias, as our duties and functions are spelt out within the law." She is also busy travelling to schools, neighbourhoods and newsrooms to hold discussions and workshops. "You can't expect people to stand up for their rights if they don't even know they have them," Ottaviano says.

Where will it go from here? Argentina's media law is bigger than the current Fernández government, but the two are very much intertwined. The president has often put a focus on human rights issues, while giving very mixed messages on the media. For example, Fernández never gives interviews, and when the public were given free access to football on television, the matches came with a running ticker of government propaganda. If a split-up of the Clarín Group is well under way before she finishes her final term in October 2015, Fernández will see it as one of her biggest legacies.

Frank La Rue, the former United Nations special rapporteur on freedom of expression, once declared Argentina's media law "an example for the entire continent". Meanwhile, the Washington Post has written of Clarín being "a newspaper under siege".

"It's complicated in Argentina," says Ottaviano, and few could argue with that. ☒

© Vicky Baker
www.indexoncensorship.org

Vicky Baker is deputy editor of Index on Censorship magazine

Turkey's "treacherous" women journalists

43(4): 88/92 | DOI: 10.1177/0306422014560506

Female reporters are being demonised, to the point that some have received death threats and one has fled the country, says **Kaya Genç**

THE TREATMENT OF Turkey's women journalists by mainstream newspapers is a good indication of recent shifts in Turkey's political culture. Over the course of the past year Turkish papers have adopted an increasingly macho attitude towards women journalists in general – and women journalists with even slightly dissident views in particular. A review of the past year's events shows us how a patriarchal tone towards women writers is in the process of becoming the norm here rather than the exception.

Women journalists are regularly told to "know their place" by state officials, newspaper editors and opinion leaders who are calling the shots in the political establishment and the media. It is as if, with every incident, a strong message is being sent to women: leave the field of politics to those who know how to handle it with the care it deserves. In other words, leave it to your male colleagues. As a male journalist who lives in Istanbul and sees the treatment of my female colleagues, I find this intimidating.

On the day right-wing newspapers called her a traitor, Ceylan Yeğinsu, Turkish correspondent of The New York Times received multiple death threats through email and Twitter messages. Yeğinsu was the most recent victim of intimidation of women writers by Turkish newspapers. Her NYT report on Islamic State's recruitment activities in Ankara, Turkey's capital, had rubbed up the authorities the wrong way. The NYT, which argued for Turkey to play a more active role in the coalition against the IS, had placed Yeğinsu's piece on its front page with a picture that showed Turkey's president and the prime minister leaving the Haci Bayram mosque. This mosque houses the cenotaph of the founder of the Bayrami Sufi sect. The selection of the picture was problematic from the start. Some pious Turks, who were irritated by the NYT's implication of a formal relationship between IS, the Republic of Turkey and the mosque in whose neighbourhood the IS recruiters allegedly worked, took to Twitter to express their frustration.

This was not exactly an extraordinary event. Every day newspapers publish articles some readers find disturbing. So it was not unusual to see outraged Turkish state officials accuse the NYT of acting shamelessly, hours after the publication of Yeğinsu's piece. The extraordinary development came the following morning when hundreds of thousands of readers saw the front pages of right-wing newspapers which announced, in capital letters, that the real culprit of the NYT debate was the reporter, Yeğinsu, rather than the NYT editors. Apparently she needed to be taught a lesson. Yeğinsu, who →

NN TÜRK CANLI YAYININDA
EÇMENİ VE MÜSLÜMANLARI
SAĞILADILAR

HAİNİ İYİ TANIYIN
BBC'nin Türk muhabirinin ihaneti

KEY BLOCKS TWITTER
Minister battling a major corruption scandal
WORLD NEWS 8 PEOPLE, INCLUDING FOUR FOREIGNERS, ARE KILLED

Selin Girit @selingirit
#Yoğurtçu forumundan bir öneri: Duran adam değil, durduran adam olalım. Ekonomiyi durduralım. Tüketmeyin. Altı ay tüketmeyin. Dinleyecekler.

İbrahim Melih Gökçek @06melih... 1h
İNGİLTERE ADINA ÇALIŞAN BBC MUHABİRİ SELİN GİRİT'in ATTIĞI TWİT...YAPILAN VATAN HAİNLİĞİNİN KARŞISINDA TÜYLERİNİZ DİKEN DİKEN OLACAK...

Haşhaşi ve yancısı hainler kudurur da

O MADENCİLER NEDEN AKP'YE OY VERDİ?

NEDEN AKP'YE OY VERDİ?

İNGİLİZLERLE PARALEL ÖRGÜT MEDYASI VE ODA TV ELELE MADENCİ KARISI PROVOKASYONU!

2. MÜFTÜ KARISI VAKASI!

ndi ülkesini karıştırmak için İngiliz'e maşalık yapan Türkler

İNGİLİZ SELİN'DEN SONRA
LDA İNGİLİZ BENGİN!

Tüketmeyin. Altı ay tüketmeyin. Dinleyecekler.

BU MU GAZETECİLİK
İngiliz patronun sana sahip çıksa ne yazar
SEN ÜLKENE İHANET ETTİN

ABOVE: Women journalists in Turkey have been subject to aggressive personal campaigns in the press and on social media

→ had carried interviews with IS recruiters for her piece, did not report that there was a connection between the mosque and the IS. But right-wing papers framed her as portraying the mosque as a recruitment centre of IS militants. She was accused of something she had not done.

Why the blatant attempt at slandering a fellow journalist? Perhaps male editors were outraged to see that a woman, in her early 30s, could write unsettling things about issues the Turkish state preferred to overlook.

Yeğinsu was subjected to a flood of emails and Twitter messages. Many tweets threatened her with drowning, and there were endless threats of rape. Having no previous experience of dealing with such a co-ordinat-

Calling a journalist a traitor, labelling her work as betrayal against her own people are the gravest accusations one can make to dishonour her

ed campaign, Yeğinsu went into hiding. She took a plane to New York and spent weeks there before heading back to Istanbul.

Although the NYT published a correction on 17 September ("Neither that mosque nor the president's visit were related to the recruiting of ISIS fighters described in the article," it read) and then removed the picture from its website ("A picture with an earlier version of this article, which showed President Recep Tayyip Erdoğan and Prime Minister Ahmet Davutoglu leaving a mosque in August, was published in error") those gestures did little to stop the intimidation campaign against her.

The way Yeğinsu was silenced had been eerily similar to other recent cases of intimidation of Turkey's women journalists. The BBC's Selin Girit had been targeted the same way, and by the same newspapers, in 2013. The crime Girit had committed was similar:

she was reporting from a forum where protestors discussed ways of fighting the state. If people stopped consuming, the protesters suggested, the state would have no other choice but to listen to their demands. Girit quoted this on her Twitter feed and this was enough to get her into trouble. She was also personally attacked by the mayor of Ankara, Melih Gökçek, on social media. She was nicknamed alternately as "English Selin" and "Agent Selin". Newspapers used her image on their front pages with the same emphasis on her treachery. This was followed by numerous rape and death threats on Twitter.

Another Turkish correspondent, the BBC's Rengin Arslan, had her moment of intimidation after she interviewed two wives of miners after the mining disaster in the city of Soma on 13 May 2014. One of the interviewees severely criticised the state for its handling of the situation. Right-wing papers accused Arslan of finding left-wing activists from another city, bringing them into Soma and donning headscarves before asking them to act as if they were wives of miners.

"As the government responds to such cases in a more muscular way, people's reactions to women journalists also began to change," says Onur Burçak Belli, a freelance journalist. "People [have] become more fearful about sharing their knowledge and opinions with women journalists. This had been my experience in the past two years. The authorities can prosecute you because of your work, and go on to prosecute your interviewees as well."

Belli, a journalist who has worked for the BBC, now files reports for Al Jazeera English and Al Monitor from Turkey's border with Syria, where she is covering the humanitarian crisis in the region. "As a women journalist 'doing a man's job', you sit at traditional coffee houses with men, smoke cigarettes with or before them, travel through hills and paths with male fighters at night ... and most of the time you are considered as weak, vulnerable, even despicable by some," she

Women under pressure

|||||||||||||||||||||||||||||||||||||||||||||||||

Incidents of intimidation of female journalists in Turkey have been reported to Index on Censorship's Mapping Media Freedom project, which has been running since February 2014. Below we include some examples of incidents that have been posted to the map.

Turkey's first and only openly transgender television reporter Michelle Demishevich was fired from Turkey's IMC TV following alleged disputes with management over her make-up and clothing, although IMC denies this. Demishevich told Bianet, an independent Turkish press agency based in Istanbul, that while she worked for IMC she was not given insurance and worked long hours for low pay.

Journalist Arzu Geybullayeva has received threats via social media over the past year. Geybullayeva writes for the Armenian-language newspaper Agos, which is based in Istanbul. The threats came after an interview she gave to an Azerbaijani website. She was then criticised by the Azerbaijani media, for working for an Armenian newspaper.

A woman journalist for Iranian broadcaster Press TV was killed in a car crash in Şanlıurfa province, near the Turkish-Syrian border, in October. Serena Shim had been reporting on Islamic State militants crossing into Turkey. According to a report on Reuters, Hamid Reza Emadi, head of Press TV's newsroom, said in an interview on the television station, "Her death is very suspect and it is likely an outcome of her critical expository reports of the adverse impact of Turkish and Saudi policies on Syrian refugees." Reuters reported that the governor of Şanlıurfa province rejected the allegations but said that Shim's death is being investigated. All cases can be viewed at mediafreedom.ushahidi.com

Aimée Hamilton

says. "I always feel that these are a reaction to our power of evaluating incidents from a woman's point of view."

Belli describes how men respond when women journalists confront issues in ways they don't agree with. "They find such things humiliating, as if they are being brought down," she says. "They react to those with counterattacks. What is even worse for them is 'being brought down' by a woman. Women are considered to have a sanctified place in gender-oriented societies as mothers, sisters and wives. This leads to harsher reactions against women. They are not expected to meddle in issues they are not entitled to. They are told to know their place in society."

People [have] become more fearful about sharing their knowledge and opinions with women journalists

Women journalists and columnists, such as Amberin Zaman, Turkish correspondent of The Economist and Nuray Mert, a vocal critic of the government, have been grilled on social media in similar cases. There appears to be few legal ramifications for those who made the threats, or the editors responsible for publishing them. The only exception so far has been the cases opened by activists, who were accused of acting as miners' wives in Arslan's report. They successfully sued newspapers that made the accusations and courts ordered the removal of the articles.

Women journalists in Turkey are not keen to make a fuss. This is understandable. After all, they are not artists, novelists or opinion leaders who voice their views about the world. They are journalists who report on it. They want to report the news in an impartial way, rather than become the news and taking sides. Women novelists have also been targeted by the same papers. The novelist →

→ Elif Shafak, for example, was subjected to media grilling when a newspaper put pictures of her and other writers on its front page, under the heading "Their sneaking, insults and arrogance know no bounds: they cannot be human." The previous day Shafak had published an article in The Guardian in which she wrote about Turkish state's long history of intimidating dissidents. It seems as if women writers, be they novelists or journalists, have become the favourite traitors of Turkish society.

"Treason is just another phenomenon in the cultures of nationalist states," Belli says. "Calling a journalist a traitor, labelling her work as betrayal against her own people are the gravest accusations one can make to dishonour her. When you accuse someone of treason, there is not much chance of a comeback from it." X

© Kaya Genç
www.indexoncensorship.org

Kaya Genç is a Turkish journalist and novelist, and a contributing editor to Index on Censorship magazine. He tweets @kayagenc

Dark arts

43(4): 93/96 | DOI: 10.1177/0306422014561945

Nargis Tashpulatova interviews three of Uzbekistan's most acclaimed artists – writer Sid Yanishev, photographer Umida Akhmedova and conceptual artist Vyacheslav Akhunov – about censorship, their desire to challenge the rules, and why restrictions are now greater than during the Soviet era

"THE SITUATION IN Uzbekistan is not likely to change unless the political system of the country changes. That means unless the state become open, the fear of creating something that can be censored will remain with most of artists here," says award-winning writer, journalist and director Sid Yanishev, ahead of the country's elections in March 2015.

Yanishev was fined 9,610,500 soms ($3,200) in June 2014 by Uzbek authorities, for researching and writing a story about residents of a demolished Tashkent housing estate receiving inadequate compensation, according to news website Uznews.net. Yanishev was charged with operating as a journalist without a licence and producing or storing materials that pose a threat to public safety. The judge handed down the maximum penalty.

During the past few years, dozens of artists, poets and musicians have faced oppression for their art or political views. Aside from Yanishev, two more artists have become symbolic of the struggle of Uzbek artists – those of celebrated photographer Umida Akhmedova and conceptual artist Vyacheslav Akhunov. All three were interviewed for this article.

Yanishev spoke of his worries about the future of Uzbek arts, particularly literature, and the restrictions on independent publishing, which, he feels, suffer more than performance and theatre.

"Theatres, including those performing in Russian, work quite successfully, and they manage to sell out their performances. But in literature we have problems: there is almost no possibility for writers to get published, and they are hardly able to get any readership even if they can. Most people nowadays read from a computer screen or e-books," said Yanishev.

Photographer and filmmaker Umida Akhmedova was charged with an "insult of Uzbek people" and "creation of a negative image of Uzbekistan" after the broadcast of her documentary The Burden of Virginity. She was also charged with defamation and damaging the country's image in her photo exhibit Women and Men: from Dusk till Dawn, which showed images of rural life in the country. She could have faced up to two to three years in a labour camp. She was found guilty in 2010, but the judge waived the penalty "in honour of the 18th anniversary of Uzbek independence". Akhmedova said she would appeal. According to Akhmedova, whose work has been published in The New York Times and the Wall Street Journal among others, she just filmed the traditions of her nation, →

ABOVE: Writer Sid Yanishev next to words that translate as meaning "if you can not prevent something, then take charge yourself"

→ taking an ethnographic approach. The photographer donated the series to Radio Free Europe, where they can be viewed: rferl.org/photogal lery/3213.html.

Akhmedova told Index she felt there are more restrictions on arts now than during the Soviet era. She said: "It seems like culture and cultural programmes have been totally forgotten during the independence era. During Soviet times there were arts, in one way or another, although they served the communist ideology. But there was the Khrushchev thaw in 1960s, and there was a powerful rise of arts in the Soviet Union, including Uzbekistan.

"During the Soviet times, the cultural elite of the republics interacted between each other, shared experiences, thus there was some development. Nowadays I don't see any perspectives for the part of young people; there is no base, no knowledge. If a young artist is worthy, he or she prefers to develop their talent abroad."

Conceptual artist Vyacheslav Akhunov, whose work includes performance and video art, has been fighting for his right to free movement for three years. In 2011 he was refused an exit sticker that would give him the right to leave Uzbekistan. At the same time he was banned from working in the country, and his name is even excluded from official list of artists of Uzbekistan, despite his numerous international awards. Akhunov says repressions against him are connected to his dissident views and to his sharp socially motivated art.

He said: "In our case the strategy of searching for a way out of the deadlock situation is defined by impossibility of going forward into the future. To get art back as a genuine cultural system, we need to have a completely new composition of public relations, a new society."

All the artists interviewed for this piece were worried about the future, and the pressure being placed on them and others to leave the country in order to be able to show or publish their work.

Yanishev said: "The biggest problem with artistic expression is that you can't earn a living in Uzbekistan, even professional actors have to survive with a poor salary. To make ends meet they have to dedicate themselves to popular culture or even perform at weddings."

Akhmedova would agree. "It is difficult for an artist to express oneself in Uzbekistan. An artist can survive if they have a powerful patron, and if they just 'go with the flow'. There are almost no programmes for support of arts, except a few provided by the Goethe Institut or Swiss Agency for Development and Cooperation. And there are no new ideas. Biennales of modern art in recent years were of very low quality, as their foreign participants say. One can see imitation of activity and the absence of professional art curators. There is simply no environment for an artist here."

Akhmedova added: "I don't see any perspectives, and I don't believe the government will be replaced. We don't have anyone courageous enough to challenge the system."

Speaking of the legal cases taken against her, and of the pressure that placed on her, she said: "Events related to a criminal case against me definitely affected my civic

position. I used to see the world in a more colourful way before. I feel like I have grown up since. There is more irony in my projects now, sometimes even sarcasm. And I feel I am 'the fifth column' now. I have always felt myself to be a national artist."

But she and others have not given up. Yanishev said: "Probably I will take up a topic of my persecution for one of my future books. I am not a revolutionary in my writing, I write in quite a traditional manner."

According to Akhmedova: "Art cannot be non-political. The question is what form an artist does this in. I don't know much about

It is difficult for an artist to express oneself in Uzbekistan. An artist can survive if they have a powerful patron, and if they just "go with the flow"

terms of the official propaganda, but whatever they say, they have no right to impose and dictate to everybody. I will never accept it. Total control is deadly not only for any art, but also for any development."

Both Yanishev and Akhmedova do not want to leave Uzbekistan to be able to work. "I would not like to leave my homeland. I feel lonely, sad and nostalgic while abroad. But if they put pressure on me … It is better to suffer being free than to die behind bars in my home country," said Yanishev.

Akhmedova also felt strongly about staying in her homeland: "I want to work here and now. I want to stay at home. And I do hope the things will not come to extremes, and I won't have to leave. It is a pity though that I cannot exhibit here, as everything is under such tight control".

Arts and culture have always reflected the pressures within society. The attitude towards culture is an indicator of the development of a society. The word of these →

→ three artists proves that it is impossible to restrict art to the borders of any state or nation. But the consequences of the isolation of artists from the rest of the world, that can be fatal both for art, and for society. ☒

© Nargis Tashpulatova
www.indexoncensorship.org

Nargis Tashpulatova curated art exhibitions in Tashkent from 2008 to 2011, and lectured at the National Institute until 2011. She is currently a visiting scholar at Harvard University's Davis Center for Russian and Eurasian Studies

Talk is cheap

43(4): 97/99 | DOI: 10.1177/0306422014560988

After years as an opposition politician, Jung Jin-woo was used to getting warnings from prosecutors and the police. **Steven Borowiec** interviews him to find out about the ominous relationship between the South Korean government and the most popular instant messaging app

ONE AFTERNOON JUNG Jin-woo, deputy leader of South Korea's Labour Party, received a letter from the police. They told him it was part of an investigation by prosecutors into his role during a press conference in June where the government's handling of the Sewol ferry sinking was criticised. He was taken into custody in July and released on bail shortly after on charges of participating in the press conference, which the government alleges was an illegal gathering.

The letter contained one shocking fact: the police said they were analysing Jung's private communications, mostly text messages sent via KakaoTalk, South Korea's main instant messaging app. Jung's communications, the letter said, were being considered as evidence in the case against him for leading the press conference.

Jung says, upon reading the letter, he felt the kind of shock and embarrassment that comes with having been unknowingly spied on during what he'd believed to be private moments. "I was shocked to hear that not just my private communications, but those of all the people I'd communicated with had been somehow brought into the open," Jung said during an interview at his Seoul office.

Jung believed the letter also suggested illegal co-operation between KakaoTalk (now Daum Kakao) and the South Korean government. If prosecutors had his chat records, KakaoTalk must have agreed to hand them over. The government and the company must have colluded as part of a relationship that had never been made public. This violated Jung's rights under South Korea's Personal Information Protection Act and if his communications had been seized, presumably he wasn't the only one.

Jung decided to go public with what he'd learned. He called a press conference in central Seoul where he argued that Daum Kakao, a company to which millions of South Koreans entrust their private communications, had been co-opted by the government and in the process sacrificed its users' privacy.

He wasn't arrested that day, but using its strongest Orwellian language, the prosecution called his announcement an incitement to "national chaos".

The consequences of Jung's revelations have been a public relations nightmare for the company that owns and operates the country's largest instant messaging service.

After launching in 2010, KakaoTalk quickly became South Korea's main platform for instant communication and now boasts more than 100 million users worldwide. It reached a large audience after making the app free to download. It also has a →

ABOVE: Millions of South Koreans use instant messaging apps. Here, passengers use mobile phones on a Seoul subway train

→ diverse range of unique and popular emoticons, the sale of which provides the company with much of its revenue.

KakaoTalk was also attractive to users for its comparatively long storage of chats. That feature is also part of what made KakaoTalk attractive to prosecutors, as it made it possible to acquire extensive chat records.

When Jung came out with his explosive allegations, the company hastily arranged a press conference at its Seoul headquarters where the chief executive Lee Sir-goo admitted to having complied with a request from prosecutors to turn over Jung's chat records in violation of South Korean law. Lee pledged that they would not co-operate

again when authorities asked for a user's chat records. He also announced that the company would cut the time chats are stored to three days from seven, and that the company had sophisticated security technology that could block any unwanted surveillance.

"When there is no social consensus on the law and privacy, our policy will put privacy first in any case," Lee said at the press conference, according to the Associated Press.

The press conference ended with Lee performing a near 90-degree bow, a customary Korean gesture of contrition.

Kim Seung-joo, a professor at Korea University Graduate School of Information Security, explained that in South Korea there are three different types of investigative warrants, and only with the type reserved for the most serious cases are prosecutors authorised to seize a citizen's private communications. Jung was arrested on a lower level warrant.

"Kakao handing over the chat records like they did in Jung's case is clearly illegal," Kim said in a telephone interview.

In an apparent illustration of users' resultant loss of trust in Daum Kakao, Telegram, a German messaging app that provides similar services, added two million new Korean users in two weeks in early October, according to market researcher Rankey.com. In South Korea this is referred to as "cyber exile", as many felt they couldn't trust Daum Kakao to keep their communications private.

Daum Kakao has refused to disclose how many users left the service in that period, and has declined to comment to Index.

For many South Koreans, the story of Daum Kakao's co-operation with prosecutors harks back to the repressive governments that ruled the country in the 1970s and 1980s. Current president Park Geun-hye is the daughter of Park Chung-hee, the military strongman who ruled the country from 1961-79 and suspended most civic and political rights, arguing this would facilitate the country's economic development.

In 2011, South Korea's Freedom House press freedom ranking fell from "free" to "partly free" and has remained there ever since. In knocking South Korea down a notch, the Washington-based watchdog pointed to "increasing official censorship, particularly of online content, as well as the government's attempt to influence media outlets' news and information content".

The rule of President Park Geun-hye, in office since February 2013, has had a further chilling effect. In September, Park held a meeting where she said that online insults against her constituted an insult to the country as a whole. Park said such rumours were "deepening divisions" in South Korean society and had to be rooted out. She made comments about the need for the government to monitor the internet in order to prevent false or harmful information being spread.

And Jung's case is evidence of how South Korea's political and social development has not kept pace with its rapid technological progress. South Korea has embraced the internet as a means to facilitate its economic development, but authoritarian political instincts sometimes clash with the freedom that widespread online access has unleashed.

Jung believes the government is trying to stifle criticism by eliminating the space for private communication. He says he no longer

South Korea's authoritarian political instincts sometimes clash with the freedom

feels comfortable discussing sensitive topics with friends or colleagues, and believes self-censorship is becoming common. "People will refrain from making any critical statements, online and even in person," he said.

Prosecutors obtained Jung's past chat records and have told him that his present communication is not being monitored. Still, Jung isn't any longer confident that he enjoys the privacy guaranteed by South Korean law. He said, "I'd been acting under the assumption that what I said was private, but now I know that wasn't the case. There's a feeling of safety that's now gone." ⌧

© Steven Borowiec
www.indexoncensorship.org

Steven Borowiec is a journalist based in South Korea

Fear of faith

43(4): 100/104 | DOI: 10.1177/0306422014561163

Persecution of Chinese Christians has included demolition of churches, removing crosses and driving services underground. As Christmas approaches, **Jemimah Steinfeld** reports on a difficult year

LIFE FOR THE inhabitants of the south-eastern port city of Wenzhou, 350 miles south of Shanghai, known as the "Jerusalem of China" because of its large Christian population and abundance of churches, 2014 has been a bad year. Many churches have been demolished by the local authorities or have had their crosses removed. Dozens of people were injured in the process as congregations defended their churches. The targets were mostly churches that had previously been tolerated by the ruling communist party and had frequently been cited as evidence of religious freedom in what is officially an atheist country.

Local government officials claimed the demolitions were part of a campaign to target illegal structures in the province. But their statement was contradicted by leaked party documents, which singled out churches and folk religious sites in a "three rectifica-tions and one demolition" campaign.

Elsewhere in China, a Chinese pastor at a church in Henan province will celebrate Christmas from a prison cell. Zhang Shaojie, who led the Nanle County Christian Church, was found guilty of fraud and of "gather-ing crowds to disturb public order" in July and jailed for 12 years. His daughter, her husband and their son fled to the US imme-diately afterwards.

Then, on the border with North Korea, hundreds of missionaries and foreign workers in Christian charity groups were forced to leave the country. Some who re-main have spoken of an atmosphere of fear, according to a report by Voice of America.

These incidents come as a recent govern-ment pledge to nationalise Christianity is believed to be a trick to bring underground churches to the surface in order to better control them. In August, Wang Zuoan, direc-tor of the State Administration for Religious Affairs, officially announced at a Shanghai conference on Christianity: "The construc-tion of Chinese Christian theology should adapt to China's national condition and integrate with Chinese culture." The great-est fear, beyond the immediate, is that both these moves are forerunners for a wider cam-paign against Christianity.

Bob Fu, founder and president of China Aid, which provides legal aid to Christians in China, has called the recent persecution of Christians under Xi Jinping's leadership the worst since the Cultural Revolution. Fu is not someone to mince his words. The US-based pastor converted to Christianity at the end of the 1980s. He then went on to start a campus church at Renmin University in Beijing and a secret bible school in Fangshan District, Bei-jing. In 1996, he and his wife were detained for illegal evangelising. Released unharmed, they soon sought sanctuary in the US.

Speaking to Index, Clay Finley at China Aid described the persecution as

ABOVE: Chinese Catholics pray during a Christmas mass at the Xishiku Cathedral Catholic church on Christmas Day in Beijing, 2011

"significantly worse under Xi Jinping than it was under his predecessor". But, he said: "The reasons for that change of policy are not entirely clear."

One suggestion is that Christianity is becoming a victim of its own success. A remarkable trend in China in recent years is the explosive growth of Christianity. The number of Christians is now estimated at between 100 million and 130 million, more than the membership of the communist party. The church has the potential to act as a unifying force for political opposition to the government's authority: it cuts across regional and class divides.

Christianity arrived in China during the Tang dynasty (618-907), establishing itself

The number of Christians is now estimated at between 100 million and 130 million, more than the membership of the communist party

from the 19th century under the influence of Western powers. The 20th century dealt the faith a series of blows. Most significantly, →

→ when Mao came to power in 1949, religion was deemed an enemy and described as "poison". During the Cultural Revolution (1966-76), the eradication of religious life became a top priority. Christians went underground.

Since the death of Mao in 1976, Christians have been able to create more space for themselves and are tolerated to a degree. There have even been encouraging sounds from the communist party. China's last president, Hu Jintao, described elements of Christianity as compatible with his vision of China as a "harmonious society".

But the government has continued to preach atheism and places restrictions on faith. All churches are required to register

Christians face jail for distributing religious materials, founding unlicensed house churches and other perceived transgressions

with the government. The printing of bibles is banned; Catholics cannot recognise the authority of the Vatican; and proselytising is an offence. Christians face jail for distributing religious materials, founding unlicensed house churches and other perceived transgressions.

Finally, membership of a church and of the communist party are mutually exclusive (though it's rumoured plenty of communist party members attend churches in secret). Given the benefits open to communist party members, this is a serious deterrent. Chen Xiaomi, who has just started university in Sichuan province, tells Index about how her grandparents converted to Christianity a few years back. Following suit is not an option for her at this stage, as she would like to join the communist party.

"Carrying on the work of the church is not easy," says Brent Fulton, president of China Source, which tracks Christian life in China.

"There is a huge grey area in terms of what is or is not allowed. I admire the ability of today's young urban Christians to walk carefully in this grey area, being willing to explore new opportunities as they arise and not giving up when they run up against obstacles. By doing so they have greatly expanded the social space which Christianity in China occupies."

Wang Meimei, a 32-year-old practicing Christian in Beijing, speaks of the hostility she experiences on a daily basis. "People mock me when I say I am Christian," she tells Index.

At university, Meimei was actively discouraged by her teacher from practising her faith. She would never attempt to convert people and would not post about her faith on social media platforms.

It's a similar story for Diane (not her real name), a young woman who attends a local church in Hebei province, near Beijing. She is not comfortable asking for 25 December off work and instead will celebrate Christmas on 27 December.

But not everyone or every part of the country appears to have had the same experience. "No, I've not noticed any increase in repression in 2014," says Meimei. Though neither Meimei nor Diane have heard of the recent crackdowns going on elsewhere in their country, a testament to how tightly controlled information is in China, and one questions to what extent their sense of security is premised on false information.

Fulton picks up on this point. He says that if the events of 2014 are part of a crackdown, it is not widespread at present. Should we be worried? "Not from the standpoint of government repression," he says.

"Christians in China do face significant restrictions and (as in the case of Wenzhou) sometimes outright hostility from officials.

However, most Christians I talk to are more concerned about the future of church leadership, the effects of materialism upon the church, and whether or not the church will be able to meaningfully engage with China's urban society."

Fulton does concede some cause for concern. While China's current president Xi has not come out as either for or against Christianity, Fulton says, "he is emphasising some themes that could have repercussion for Christians". Nationalism is one such example. Christianity is often portrayed as foreign, so campaigns to increase nationalist sentiment could be married to campaigns against Christianity.

Fulton also explains how the regime is getting tougher on dissident voices (see Index's previous report on the crackdown on human rights lawyers, Guarding the Guards, Volume 43, 3/2014) and the effects could spill over into the church. This has happened during previous anti-crime and anti-dissident campaigns.

As Christmas trees go up in shopping hubs across the country (with many missing the religious significance and leaving them up way into the new year), Christians wait with bated breath to see what the future will bring. ☒

© Jemimah Steinfeld
www.indexoncensorship.org

Jemimah Steinfeld is a contributing editor to Index on Censorship, and formerly reported for CNN and Time Out in Beijing. She tweets @JFSteinfeld

A Christian in Hong Kong

....

*Journalist **Hannah Leung** on her experiences as a Christian living in the city, and fears Christians have about the future*

Being a Christian in Hong Kong comes at the ease you would expect in any open society. Perhaps the difficult task would be finding a church that suits your needs. Even among the expat community, there are plenty of options.

In Hong Kong, a friend introduced me to Alpha (a beginner's guide to Christianity), and the sessions are open to all English speakers living in Hong Kong. I found the mix of locals and expats a welcome and stark contrast from China. In the mainland, locals and foreigners are not allowed to gather together for purposes of worship, unless the service is state-approved ahead of time.

But now Christians from Hong Kong are grappling with a new feeling: a fear that one day, the landscape could resemble what's across the sea in the mainland, the other half in the "one country two systems".

That may be one of the reasons that some Christians are key players in the pro-democracy protests, including self-identified Christian Josh Wong, who at only 17 years old has become the face of the movement.

The Occupy Central campaign may have started as a protest for greater democracy in Hong Kong, but it's now encompassing issues such as religious freedom.

In Beijing, a foreigner can enjoy the privilege of choosing a church, but this requires bringing something else to a place from worship aside from curiosity: a foreign passport.

That is what deterred me from finding a church during my four years living in Beijing, a city where churches often function as decorative backdrops for wedding photos. Having grown up in a Christian family in the United States, I considered re-exploring my faith. The notion, however, that only those with a foreign identity could benefit from religious freedom discouraged me.

This isn't to say that access to Christianity is unattainable. For example, Beijing International Christian Fellowship is one of the main churches for foreigners, with over 3,000 members.

The website comes with this disclaimer though: "As an international church in the People's Republic of China, the local authorities have given us permission to meet together for worship each Sunday, however, our religious activities are limited to foreign photo ID holders ... We encourage Beijing International Christian Fellowship members to actively seek friendships within the local Chinese communities and pray for opportunities to invite them to a local Chinese church."

In the Alpha group I currently attend in Hong Kong, of the dozen or so participants, around half hail from Hong Kong. The other half is a mixture of Americans, British Taiwanese, and everyone in between. Grace Fan, head of one of the Alpha groups at Soloman's Porch, is from Hong Kong but spent a year in Beijing.

"I had just started going back to church again when I was based in China, I went to several churches and underground churches while I was there. The passport-for-entry type churches did feel really segregated and classist, but that's really the only way that China can control 'outside' thinking," she said.

Not all Christians support the protest and some churches have been divided over the issue. Reverend Tin Yau Yuen of the Methodist Congregations of Hong Kong issued an open letter, A Church at Crossroads, which explained he was opening the church as a refuge to people who were hurt in the demonstrations, and why he felt he should.

For now, what is at stake is the future for Hong Kong schools and churches? Is the fight for democracy so intricately intertwined with Christianity that churches should feel obliged to take a stand? For schools that are religiously affiliated, do they have an obligation to protect students? Or, is the cause so muddled that churches should just maintain their silence? Either way, the religion and the pro-democracy movement are both grappling with the Communist Party of China's limitations on their currently enjoyed freedoms. X

© Hannah Leung
www.indexoncensorship.org

Hannah Leung is a journalist based in Hong Kong

COUNTERPOINTS ARTS

Paper Project 2014, photo: Diana Varveropoulou

WE ARE A CREATIVE ARTS AND CULTURAL ORGANISATION EXPLORING REFUGEE AND MIGRANT EXPERIENCES

OUR MISSION IS TO SUPPORT, PRODUCE AND PROMOTE THE ARTS BY & ABOUT MIGRANTS AND REFUGEES, SEEKING TO ENSURE THAT THEIR CULTURAL AND ARTISTIC CONTRIBUTIONS ARE RECOGNIZED AND WELCOMED WITHIN BRITISH HISTORY AND CULTURE.

WE DO THIS BY DEVELOPING CREATIVE PROJECTS TO REPRESENT THE STORIES AND EXPERIENCES OF REFUGEES AND MIGRANTS. WE COLLABORATE WITH ARTISTS, ARTS/CULTURAL AND EDUCATIONAL ORGANIZATIONS AND CIVIL SOCIETY ACTIVISTS. WE WORK NATIONALLY AND INTERNATIONALLY.

Information about our many projects and unique way of working with partners can be found at: www. counterpointsarts.org.uk
Contact us on: 0044 (0) 20 7012 1761; or at hello@counterpointsarts.org.uk
Visit us at: Unit 2.3 Hoxton Works, 128 Hoxton Street, London N1 6SH.
Follow us at: @CounterArts

Time travel to web of the past and future

43(4): 106/109 | DOI: 10.1177/0306422014561180

More than 20 years ago, Index asked **Mike Godwin** to write about the arrival of the online world and tell us what the future looked like. In this issue we ask him to revisit his article and assess what he got right, and what challenges remain today

WHEN I LOOK back at the piece now, I'm a little startled to find that it holds up well enough: yes, the internet – we capitalised it as "Internet" back then – did become a worldwide forum for freedom of expression, as I predicted, and, yes, ordinary citizens in open societies have already become accustomed to claiming freedom of the press just as much as they have long claimed freedom of speech.

My daughter, who was not yet born when I wrote that article two decades ago (extracts of which can be seen in the graphic opposite), has been accustomed her whole life to speaking to the rest of the world easily and cheaply. Mass-media audiences are no longer reserved for highly capitalised, highly centralised media institutions such as newspapers and broadcasters. Audiences are now reachable by ordinary individuals, who may be equipped with little more than a mobile phone.

Although one could foresee the democratic potential of the internet in 1993, it was by no means clear that debates over internet censorship and government anxiety over internet communications would extend more than two decades into the future. As

it happens, 1993 – a year that marked the internet's transition from something that few folks talked about into something that one's parents, grandparents and children used to stay in contact – also turned out to be a pivotal year for internet freedom of expression. This was the last full year in which governments around the world seemed mainly to ignore the disruptive potential of a hugely democratic new mass medium. As I was instinctively aware at the time, it was a golden age that couldn't last.

The following year, 1994, saw the beginning of a series of legal and policy battles in the United States and around the world over internet freedom. Unsurprisingly, given the USA's cultural roots in Puritanism, the most public of the early internet policy debates centred on the censorship of sexual content. Cultural conservatives were confronted with a medium where individual computer hobbyists enthusiastically published sexual content online in ways that couldn't easily be censored. Plus there was the ever-decreasing and sometimes nonexistent cost of duplication and redistribution.

A few early hobbyist pornographers – or mom-and-pop entrepreneurs like Robert →

first it does not seem like speaking or ng at all: you invoke a command at computer keyboard, and after a short e you hear a dialtone and a rapid series nes coming from your modem. One or ings later, the modem on the other end

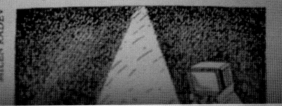

article would be inaccurate, or the facts to reflect a particula recently, opinion polls showed be unsympathetic to media con press-pool reporting during On the sexual expression

At first it does not seem like speaking or writing at all: you invoke a command at your computer keyboard, and after a short pause you hear a dialtone and a rapid series of tones coming from your modem.

It may be a hobbyist's bulletin board system, a university's mainframe computer or a commercial information service. But no matter what you are connected to, you have just become another explorer on the newest frontier in the exercise of the freedom of expression: the electronic frontier. Coming to grips with this frontier — and the stories and issues that it will generate — will be a major challenge for everyone committed to the spread of freedom of speech, writing and thought.

But for all the accelerating presence of the computer in newsrooms, at universities, in publishing houses, at broadcasting studios and, perhaps most important, in the home, too many of us still think primarily of words printed on paper when we hear the term 'freedom of the press'.

Since most US citizens don't own a newspaper or radio station, the nearest they can come to public debate is through writing a letter to the editor, taking part in a demonstration or soliciting signatures on a door-to-door petition drive.

The new computer-based fora for debate and information exchange are witnessing perhaps the greatest exercise of freedom of expression that the USA and the rest of the world has ever seen.

Increasingly, ordinary people will use online communications as an integral part of their daily activities. Citizens' groups will rely on electronic fora to organise events, develop policies, conduct meetings and lobby public and private organisations.

MILEN RADEV

→ and Carleen Thomas who sold access to pornographic pictures on an online bulletin board – were prosecuted in the early 1990s. But it was quickly apparent to the USA's religious-right anti-porn activists that the deterrent aspects of such prosecutions weren't going to be enough. So they soon moved to design US Senator Jim Exon's Communications Decency Act, which mutated only slightly before being incorporated into Congress's Telecommunications Reform Act of 1996.

Ironically, the anti-porn crusaders' legislative triumph unwittingly did internet-freedom activists like me a favour; the CDA's scope was so broad, so ungrounded in constitutional doctrine, that it was quickly and effectively challenged in US courts in 1996, with a decisive Supreme

The anti-porn crusaders' legislative triumph unwittingly did internet-freedom activists like me a favour

Court victory for internet freedom in 1997. The case, Reno v. ACLU, overwhelmingly affirmed a lower court's finding that the CDA was unconstitutional and the Supreme Court judges squarely classified the internet as a medium protected by the first amendment.

In a very short space of time, the moral panic about sexual content on the internet had led to judicial recognition that expression on the internet was as deserving of first amendment protection as expression in newspapers or in books. Maybe even more so, since the first amendment's "freedom of the press" prerogatives had been technologically expanded beyond traditional publishers to ordinary citizens with internet access.

Of course, a freedom of expression victory in the USA does not guarantee freedom

elsewhere around the world. And, in fact, it did not even permanently guarantee US internet freedom. Although constitutional lawyers, like me, had long believed that freedom of expression depends from time to time on the right of individuals to speak and publish anonymously and privately, we also knew that police and intelligence agencies in the US and worldwide had grown accustomed – I actually prefer the word addicted to using technology to intercept and capture private conversations.

The signals intelligence (SIGINT) mavens at the National Security Agency essentially intercepted information above or about electronic communications and they weren't dummies. They knew that digital communications, and especially those protected by encryption, had the potential to force the NSA and like-minded folks at the Federal Bureau of Investigation and other law-enforcement agencies into withdrawal. So even as the public debate in the 1990s centred on internet pornography, or the publication of bomb-making instructions, or digital copyright infringement, a more private debate was being played out, as the US government made efforts to guarantee their right to what one may call the "wiretappability" of internet communications. The NSA and like-minded agencies correctly guessed that the internet would increasingly be central to how we all communicate. These agencies' reaction to this development, though cloaked in sober pronouncements about "national security" and law-enforcement needs, were driven by panic, similar to how an addict might react to the prospect of involuntary detox in a jail cell.

And, clearly, this response to the prospect of losing the ability to engage in bulk surveillance has haunted the NSA and its partner in the UK, GCHQ to the present day. Even as activists like Cindy Cohn, currently legal director of my first employer, the Electronic Frontier Foundation, have continued to litigate for freedom to use encryption to guarantee privacy, as well as for legal limitations on intelligence and law enforcement agencies' power to snoop, the agencies have continued to labour in secret to expand their legal and some arguably illegal powers to capture private communications. The same technological advances (powerful digital devices and mass digital storage connected to worldwide networks) that have expanded individuals' ability to exercise their mass medium freedom of expression, have also expanded the agencies' ability to gather and search the world's public and private conversations.

It's compelling to note, in this post-Snowden revelations era, that the two developed nations that have proudly committed themselves, as a matter of political doctrine, to being open societies are also the first to have the sheer monumental scope of their surveillance practices exposed to public review and criticism. The Snowden revelations have succeeded where many activists had failed, in putting the issues squarely at the centre of public debate in these developed democratic countries.

Now that the debate has begun, we must labour to make sure the right balances are struck, not just in the UK and USA, but also, to vindicate our belief in individual freedom, privacy and dignity, to the rest of the world.

As my own work has increasingly grown more international especially my recent work for Wikipedia and for Internews, I've seen the same governmental moral panics about disruptive speech and disruptive limitations on surveillance begin to emerge in other countries. With the possible exception of Antarctica, no continent is immune to this general panic, although it may manifest itself in a range of particular, idiosyncratic forms. But whether one is discussing digital copyright in Latin America's free-trade agreements, the lamentable "right to be forgotten" in Europe, the suppression of purported blasphemy in Islamic countries,

the investment in surveillance infrastructure in Nigeria, the post-Mumbai terror attack amendments to India's Information Technology Act, the Great Firewall of China, or the targeting of social media dissenters in Thailand, Cambodia and now Hong Kong, one thing is clear: in sharp contrast to the world of 1993, today's governments have moved regulation of expression on the internet to the top of their agendas.

That's frightening, but there's a silver lining to what's currently happening in the "cloud" – it turns out that the democratising potential of internet communications is actually living up to my 1993 hype. And activists around the world, such as the ones who passed the Marco Civil da Internet in Brazil or those who have crafted the Magna Carta for Philippines Internet Freedom, know that

Today's governments have moved regulation of expresssion on the internet to the top of their agendas

they can no longer merely react to threats of governmental censorship and surveillance. They must proactively set the agendas for the governments in this century in terms that guarantee individual freedom and dignity. Fortunately, the internet itself has given us the tools we need to do just that. ☒

© Mike Godwin
www.indexoncensorship.org

For the original article, see New Frontiers: A Visitor's Guide, Volume 22, 2/1993.

Mike Godwin has served as first staff counsel for the Electronic Frontier Foundation, as general counsel for the Wikimedia Foundation, and as senior legal adviser for Internews

ABOVE: Access to books is limited in China. Here, children learn to read in Xin Zhou Zhen village

CULTURE

In this section

Language lessons

43(4): 112/114 | DOI: 10.1177/0306422014561392

Author **Chen Xiwo** on the value of being published in translation, but why he mostly cares about his books being read by Chinese people

TWENTY YEARS AGO, I left China to go to Japan, but then I returned in order to write. One result of that was that I came in for a lot of stick from family and friends. They felt I was deliberately walking into trouble. But this is my country and these are hard times. I need to be here, to bear witness to the hard times, and to resist. So that's why I've got involved in supporting people fighting for their legal rights, something a lot of people thought was a strange thing to do. Why would a writer get involved in politics? Well, I feel that writers are, to some degree, a bit like politicians in that they cannot leave their country, no matter how dangerous or hard life is, because that is where they "operate". As soon as writers go into exile, they wither and die, like a tree without soil. Take Thomas Mann, for example. When he left Nazi Germany for United States in 1938, he confidently declared: "Where I am, there is Germany!" Unfortunately, his life as a writer withered from then on; Germany was not where he was but where Hitler was.

A comparison between writers and politicians may seem strange. But in a dictatorship such as China, politics is everywhere, it undermines basic human dignities, even threatens life itself. Chinese writers do not have the luxury of standing aloof from politics. They have to confront political questions first and foremost. If they do skirt around them, they are not true writers. In the UK, a writer without any political consciousness can still be a good one, but in China, a writer who lacks political consciousness is bogus.

The same goes for publishing. When I say that there is no freedom to write in China, I actually mean no freedom to publish. Of course one can write, but that writing means nothing if it ends up in a drawer. Writing is, after all, speaking out. The authorities in China know this perfectly well, so they enforce strict controls over publication. They do this by forcing publishers to 'self-regulate', that is, to act as their own censors.

Under these circumstances, it is, of course, a good thing that works can be published, and published in their entirety, outside China. However, any book of mine published outside China is set within China, where I "operate", and there is no doubt that overseas readers can find it hard to comprehend what I am writing about. They may even not care very much. As I have said before, I can say what I want outside China, but how many people are listening? And how many of them understand what I am saying? This is the question we really need to ask.

It is the same with publishing. Since publishing is not free in China, a published writer who says he or she is "speaking out" is just talking nonsense. This is what it means to be a writer in China today. Huge

ABOVE: Access to books and the internet are limited in China. Here, a man uses his iPad inside a Shanghai coffee shop

numbers of books are published but they are not real literature.

To be quite honest, when I talk to foreign readers, I often feel there is a gulf between us. This is inevitable, because we live in different cultures, and confront different problems and realities. There are foreign readers who care deeply about China's problems but if they have not lived there, then China's complex problems just seem impenetrably weird and hard to fathom. I can only convey very simple concepts to them. There are, of course, some Chinese writers who consciously aim their writing at a foreign readership, tailoring it to things they are interested in.

The result is that much of what is published outside China is of questionable value.

Without question, Chinese writers should write primarily for Chinese readers, because

I can say what I want outside China, but how many people are listening?

only they can fully understand the life these stories describe. The best thing that can happen to a Chinese writer is that you write a sketch and the readers immediately get →

→ the subtleties of the joke and burst out laughing with you; or you have a dig at something and they get the point without needing any explanations, and you know that because you see the intuitive understanding in their eyes. Or you tell a story of suffering, and there is instant empathy, at the deepest emotional level.

For a writer not to be published in their own country is the greatest tragedy they can face. But that is precisely the situation in China, one that genuine writers face all the time. So, for them, it is really important to be able to publish outside China. Firstly, it allows good writing which cannot come out in China, to see the light of day and be preserved. Secondly, these works may have an impact overseas and that impact will

their values are pro-Western. If they had the choice between a CCP-approved novel and a Chinese novel which was selling well outside China, they would undoubtedly go for the latter. So from this point of view, publishing overseas is important because there is a chance it will exert some influence even within official circles. ⊠

© Chen Xiwo
www.indexoncensorship.org

Translated by Nicky Harman

For a writer not to be published in their own country is the greatest tragedy they can face

gradually percolate back to China. We live in the information age, and the internet is essential to this. Even though the communist party does its best to control the internet and blocks many foreign-based web sites, people have software that enables them to breach the party's "Great Firewall". Once they reach those sites, they read what has been published outside China.

No thinking person in China trusts party propaganda any more. They prefer to believe news and information from overseas. It is worth pointing out that those who wield power in China do not believe the party line either. I know many party members, who privately say worse things about their party than ordinary non-party people do because, from their position at the centre of the system, they can see its evils only too clearly. They want to protect that system in order to protect their own vested interests. But

Chen Xiwo teaches comparative literature at Fuijan Normal University and has published seven major novels. The English translation of I Love My Mum (Make-Do) was published in 2010

Spirit unleashed

43(4): 116/124 | DOI: 10.1177/0306422014560675

Award-winning Australian poet **Diane Fahey** was prompted to write her latest work by the tragic and horrific death of a young asylum seeker. The poem is published here for the first time

LEO SEEMANPILLAI WAS born in a village in northern Sri Lanka. When he was a baby his father, a fisherman, wrapped him in banana leaves and hid him in the rainforest to keep him safe from the violence of the civil war. Leo's family, who are Tamils, fled to India when he was six; his parents and three brothers still live in a refugee camp in Tamil Nadu. Because of the harassment of Tamils by the Indian authorities in the camp, Leo returned to Sri Lanka when he was 18 and stayed for two years, but during that time he was tortured by the military and, at the end, beaten by police and left for dead after a blow with a rifle butt to his head.

Leo returned to India but was again harassed, and so undertook the long journey to Australia, during which he was placed in a detention camp in Sumatra, Indonesia, for six months, and was also tortured there.

When he reached Australia by boat he lived in Darwin, before settling in Geelong. His abiding hope of becoming an Australian citizen, and eventually bringing his family to Australia, was rendered impossible by the announcement in October 2013 by Scott Morrison, the minister for immigration and border protection, that all Tamil asylum seekers would eventually be returned to Sri Lanka.

While living in Geelong, Leo, who had wanted to be a Catholic priest earlier in his life, became part of a church community, volunteered in an aged care facility, joined Amnesty International, donated blood to the Red Cross and registered as an organ donor; his friends sometimes needed to persuade him not to give what money he had away.

Leo took his own life, by self immolation, in June 2014.

A Death in Winter
In Memory of Leo Seemanpillai

1.
Let me, first, take my bearings
by speaking of weather, the season.
A spell of summer in late autumn
has lasted until this first day of winter,
will last beyond it.
I step outside, tilt my face up
to receive the sun.

Inside the cave of my closed eyes
a cloudy webbed white
is set against lava-red;
as in a lit cavern
there are many flashpoints of mica,
each a single flare then gone.
Soon my eyes will hold
the image of a burning man.
On this day, at 9.15 a.m.
Leo Seemanpillai
died in a Melbourne Hospital
after an act of self-immolation.

2.
I read the newspapers,
learn of Leo's life:
of how, when he was six,
his family fled from Sri Lanka
to a camp for refugees in India.
Returning as a young man to Sri Lanka
he was tortured by the military;
beaten by police and left to die.
Back in India, more persecution.
Then the journey to Australia –
en route, detention in Sumatra,
grave abuse and cruelty there.
In sum, a tidal wave of suffering
has broken over Leo Seemanpillai
and left him on an unlit shore.
Once here in Australia
he responds to others in need
with generosity, kindness,
turns his suffering into hope,
sows hope in others.
When, two days before his death,
a loved gift, a turquoise tile
painted with a butterfly, breaks,
he laughs it off.

3.
Leo Seemanpillai arrived in Darwin from India on 9 January 2013,
and was held in detention before being granted a bridging visa
with work rights in June of that year.

When he settles in Geelong
Leo, who knows English well,
may have seen the bumper stickers –

ABOVE: Diane Fahey

They came. They saw. They sank.
But here he will find friendship,
enter the life of his community.
In the week after Leo's death
a workmate will speak of his keenness
to do his job – one day a week
cleaning trucks, mowing the lawn;
of how he'd lay out his uniform with care,
finish his lunch break five minutes early
to return to work.

4. *"Anyone who may have come from Sri Lanka should know that*
they will go back to Sri Lanka."
– Scott Morrison, Australian minister for immigration and border
protection, October 2013

ABOVE: A memorial for asylum seeker Leo Seemanpillai, with members of the Queenscliffe Rural Australians for Refugees group

A man on fire
is running from the front garden
of the house where he lived
into the street.
A neighbour who is a nurse
tries to help him.
Later that day, in a Melbourne hospital
dying in agony
he asks for his organs to be donated.
His parents, speaking from their refugee camp,
support his wishes.
Five people will benefit
from the gift of
an eye, both kidneys, his liver and one lung
from Leo Seemanpillai.

5. A man casts off and rows
across a lake of fire

in the small boat of his body
because he feels, because
everything he knows now tells him,
that he can do no other.
This last act of torture
that will end all torture.

6.
How can I venture
to speak of such things?
I step back now,
insist that I do not know
what Leo's sufferings might have been like.
I can only create –
for myself, for others –
a space for imagining.

7.
A friend rings in the night from England.
Of the terrifying mayhem
that is now, (again), Iraq, she says:
"When we can see no clear way forward,
no way to offer help or hope,
the way forward
is to travel within
and dwell inside the cave of stillness.
There will be found the peace we can offer."
But here, now, in Australia
new choices can be made,
bad decisions reversed,
so that the tortured, the persecuted,
will not be sent back to the hellholes –
old ones, new ones –
where persecutors hold sway.

8.
"If I'm deported back to Sri Lanka, torture is certain because I'm a Tamil."
– from the journal of Leo Seemanpillai

In a class on Mindfulness
I take to heart these words:
Be aware of each breath; treasure it.
You will never have this breath again.
I have started to imagine
all the breaths Leo might have had,
the days and years he might have had,
and the kindness friends and others

would have known from him,
and he from them.

9.
Leo had, pinned to his wall, a slip of paper that read,
"It is our light, not our darkness, that most frightens us."
Leo, one of the light-bearers,
had reason, though, to fear the dark.
When a friend gave him a night-light
to help him sleep, he told her
it was like "a shiny moon"
always there inside his room.

10.
I watch a mica-cloud of midges
above the winter sun –
small winter suns themselves;
their shaped flux set against
that far-off cypress, like dust motes
in a green-walled room.
I think of sky-loving murmurations,
of spaces within the mind, the heart,
drawn tightly close
then flowing outwards, oceanic,
within a split second.
When I look up again
the clouds are seamed with chrysolite;
no sun; the air blank.

11. *During a stay in a mental hospital early in 2014 because of*
severe depression, Leo tried to hang himself with a towel.

Who, exactly, is ill here?
Doctors sometimes forsake
medical language, to speak of
heart murmurs, shadows on a lung.
We live now with fear,
its murmurs, its shadows,
carried in the heart, the lungs:
the fear of losing –
even of sharing –
the smallest part of what we possess.
Some of us have
plighted our troth with fear:
in the caves of the heart, the lungs,
loving our fear.
It is time to breathe freely, to feel.

12.
On the day I hear of Leo's death
I pass a tall maple,
its star-like leaves, blood-red
and flame-red, irradiated.
Many leaves have fallen,
many leaves are still hanging;
all will be gone by the Solstice.
Tree of fire, tree of blood.

13.
In search of spiritual composure,
I walk the cliff path
under a cloud-marbled white dome –
having just missed, I'm told,

They carry their bodies, their spirits, so quietly. Some of them, I know, have cigarette burns on their backs and many other scars

two sea-eagles flying around the bay,
their eyes mapping the coast.
Back home I listen to Early Choral music
that has echoed inside cathedral domes,
caves of light mixed with incense,
each note a mica glint
ascending into the light beyond the light we see –
that further light
that presses back on us.
We live,
sub specie aeternitatis –
"under the aspect of eternity".

14. *"We get to listen to the silence in the cave,*
and perhaps we can even hear our own heartbeats."
– *Werner Herzog*

And now I watch
Herzog's *Cave of Forgotten Dreams* –
a film that takes me inside the Chauvet Cave:
sealed by a rockslide for twenty thousand years,
newly discovered.
A held light presses into the darkness

and that ancient darkness,
pricked with mica glints,
presses back against the light.
There are scratches from bear claws
on walls painted with horses,
wild and strange,
in the mystery of their nature,
the light in their eyes
preserved through thirty millennia.
And, among bones on the floor of the Cave –
the province now of archaeologists,
forensic scientists – there is
the skeleton of a golden eagle.
Outside, in this present world,
and less than twenty miles from Chauvet Cave,
run-off from a nuclear power station
has formed toxic lagoons where crocodiles
multiply, mutate.
A white crocodile with white eyes
curves up to the surface, to breathe.

15.
Spirit of Life
may you guard the afflicted,
those who have suffered
beyond reason, beyond imagining,
those who fear certain persecution –
may a haven be found for them
somewhere this side of death.
Spirit of Life
save us from the white crocodiles.

16.
Some speak of
the solace of eternity
some believe that in death
we become part of everything,
our spark of awareness
carried by all the winds that blow,
then above them
into the light beyond light.
May Leo
rest in peace
May his mother and father, his brothers,
know peace
May the many people here who loved him
know peace.

17.
"We want to be by our son's side when his funeral takes place.
That way our lives will be more peaceful."
– Leo's father

The Australian government refused the visas applied for by Leo's family
so that they might attend his funeral.
As three Tamil men at a microphone
sing a long hymn in Tamil
the Basilica fills with an undertow of sound,
a faint bass humming by many voices
that I cannot account for until, at the end,
Leo's coffin is carried out
followed by a long procession of Tamil men
who'd sat, unseen by me, at the front.
They carry their bodies, their spirits, so quietly.
Some of them, I know,
have cigarette burns on their backs
and many other scars.
We all wait in the clear winter light.
It is achieved.
The funeral car starts its slow journey.
The elderly woman I had sat beside,
who'd travelled three hours to be here,
turns down my offer of a lift,
chooses, despite her damaged leg,
to walk with her stroller
to the railway station.
"It'll be thinking time,' she says,
calmly passionate.
'There is a lot to think about". X

© Diane Fahey
www.indexoncensorship.org

Diane Fahey is the author of 12 poetry collections, most recently The
Wing Collection: New & Selected Poems and The Stone Garden: Poems
from Clare, both shortlisted for major poetry awards. In 2013 she took
part in Australian Poetry's International poetry tour of Ireland. She lives
in Clifton Springs, Victoria, Australia

Diary unlocked

43(4): 125/127 | DOI: 10.1177/0306422014561167

Israeli playwright **Hanoch Levin**'s play The Patriot was banned for damaging his homeland's values. His response, the short story Diary of a Censor, is translated for the first time into English for Index

MARKING THE FIVE-YEAR anniversary of Hanoch Levin's death, Michael Handelzalts wrote in the Israeli newspaper Haaretz, in 2004, that Levin's works had an impact on his country. "In all of his writings, both satirical and dramatic, he dissected Israeli society and described it in detail: the crudeness, the insensitivity, the interpersonal violence, the oppression, the gluttony, the intolerance and the cruelty."

Levin, who maintained a certain distance from the public by refusing to give interviews, was frequently in the cross hairs of censors including political groups, who forced the closure of 1970s play The Queen of the Bathtub – which mocked Prime Minister Golda Meir – after just 18 performances. Israel's Film and Censorship Board later banned his 1982 play The Patriot for being damaging to Israeli values and Judaism. The ban was defied in Tel Aviv and it had rave reviews, provoking a parliamentary debate on arts censorship.

In The Patriot, Levin portrayed a Palestinian being tortured with Sabbath candles. Diary of a Censor, published here, was his rejoinder to the ban.

When Levin died from cancer in 1999, aged 55, Israel's Prime Minister Ehud Barak was quoted in The New York Times as having called him "one of the greatest playwrights that Israel has ever had".

Diary of a Censor

Dear Diary,

As is my habit of an evening – a few heartfelt words before I sleep. Today once again, dear Diary, as happens day by day, I saved a Jewish life. He was some tragic figure in an antique play, a negro, army general, brave, but pathologically jealous. He took to wife this white nobleman's daughter, who loved him, but suffered bitterly from his jealous outbursts to the bitter end, when he strangled her. Dear Diary, I don't quite know how the idea suddenly came up for me, but right after the start of the play it dawned on me beyond a shadow of a doubt that the source of all evil was the untrammelled and overflowing urges of the poor negro. In light of his suffering I could no longer contain my compassion, got my scissors, and right at the end of his first scene two Turkish soldiers entered and cut off his balls and sexual organ altogether. In half a minute flat the poor negro calmed down, all his outbursts of jealousy throughout the play vanished as if they never were. While I was at it, dear Diary, I couldn't very well leave his wife as she was with her husband short of a sexual organ, in case her own urge bestir itself and she should be unfaithful to him. So I inserted into the next scene two further Turkish soldiers who cut

ABOVE: High school students produce, direct and perform Hefetz by Hanoch Levin in Jerusalem in 2012

→ off her breasts, amputated her womb and filed away her clitoris with a nail file. Diary, their love scene was now so tranquil and serene. But the job wasn't done yet. There was this conspirator there too, hatching plots, looking to disrupt the cute couple's matrimonial bliss. In his soliloquy, where he confesses his schemes, I inserted another two soldiers, Turkish naturally, and they grabbed him and cut off his balls. All his motivation for wickedness and malice instantly disappeared. Against a backdrop entirely filled with Turkish soldiers he now stood, weak, passive and indifferent, barely completing his soliloquy before he got off stage.

Straight off the second act began, and our negro went up on stage, pure, free of contamination, with no nonsense in his head, with no secreting or sexual organs, and the entire lower half of his body covered in sterile white bandages, to sit down and drink a nice cup of tea with his wife, whose lower half was also covered in identical bandages. And so they sat quietly drinking tea with the Turks standing behind them waiting, till toward the end of the second act there was nothing left for me to do but the natural and rational thing appropriate to their condition, that is – convert them. First I whitened the negro, introduced a rabbi, but as the rabbi was standing before that fortress in Cyprus, I realised it was an impossible proposition because I'd already amputated the negro's sexual organ. I instantly added an extra operating theatre scene to the third act, ten surgeons grafted a new sexual organ on to the white negro, then the rabbi appeared to circumcise him, and just at the end of the circumcision ceremony two more Turkish soldiers appeared to cut his circumcised organ off again. I'll grant you we got in a bit of a muddle with sexual organs in that act, but at least we were now left with a white, kosher Jew on stage, converted by the book, and with no evil urge.

The fourth act opened with a bang. I gave our Jew a handsome beard, yarmulke, and so, as he was now, a good-looking Jew with a high, sweet voice, how could I leave him an army commander in Cyprus? What has a Jew, one of ours, to do with the Turks and their conflicts? Quick as a flash I turned him into a cantor and changed his name from Othello to Otl, Reb Otl the Cantor. And what remained for a renowned cantor like Reb Otl to do in Cyprus? Why there's no Jewish community at all there! I also had to get rid of the battalion of Turkish soldiers on stage. In the twinkling of an eye, right at the end of act four, I had him emigrate to the land of Israel, him and his humble spouse, formerly known as Desdemona, and as of today – Mrs Dina daughter of Mina, long may she live.

The fifth act, dear Diary, opened on our couple atop the hilltop cliff of a new settlement in the West Bank. And who drop in on them there suddenly towards evening, around the end of the play? Hugo, formerly known as Iago, Hugo Cohen, a one time Argentinean left-wing journalist born again due to anti-Semitic persecution as an ardent Zionist, turned religious and just arrived in the new settlement in the West Bank with his spouse – formerly known as Emilia, now Malka. And so they are standing at the end of the play all four: Reb Otl, Dina daughter of Mina, Hugo and Malka, with white sterile bandages on the lower halves of their bodies and mouths bespeaking songs of praise, the stage cleansed of Turks.

Dear Diary, that's all for today. Tomorrow I've got a play about some prince of Denmark, with a murdered father, lust for vengeance and the devil knows what. It seems to me, dear Diary, it may be advisable to remove the balls right away in that case too and pour oil over troubled waters. We'll see after that. The West Bank is hungry for settlers. Sweet dreams, dear Diary. ☒

October 1982
www.indexoncensorship.org

Published with permission from the Hanoch Levin Institute of Israeli Drama

Translated by Atar Hadari

CULTURE

Oz on trial

43(4): 128/130 | DOI: 10.1177/0306422014560972

Poet John Kinsella talks to **Aimée Hamilton** about Australia's new era of censorship, and, below, Index exclusively publishes two new poems

POET JOHN KINSELLA describes Australia as "collapsing into a 'dark age' of censorship". He says: "I have experienced censorship in many forms. But the Australia of today is even more extreme – the limitation on reporting of things considered a threat to the nation has frightening implications."

Kinsella's comments on his homeland come after the board of the World Association of Newspapers and News Publishers called on Australian prime minister Tony Abbott to protect press freedom by revising the initial part of new national security laws, which stipulated that journalists could face 10 years in jail for reporting on a "special intelligence operation".

Kinsella says: "The government impositions on journalism, internet and personal liberties are only part of a complex picture of suppression. There are many Australians who censor each other, oppress their fellows by demeaning their religious, social, identity and political freedoms."

Has he ever had his own poetry censored? "Never by my book editors or publishers, but I have been in many other ways – including by literary and other journals who have dropped overtly politicised poems 'on advice'. And I had a 'rewording' issue for legal reasons with another journal."

When asked if self-censorship is a problem, Kinsella says: "Too often, review-culture is praise or hate, and is driven by fear that

Australian identity (that is, the nationalist version) will be undermined or especially shamed overseas."

Kinsella considers himself an "activist poet". "I use all 'methods' in my poetry, from the lyric to the rant, from figurative language to factual details. I don't wish to 'tell' anyone how or what to think, but rather to prompt discussion and concern, to open different ways (maybe) of seeing and hearing."

He calls the two poems Index is publishing here "direct indictments of the loss of rights to an increasing militarisation of Australian society". He adds: "I don't need to provide statistics to show the impoverishment and exploitation of Australian indigenous peoples – mining companies have become very adept at manipulating and claiming rights where they should have no rights. It is indigenous land, and usage needs constant negotiating. Of course, 'we' are all part of the place now, and we have rights, but those rights should not occlude or deny the rights of traditional peoples."

© John Kinsella
www.indexoncensorship.org

John Kinsella has published more than 50 books. His book Armour was the winner of the Victorian Premier's Award for Poetry. His new volume of poetry, Sack, was published in November. He is a professor of literature and sustainability at Curtin University

ABOVE: Prime Minister Tony Abbott is accused of pushing Australia into a new age of censorship in the name of national security

Warrant: Pssst (National Security Legislation Amendment Bill)

All you see
will be seen
or, say, unsaid –
your words
another's
a cluster's.
Seen and not
heard is an old way
few of us would raise
our children by – history?
Incognito (mode)?
Obliterate?
Following

in the footsteps.
I watched blue butterflies
for so long in summer
they hurt my eyes
and yet they have
such short lives –
these, their last lives?
Sifting for the well-
being. Of me.
You. Blue
Butterflies.
I warrant
we won't think
further; giving up
what you can't see
won't hurt.

ABOVE: Poet John Kinsella

→ Delicate Balance

'The delicate balance between freedom and security
may have to shift' – Tony Abbott, Australian Prime
Minister

Tilting
on edge,
the fall.
Point
of return
profitable
as security.
Butterfly
with its effect
torn off —
as brutal
as the cruel
child, bitter
adult.
Sets the gallery's
seismographs off
before walls
even move, art
stable as iron
ore.
Sovereign
with self-styled
head, done
in coal.
Doesn't require
comparison
with other
titular heads:
needs no precedent,
is its own pedestal.
Your signature,
elusive and solid
as its digital record.
You've created
a placebo,
ephemera:
together we can
keep an eye on
each other,
push the shift
key.

Credit: Tracy Ryan

Index around the world

by **Aimée Hamilton**

INDEX NEWS

43(4): 131/133 | DOI: 10.1177/0306422014560521

THE PAST FEW months have been a typical whirl of activity at Index, with visits from human rights activists, the launch of our awards and a mix of campaigns and events.

In September, Index had a meeting with the human rights activist and president of the Bahrain Centre for Human Rights Nabeel Rajab, about how the organisation could help the fight to improve human rights in his country. Following a month-long stay in Europe, Rajab was arrested on his return to Bahrain for insulting government institutions on Twitter. Index took up his case in a social media campaign to help increase awareness of both the poor treatment of political prisoners in Bahrain, and the conditions of Rajab's arrest. In October, Index co-hosted a press conference with Bahrain Institute for Rights and Democracy (BIRD) for the prominent activist and co-director for the Gulf Centre for Human Rights, Maryam Al Khawaja. Al Khawaja, who had only just been released from prison herself and visited London after a travel ban was lifted, called on the UK authorities to speak out about human rights abuses in Bahrain.

The year 2014 marked the 25th anniversary of Sir Tim Berners-Lee releasing the World Wide Web, a tool, now a basic of life, which has changed the face of journalism forever. On 22 October, Index launched its autumn magazine with its special report Seeing The Future of Journalism, at the Frontline Club in London. The event was chaired by author, columnist and chairman of Index, David Aaronovitch and speakers included professor of journalism at the Cardiff School of Journalism Richard Sambrook; data journalist and former regional editor of the South African Sunday Times Raymond Joseph; director of Hostage UK Rachel Briggs and Amie Ferris-Rotman, John S Knight Journalism Fellow at Stanford University. Debate from the panel and speakers covered subjects as diverse as the decline in foreign correspondents, the risks citizen journalists take, the line between propaganda and news, and sourcing facts.

Also in October, Index launched the nominations for the 15th annual Index Freedom of Expression Awards, which will be held in March 2015 at The Barbican in London. The awards categories are journalist, digital activist, campaigner/advocate and artist. The nominations closed on 20 November and the shortlist will be announced on 27 January. Just a few days before the nominations were launched, it was announced that previous Index award winner Malala Yousafzai was given the 2014 Nobel Peace Prize, along with Indian children's campaigner, Kailash Satyarthi. Yousafzi was awarded the Index/Doughty Street Chambers Advocacy award in 2013.

At the beginning of October, Index's arts associate Julia Farrington attended the Frankfurt Book Fair along with Turkish playwright Meltem Arikan as guests of the German PEN Centre. Arikan was invited to speak about the difficulties writers in Turkey face today. The political fallout of →

ABOVE: Debating the future of journalism, participants at the autumn magazine launch in London

→ one of her plays, Mi Minor, forced her into exile. The event also looked at Arikan's writing. Her book Stop Hurting My Flesh was banned in Turkey in 2004. Dr Josef Haslinger, president of the German PEN centre, said he was delighted to give a platform to Arikan, so that more people knew the story of how she was forced into exile. Sascha Feuchert, vice-president of the German PEN Centre also spoke. Arikan was shortlisted for the Index 2014 arts award and is a contributor to the Index website and magazine.

In November Index held a one-day Arts-FreedomWales event at the Chapter Arts Centre in Cardiff. The day's activities, supported by Arts Council Wales, explored whether the space for free expression in Wales was shrinking or expanding. Guest speakers included David Anderson, director general of National Museum Wales; John McGrath, artistic director of National Theatre Wales; Elen Ap Robert, artistic director of Bangor University's arts and innovation centre Pontio; Dai Smith, chair of Arts Council Wales.

The youth programme has been a prominent feature of Index's work over the past few months, with the second youth advisory board being selected this month. Each month, the youth advisory board choose a free expression topic for Draw the Line, a free speech debate brought together via the Twitter hashtag #IndexDrawTheLine, and culminating in a monthly event. Index's youth officer Fiona Bradley also attended the British Youth Council Convention for the North East, which was held near Newcastle. At the conference, Index discussed whether the police have a role in controlling free speech. Index also held a workshop for the Ovalhouse young associates' programme, a group affiliated with the Ovalhouse theatre in London. Artistic repression was discussed and the group talked about whether laws protect or restrict freedom of expression. In preparation for a model United Nations debate held by Buckinghamshire schools in December, Index talked to a group of sixth formers about freedom of expression.

Index also attended the annual South East Europe Media Forum (SEEMF) in

Skopje, Macedonia. The forum discussed how most countries in south-east Europe are experiencing a decline in media freedom, a finding supported by the Media Freedom Map, which Index is compiling in conjunction with Osservatorio Balcani e Caucaso. At the forum, a panel discussion also explored censorship across western Europe. During the debate panellists discussed the worrying number of journalists all over Europe who are now facing intimidation.

Index recently launched Frontline Free Speech, a pilot project seeking to amplify the voice of individuals under pressure. The project was launched with a series of free speech hearings in India, Tunisia and Senegal bringing together activists and leading free expression campaigners to ask, which subjects and debates were not being heard in each country. The hearings explored what the situation is for free speech in each country and then went on to discuss how the internet and mapping could be used as a tool to help. ☒

© Aimée Hamilton
www.indexoncensorship.org

Aimée Hamilton is on the full-time year-long post graduation internship programme at Index on Censorship. She is an editorial assistant

Humour on record

43(4): 134/136 | DOI: 10.1177/0306422014560520

Parody videos that splice together footage of world leaders and other powers should be enjoyed and protected, says **Vicky Baker**. Here she speaks to one half of artistic duo Cassetteboy about a change in UK law that relaxes rules for such montages – but only if they are funny

UK PRIME MINISTER David Cameron burst on to the stage at the 2014 Conservative Party conference and started to rap to a hip-hop beat. "I am hardcore and I know the score. And I am disgusted by the poor." Sadly, it wasn't a career change, but a video parody, which very cleverly spliced different words of his speech. Over the following month, the two-minute montage – created by video artists Cassetteboy – racked up close to four million views on YouTube, while Cameron's real speech only reached around 50,000. Now, with a general election coming up in 2015 and a relaxation of UK copyright laws, this should be a fruitful time for political parodies.

As of 1 October this year, UK copyright law allows for creative montages made from existing material "for the purposes of parody, caricature or pastiche". "Seriously though Dave, thanks for legalising parody videos," read the subtitle underneath Cassetteboy's Cameron video, which was posted on the same day as the amendment was announced.

Was the video funny? I certainly thought so – partly for the political satire, partly just for the incongruity of hearing "let the beat drop" from a world leader. Judging by the number of times it was posted and reposted on social networks, many more felt the same.

But the twist in the tale is that if the video ends up being challenged in court under copyright laws, it's a judge who must rule whether it is funny or not. And if it's not funny, it's not parody.

This opens all sorts of grey areas. What if someone intends it to be funny, but doesn't pull it off? What if something is deemed offensive and therefore, according to some tastes, not funny? And what if a mash-up, as these video montages are known, is done to make a point rather than score laughs?

"Not only is it crazy to legally judge humour, with this amendment, they've also ended up prioritising parody over all forms of artistic expression," says one half of the semi-anonymous duo Cassetteboy, who wishes to be known only as Mike. "These videos can also be moving, or make you cry, and that should be equally valid." He refers me to a video they once made for Amnesty International, which involves splicing together footage of President Barack Obama so it looks as if he is giving a speech about the hypocrisy of the international arms trade. ("Anyone buying a gun must at least have to prove they are not ... President Assad".) The result is powerful, close to the bone and quite depressing.

One key difference between the Obama video and the Cameron video is the White

ABOVE: Parody specialist Cassetteboy

House allows users to manipulate footage as they wish. "If we'd done the same with David Cameron, I don't know what would happen," admits Mike. "Cameron is not likely to sue Amnesty International, but it mashes up content I don't own to make a serious point, which I believe is still illegal." (It is, although he could lean on the fair-dealing exception for news reporting and criticism.)

"You could say that everything we do is political," he adds. "We want to annoy the people we feature in our videos. Although it's only funny when you are taking the piss out of people more powerful than you. People like David Cameron, [businessman] Alan Sugar, even [television chefs] The Hairy Bikers. If we were to do this with people's home videos, it wouldn't be funny." Although perhaps another artist could argue it was …

I called the Number 10 press office to find out if Cameron had commented on the video montage. He hasn't and any comment would have surely been anodyne (as Max Wind-Cowie writes on page 81). But it strikes me afterwards that I'd just had a frank chat with the prime minister's office about a video that ridiculed him, while giving my real name and number. And why wouldn't I? It's such an obvious thing to do that it seems ridiculous to write it here. So why did I even think of this?

Fresh in my mind was a visit to the Index on Censorship offices from Maryam Al Khawaja, the Bahraini co-director of the Gulf Center for Human Rights. She has recently been released from jail, and fully expects to end up there again, for criticising the state. Her sister was also recently incarcerated and faced up to seven years in prison and a hefty fine for tearing up a picture of the king.

I asked Mike if he ever considered this difference. "It's not something I think about, but it's true that in the UK we have a long tradition of satire, of mocking royalty and the political establishment. And if you stop to think about the sort of trouble we could be getting into if we did this in China or North Korea … then we are very lucky."

Of course, it's not really down to luck, although that's a turn of phrase that we all use. It isn't an accident that we have freedom to do this and, despite our long history, it's not guaranteed forevermore. This recent amendment only comes after years of active campaigns by organisations such as Open Rights Group. And we were reminded recently that the British don't always protect – or even understand – satire, when a mural

Not only is it crazy to legally judge humour, with this amendment, they've also ended up prioritising parody over all forms of artistic expression

of some racist pigeons by street artist Banksy was erased by the local district council in Clacton-on-Sea in Essex. The grey pigeons were holding placards towards a parrot, reading "Go back to Africa" and "Keep off our worms".

Video artists will still need to be careful, says Arty Rajendra, a lawyer on the committee of the Intellectual Property Lawyers' Association: "This is not a get-out-of-jail-free card." Rajendra explains artists still can't use entire music tracks as they might compete with the original; defamation remains a risk; and they can still be challenged over copyright if the parody exception does not apply to the specific usage.

→ This leaves artists such as Cassetteboy still walking a fine line and often having to draw up their own boundaries. Mike cites a video that reworked BBC footage of the royal family so they seemed to make smutty remarks about the Queen's sex life. It was taken down from YouTube after complaints. "It really was quite filthy. The BBC has been very good about tolerating a lot of stuff from us, but with that video, we found the line and went a long way over it. It seems you can't mess with her majesty." ⊠

© Vicky Baker
www.indexoncensorship.org

Vicky Baker is deputy editor at Index on Censorship magazine

Kirsten.
07737249222

Certificate Paper

GW00601617

FUNDAMENTALS OF ETHICS, CORPORATE GOVERNANCE AND BUSINESS LAW

For assessments in 2006 and 2007
Computer based assessment

CIM

Practice & Revision Kit

In this June 2006 new edition

- Banks of multiple choice and objective test questions on every syllabus area
- Answers with detailed feedback
- Two mock assessments with answers
- Fully up to date as at 1 May 2006

BPP's **i-Pass** product also supports this paper

PROFESSIONAL EDUCATION

First edition June 2006

ISBN 0 7517 2656 7

British Library Cataloguing-in-Publication Data
A catalogue record for this book
is available from the British Library

Published by

BPP Professional Education
Aldine House, Aldine Place
London W12 8AW

www.bpp.com

Printed in Great Britain by
WM Print
45-47 Frederick Street
Walsall
WS2 9NE

We are grateful to the Chartered Institute of
Management Accountants for permission to reproduce
past examination questions. The answers to past
examination questions have been prepared by BPP
Professional Education.

Contents

Revising with this Kit

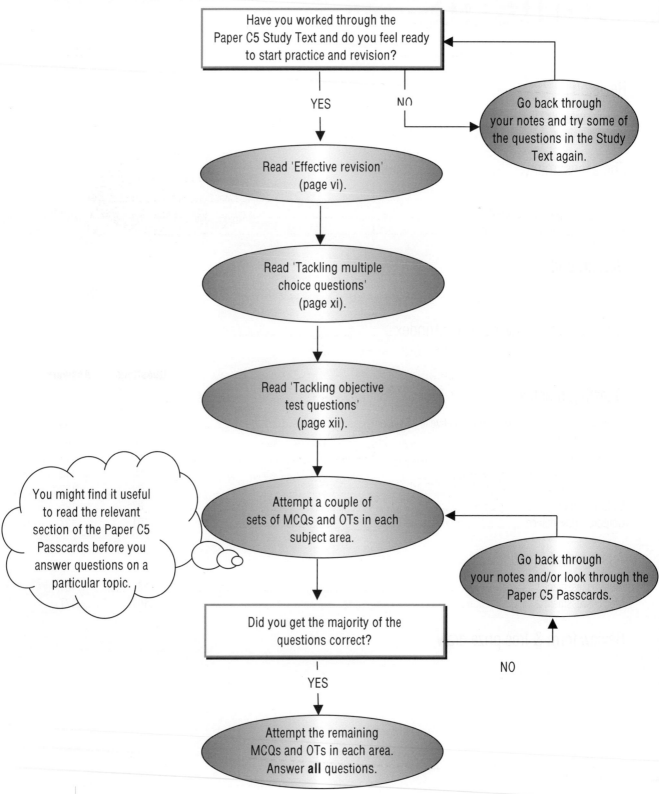

Have you worked through the Paper C5 Study Text and do you feel ready to start practice and revision?

YES

NO

Go back through your notes and try some of the questions in the Study Text again.

Read 'Effective revision' (page vi).

Read 'Tackling multiple choice questions' (page xi).

Read 'Tackling objective test questions' (page xii).

You might find it useful to read the relevant section of the Paper C5 Passcards before you answer questions on a particular topic.

Attempt a couple of sets of MCQs and OTs in each subject area.

Go back through your notes and/or look through the Paper C5 Passcards.

Did you get the majority of the questions correct?

YES

NO

Attempt the remaining MCQs and OTs in each area. Answer **all** questions.

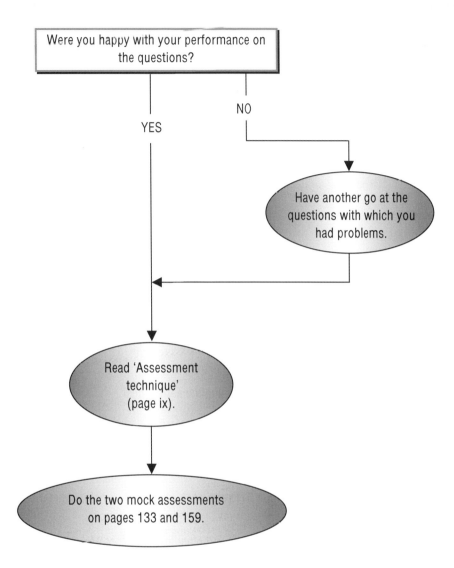

Were you happy with your performance on the questions?

YES

NO

Have another go at the questions with which you had problems.

Read 'Assessment technique' (page ix).

Do the two mock assessments on pages 133 and 159.

Effective revision

This guidance applies if you have been studying for an assessment over a period of time. (Some tuition providers are teaching subjects by means of one intensive course that ends with the assessment.)

What you must remember

Time is very important as you approach the assessment. You must remember:

> **Believe in yourself**
>
> **Use time sensibly**

Believe in yourself

Are you cultivating the right attitude of mind? There is absolutely no reason why you should not pass this **assessment** if you adopt the correct approach.

- **Be confident** – you've passed exams before, you can pass them again

- **Be calm** – plenty of adrenaline but no panicking

- **Be focused** – commit yourself to passing the assessment

Use time sensibly

1   **How much study time do you have?** Remember that you must **eat**, **sleep**, and of course, **relax**.

2   **How will you split that available time between each subject?** A revision timetable, covering what and how you will revise, will help you organise your revision thoroughly.

3   **What is your learning style?** AM/PM? Little and often/long sessions? Evenings/ weekends?

4   **Do you have quality study time?** Unplug the phone. Let everybody know that you're studying and shouldn't be disturbed.

5   **Are you taking regular breaks?** Most people absorb more if they do not attempt to study for long uninterrupted periods of time. A five minute break every hour (to make coffee, watch the news headlines) can make all the difference.

6   **Are you rewarding yourself for your hard work?** Are you leading a **healthy lifestyle?**

What to revise

Key topics

You need to spend **most time** on, and practise **lots of questions** on, topics that are likely to yield plenty of questions in your assessment.

You may also find certain areas of the syllabus difficult.

Difficult areas are

- Areas you find dull or pointless
- Subjects you highlighted as difficult when you studied them
- Topics that gave you problems when you answered questions or reviewed the material

DON'T become depressed about these areas; instead do something about them.

- Build up your knowledge by **quick tests** such as the quick quizzes in your BPP Study Text and the batches of questions in the i-Pass CD ROM.

- Work carefully through **examples** and **questions** in the Text, and refer back to the Text if you struggle with questions in the Kit.

Breadth of revision

Make sure your revision covers all areas of the syllabus. Your assessment will test your knowledge of the whole syllabus.

How to revise

There are four main ways that you can revise a topic area.

Write it!

Read it!

Teach it!

Do it!

Write it!

Writing important points down will help you recall them, particularly if your notes are presented in a way that makes it easy for you to remember them.

Read it!

You should read your notes or BPP Passcards actively, testing yourself by doing quick quizzes or Kit questions while you are reading.

Teach it!

Assessments require you to show your understanding. Teaching what you are learning to another person helps you practise explaining topics that you might be asked to define in your assessment. Teaching someone who will challenge your understanding, someone for example who will be taking the same assessment as you, can be helpful to both of you.

Do it!

Remember that you are revising in order to be able to answer questions in the assessment. Practising questions will help you practise **technique** and **discipline**, which can be crucial in passing or failing assessments.

1   Start your question practice by doing a couple of sets of objective test questions in a subject area. Note down the questions where you went wrong, try to identify why you made mistakes and go back to your Study Text for guidance or practice.

2   The **more questions** you do, the more likely you are to pass the assessment. However if you do run short of time:

   •   Make sure that you have done at least some questions from every section of the syllabus

   •   Look through the banks of questions and do questions on areas that you have found difficult or on which you have made mistakes

3   When you think you can successfully answer questions on the whole syllabus, attempt the **two mock assessments** at the end of the Kit. You will get the most benefit by sitting them under strict assessment conditions, so that you gain experience of the vital assessment processes.

   •   Managing your time
   •   Producing answers

BPP's *Learning to Learn Accountancy* gives further valuable advice on how to approach revision.
BPP has also produced other vital revision aids.

•   **Passcards** – Provide you with clear topic summaries and assessment tips

•   **i-Pass CDs** – Offer you tests of knowledge to be completed against the clock

•   **Success Tapes and Success CDs** – Help you revise on the move

You can purchase these products by completing the order form at the back of this Kit or by visiting www.bpp.com/cima

---

BPP
PROFESSIONAL EDUCATION

Assessment technique

Format of the assessment

The assessment will contain 75 questions to be completed in 2 hours. The questions will be a combination of multiple choice questions and other types of objective test questions.

Passing assessments

Passing assessments is half about having the knowledge, and half about doing yourself full justice in the assessment. You must have the right approach to two things.

> The day of the assessment
>
> Your time in the assessment room

The day of the assessment

1   Set at least one **alarm** (or get an alarm call) for a morning assessment.

2   Have **something to eat** but beware of eating too much; you may feel sleepy if your system is digesting a large meal.

3   Allow plenty of **time to get to the assessment room**; have your route worked out in advance and listen to news bulletins to check for potential travel problems.

4   **Don't forget** pens and watch. Also make sure you remember **entrance documentation** and **evidence of identity**.

5   Put **new batteries** into your calculator and take a spare set (or a spare calculator).

6   **Avoid discussion** about the assessment with other candidates outside the assessment room.

Your time in the assessment room

1   **Listen carefully to the invigilator's instructions**

Make sure you understand the formalities you have to complete.

2   **Ensure you follow the instructions on the computer screen**

In particular ensure that you select the correct assessment (not every student does!), and that you understand how to work through the assessment and submit your answers.

3   Keep your eye on the time

In the assessment you will have to complete 75 questions in 120 minutes. That will mean that you have roughly 1.6 minutes on average to answer each question. You will be able to answer some questions instantly, but others will require thinking about. If after a minute or so you have no idea how to tackle the question, leave it and come back to it later.

4   Label your workings clearly with the question number

This will help you when you check your answers, or if you come back to a question that you are unsure about.

5   Deal with problem questions

There are two ways of dealing with questions where you are unsure of the answer.

(a)   **Don't submit an answer.** The computer will tell you before you move to the next question that you have not submitted an answer, and the question will be marked as not done on the list of questions. The risk with this approach is that you run out of time before you do submit an answer.

(b)   **Submit an answer.** You can always come back and change the answer before you finish the assessment or the time runs out. You should though make a note of answers that you are unsure about, to ensure that you do revisit them later in the assessment.

6   Make sure you submit an answer for every question

When there are ten minutes left to go, concentrate on submitting answers for all the questions that you have not answered up to that point. You won't get penalised for wrong answers so take a guess if you're unsure.

7   Check your answers

If you finish the assessment with time to spare, check your answers before you sign out of the assessment. In particular revisit questions that you are unsure about, and check that your answers are in the right format and contain the correct number of words as appropriate.

BPP's *Learning to Learn Accountancy* gives further valuable advice on how to approach the day of the assessment.

Tackling multiple choice questions

The MCQs in your assessment contain a number of possible answers. You have to **choose the option(s) that best answers the question**. The three incorrect options are called distracters. There is a skill in answering MCQs quickly and correctly. By practising MCQs you can develop this skill, giving you a better chance of passing the assessment.

You may wish to follow the approach outlined below, or you may prefer to adapt it.

Step 1　**Note down how long** you should allocate to each MCQ. For this paper you will be answering 75 questions in 120 minutes, so you will be spending on average 1.6 minutes on each question. Remember however that you will not be expected to spend an equal amount of time on each MCQ; some can be answered instantly but others will take time to work out.

Step 2　**Attempt each question**. Read the question thoroughly.

You may find that you recognise a question when you sit the assessment. Be aware that the detail and/or requirement may be different. If the question seems familiar read the requirement and options carefully – do not assume that it is identical.

Step 3　Read the four options and see if one matches your own answer. Be careful with numerical questions, as the distracters are designed to match answers that incorporate **common errors**. Check that your calculation is correct. Have you followed the requirement exactly? Have you included every stage of a calculation?

Step 4　You may find that none of the options matches your answer.

- **Re-read the question** to ensure that you understand it and are answering the requirement

- **Eliminate any obviously wrong answers**

- **Consider which of the remaining answers** is the **most likely** to be correct and select the option

Step 5　If you are still unsure, **continue to the next question**. Likewise if you are nowhere near working out which option is correct after a couple of minutes, leave the question and come back to it later. Make a note of any questions for which you have submitted answers, but you need to return to later. The computer will list any questions for which you have not submitted answers.

Step 6　**Revisit questions** you are uncertain about. When you come back to a question after a break you often find you are able to answer it correctly straight away. If you are still unsure have a guess. You are not penalised for incorrect answers, so **never leave a question unanswered!**

Tackling objective test questions

What is an objective test question?

An objective test (**OT**) question is made up of some form of **stimulus**, usually a question, and a **requirement** to do something.

- **MCQs.** Read through the information on page (xi) about MCQs and how to tackle them.

- **True or false**. You will be asked if a statement is true or false.

- **Data entry**. This type of OT requires you to provide figures or missing words.

- **Hot spots**. This question format might ask you to identify which area of the screen contains the correct answer to a question.

- **Multiple response.** These questions provide you with a number of options and you have to identify those that fulfil certain criteria.

- **Matching.** This OT question format could ask you to match information from the syllabus, for example you may be asked to match the names of corporate governance reports with the area of governance they reported on.

OT questions in your assessment

CIMA is currently developing different types of OTs for inclusion in computer-based assessments. The timetable for introduction of new types of OTs is uncertain, and it is also not certain how many questions in your assessment will be MCQs, and how many will be other types of OT. Practising all the different types of OTs that this Kit provides will prepare you well for whatever questions come up in your assessment.

Dealing with OT questions

Again you may wish to follow the approach we suggest, or you may be prepared to adapt it.

Step 1   Work out **how long** you should allocate to each OT. Remember that you will not be expected to spend an equal amount of time on each one; some can be answered instantly but others will take time to work out.

Step 2   **Attempt each question**. Read the question thoroughly, and note in particular what the question says about the **format** of your answer and whether there are any **restrictions** placed on it (for example the number of words you can use).

You may find that you recognise a question when you sit the assessment. Be aware that the detail and/or requirement may be different. If the question seems familiar read the requirement and options carefully – do not assume that it is identical.

Step 3   Read any options you are given and select which ones are appropriate.

Step 4   You may find that you are unsure of the answer.

- Re-read the question to ensure that you understand it and are answering the requirement

- Eliminate any obviously wrong options if you are given a number of options from which to choose

Step 5   If you are still unsure, **continue to the next question**. Make a note of any questions for which you have submitted answers, but you need to return to later. The computer will list any questions for which you have not submitted answers.

Step 6   Revisit questions you are uncertain about. When you come back to a question after a break you often find you are able to answer it correctly straight away. If you are still unsure have a guess. You are not penalised for incorrect answers, so **never leave a question unanswered!**

Useful websites

The websites below provide additional sources of information of relevance to your studies of the *Fundamentals of Ethics, Corporate Governance and Business Law.*

- BPP   www.bpp.com

  For details of other BPP material for your CIMA studies

- CIMA   www.cimaglobal.com

  The official CIMA website

- The Times   www.timesonline.co.uk

- Financial Times   www.ft.com

- The Economist   www.economist.com

- Law Society   www.lawsociety.org.uk

- Department of Trade and Industry   www.dti.gov.uk

- UK Government   www.direct.gov.uk

- The Incorporated Council of Law Reporting   www.lawreports.co.uk

- UK Law Online   www.leeds.ac.uk/law/hamlyn

- Law rights   www.lawrights.co.uk

Relevant articles

Examiners often base questions on articles which have appeared in *Financial Management* and *CIMA Insider.* Students would therefore be well advised to read them and watch for relevant articles.

Students are also advised to keep an eye on the 'Business and Law' section of the Monday edition of the *Financial Times* and the law supplement which appears in *The Times* on Tuesdays.

Question and Answer checklist/index

The headings in this checklist/index indicate the main topics of questions, but questions often cover several different topics.

Questions

1 English and alternative legal systems 1

1   In a criminal case, what is the normal burden of proof placed upon the prosecution?

   A   Beyond any doubt
   B   Beyond reasonable doubt
   C   Beyond every reasonable doubt
   D   Balance of probabilities

2   All the following statements refer to sources of law.

   (i)   The principle that once a court has made a ruling on a particular case, then the same decision will be reached in any future similar case, forms the basis of delegated legislation.

   (ii)   The term 'case law' is used to describe judge-made laws stemming from courts' decisions.

   (iii) European Community regulations become law in member nations without the member nation having to pass legislation.

   (iv)   In the United Kingdom, legislation is introduced into Parliament by the Crown.

   Which of the above statements is **correct**?

   A   (i), (ii) and (iii) only
   B   (ii) and (iii) only
   C   (ii) and (iv) only
   D   (ii), (iii) and (iv) only

3   Which of the following statements about the structure of the English court system are correct?

   (i)   All criminal cases, regardless of their gravity, are introduced in the Magistrates' court.
   (ii)   The County Court hears civil cases involving contracts worth up to £100,000.
   (iii) The Court of Appeal binds all courts below it and also normally itself.
   (iv)   The House of Lords has to give its consent before a case can be heard before it.

   A   (ii), (iii) and (iv) only
   B   (i), (ii) and (iii) only
   C   (i), (ii) and (iv) only
   D   (i), (iii) and (iv) only

4   Which of the following EC pronouncements does not have the force of legislation?

   A   Regulation
   B   Recommendation
   C   Decision
   D   Directive

5   Which of the following statements does **not** describe an aspect of tort?

   A   Certain acts constitute an infringement of a person's rights and their commission leads to a claim for compensation by the wronged party.

   B   A person has a number of separate legal rights and an action may be brought at law to assert that a particular right has been infringed.

   C   Certain acts are prohibited by law and their commission leads to prosecution by the state.

   D   A person has a duty at civil law not to infringe the rights of other persons.

6   The Court of Appeal is bound by the previous decisions of:

   A   The House of Lords only
   B   The House of Lords and a Divisional Court of the High Court only
   C   The House of Lords and the Court of Appeal only
   D   The House of Lords, the Court of Appeal and a Divisional Court of the High Court only

7   All the following statements relate to criminal and civil law. Which one of the statements is **correct**?

   A   A criminal case may subsequently give rise to a civil case, but a civil case cannot subsequently give rise to a criminal case.

   B   The main purpose of civil law is to compensate the injured party and to punish the injuring party.

   C   A custodial sentence can be passed on the defendant in a civil case, providing the defendant is a natural person and not an incorporated body.

   D   Trial by jury is sometimes possible in a civil court.

8   Before a High Court judge is required to apply a previous decision to the case actually before him, he must:

   (i)   Decide whether the decision is binding or merely persuasive

   (ii)   Distinguish the **obiter dicta** from the **ratio decidendi** and apply the former in his reasoning

   (iii) Determine that the material facts of the two cases are similar

   (iv)   Be convinced that the decision was made by a court of higher status than the County Court or Magistrates' Court

   A   (i) and (iii) only
   B   (ii) and (iv) only
   C   (i), (ii) and (iii) only
   D   (i), (iii) and (iv) only

9   Which of the following is **true** of a criminal case?

   A   A convicted person must pay compensation to his victim.
   B   The case must be proven beyond reasonable doubt.
   C   The Crown Prosecution Service is the claimant.
   D   Law reports of criminal cases are confidential.

10 An auditor appointed to audit a company owes a contractual duty of care to:

    A   The company
    B   The directors
    C   The shareholders individually
    D   The general public

2 English and alternative legal systems 2

1 In which of the following would a claim by an employee for discrimination by an employer be heard?

    A   The Court of Appeal
    B   A court of first instance
    C   A Crown Court
    D   An Employment Tribunal

2 The criminal law aims to:

    A   Compensate injured parties
    B   Recover property which has been taken from the true owner
    C   Enforce legal obligations
    D   Penalise wrongdoers

3 All the following statements relate to sources of law. Which one of the statements is **true**?

    A   Under the principle of judicial precedent, a judge must follow all previous decisions.
    B   The House of Lords is the main original source of legislation in the United Kingdom.
    C   The European Court of Human Rights is an important source of European Community law.
    D   A by-law made by a local government organisation is an example of delegated legislation.

4 Which of the following best describes the meaning of **ratio decidendi**?

    A   A statement of the law applicable to the facts of the particular case which forms the basis of the judge's decision.

    B   The verbatim text of the judgement in a full law report.

    C   A rule of evidence whereby a court will assume the existence of a certain state of affairs without the need for proof.

    D   The approval by or on behalf of the Crown to a bill which has been passed in both Houses of Parliament.

5   All the following statements about sources of law are untrue except one. Which one of the statements is **true**?

   A   Common law is the name used for all laws stemming from the decisions of the House of Commons.

   B   Some statutory bodies possess the delegated power to enact bye-laws.

   C   Judicial precedent requires that once any court has made a ruling, the same decision must be reached in all other similar court cases where the material facts are the same.

   [handwritten: when excluding MC, C-C, C-C]

   D   Decisions of the European Council of Ministers, each of which is binding on all businesses operating within the European Union, are an important source of European Community law.

6   An investor invests in a company on the basis of its annual accounts. Why does the auditor of a company not owe him a legal duty of care?

   A   Damage is too remote.
   B   The purpose of the audit is not to help people make investment decisions.
   C   There is no general liability for loss suffered by third parties.
   D   Third party claims are excluded by company law.

7   Which one of the following statements concerning European Community Regulations is **correct**?

   A   An EC Regulation is an example of primary legislation created by the European Community.
   B   An EC Regulation is binding in its entirety for all member states.
   C   Member states are free to decide how to apply an EC Regulation.
   D   All EC Regulations derive from the judgements of the European Court of Justice.

8   Which of the following elements must be present for a duty of care to exist?

   (i)   There must be a sufficient relationship of proximity between defendant and claimant.
   (ii)   It must be reasonable that the defendant should foresee that damage might arise from his carelessness.
   (iii) The claimant must have acted in good faith and without carelessness.
   (iv)   It must be just and reasonable for the law to impose liability.

   A   (i) and (ii) only
   B   (iii) and (iv) only
   C   (i), (ii) and (iii) only
   D   (i), (ii) and (iv) only

9   Nicholas works as a foreman in a cement processing factory. Vats of chemicals are used to clean the raw materials entering the process. The materials are kept in asbestos containers in a separate part of the plant. During processing the lid of one of these containers falls into a vat near to Nicholas. He is splashed by the chemical and, before he can get away, the vat explodes following a reaction between the asbestos and the chemical previously unknown to science. Nicholas, barely alive after the explosion, brings a claim in tort against the employers. Will he succeed?

	Splash	*Explosion*
A	No – too remote	No – too remote
B	Yes – foreseeable	Yes – foreseeable
C	Yes – foreseeable	No – too remote
D	No – too remote	Yes – foreseeable

10   When an auditor audits a limited company, what standard of care does he owe?

    A   That of the common man

    B   That of a reasonable and competent auditor

    C   That which can be reasonably expected from him, personally, as an auditor

    D   Foreseeable care

3 English and alternative legal systems 3

1   All the following statements about sources of English law are true **except** one. Which one is **untrue**?

    A   The Crown is the ultimate source of English law.

    B   A European Community treaty provides an example of legislation.

    C   A local authority by-law provides an example of delegated legislation.

                                 HL, COA, HC

    D   Judicial precedent <u>involves</u> the principle that once a court has made a ruling on a particular case, the same decision will be made in a future similar case.

2   Melanie and Jane go out to lunch together at Rumsey's Restaurant. Melanie is buying lunch for Jane as a treat, so Melanie orders and also pays the bill. The same night Jane has to be admitted to hospital as she is suffering severe food poisoning as a result of eating a negligently prepared mussel at the restaurant. Jane wishes to claim damages for the distress suffered and the fact that she had to take three weeks away from her self-employment.

    What is the legal position?

    A   Jane cannot sue Rumsey's Restaurant as she does not have a contract with it.

    B   Jane can sue Melanie, as it is Melanie who ordered and paid for the bad mussel. Melanie must then sue the restaurant.

    C   Jane can sue Rumsey's Restaurant as she was owed a duty of care by the restaurant, which has breached that duty.

    D   Jane cannot sue either the restaurant or Melanie, as by eating the mussel she consented to the risk of food poisoning.

3   Only one of the following actions lies within the jurisdiction of the County Court. Which one?

    A   A claim of £60,000 for negligent advice given by a solicitor

    B   A prosecution for a driving offence

    C   A debt action for £7,000 which is expected to last for a day

    D   A debt action for £70,000 which is expected to last for several days

4   Which of the following are types of delegated legislation?

    (i)   Orders in Council
    (ii)   Regulations of the European Union
    (iii)   Statutory instruments
    (iv)   Acts of Parliament
    (v)   Local authority bye laws

    A   (i), (ii) and (iii)
    B   (i), (iii) and (v)
    C   (ii), (iii), (iv) and (v)
    D   (ii), (iii) and (v)

5   In negligence for misstatements which result in economic loss to the claimant, what forms the basis of the existence of a legal duty of care?

    A   Foreseeability
    B   Proximity
    C   Foreseeability and proximity
    D   Foreseeability and damage

6   Statements made *obiter dicta* are:

    A   Principles of law relating to the facts of the case
    B   Binding in courts 'at the same level' hearing similar cases
    C   Not binding unless they are made by the European Court
    D   Not binding at all, but judicial authority

7   In order to show that there exists a duty of care not to cause financial loss by negligent misstatement, the claimant must show that:

    (i)   The person making the statement did so in an expert capacity of which the claimant was aware.
    (ii)   The context in which the statement was made was such as to make it likely that the claimant would rely on it.
    (iii)   In making the statement the defendant foresaw that it would be relied upon by the claimant.
    (iv)   The claimant had actually relied on the statement.

    A   (i) and (ii) only
    B   (i), (ii) and (iii) only
    C   (ii), (iii) and (iv) only
    D   All of them

8   Which of the following are criminal proceedings?

    A   A divorce action
    B   An action by a claimant for £1 million damages for fraudulent misrepresentation
    C   An action by a claimant for breach of contract
    D   A prosecution by the Inland Revenue for non-payment of tax

9   Delegated legislation is drawn up under powers conferred by the full Parliament in Acts. Which of the following statements concerning delegated legislation are **true**?

    (i)   The power to make such legislation may be delegated to local authorities.

    (ii)   Ministerial powers are exercised by Orders in Council, a common form of delegated legislation.

    (iii)   All delegated legislation must be laid before Parliament.

    (iv)   Legislation laid before Parliament for 40 days without a negative resolution being passed in respect of it automatically comes into force.

    A   (i) and (iv) only
    B   (ii) and (iii) only
    C   (i), (ii) and (iv) only
    D   (i), (iii) and (iv) only

10   Which of the following presumptions are 'canons of statutory interpretation'?

    (i)   An Act of Parliament applies only to England and Wales unless otherwise stated.
    (ii)   An Act of Parliament does not have retrospective effect.
    (iii)   For a criminal offence to be committed, there must be intention on the part of the accused.
    (iv)   An Act of Parliament does not repeal a previous act.

    A   (i) and (iii) only
    B   (ii) and (iv) only
    C   (i), (ii) and (iv) only
    D   (ii), (iii) and (iv) only

4 English and alternative legal systems 4

1   What is Istishab?

    A   The theory that no more interpretation is needed
    B   The theory that local custom maybe subsumed into the law if it is not contrary to Sharia
    C   The legal presumption that a state of affairs continues until the contrary is proved
    D   The concept of equity or fairness

2   Under Sharia law actions are permitted until shown to be forbidden.

    True/False?

3   The Ahadith that comprise the Sunnah are classified according to reliability as they are recorded some time after the death of the Prophet.

    Match the name to the level of reliability.

Name		Level of reliability	
(a)	Ahad	(i)	virtually guaranteed
(b)	Muwatir	(ii)	less certain
(c)	Mashtur	(iii)	little certainty

4 Fill in the missing words

'The two main principles of civil law are C.................................... and C... '

5 A problem with codified or civil law systems is that statutes have to be complex to cover many eventualities.

True/False?

6 Which statement is correct?

A The International Court of Justice can be used to arbitrate between two parties if they both agree, but its decision is not legally binding.

B One country can take a dispute with another to the International Court of Justice without the other party agreeing, but its decision is not legally binding.

C The International Court of Justice can be used to arbitrate between two parties if they both agree, and its decision is legally binding.

D One country can take a dispute with another to the International Court of Justice without the other party agreeing, and its decision is legally binding.

7 International customary law is based on principles known as:

A Common principles
B Common custom
C Binding norms
D Accepted practice

8 Which statement(s) concerning the role of Judges is/are correct?

A Judges under Sharia law cannot create law.
B Judges under codified systems cannot create law.
C Judges under common law and codified systems can both be involved in judicial review.
D All of the above.

9 Codification of law is exclusive to codified or civil law systems.

True/False?

10 Unlike common law or codified systems, states following Sharia law never have a concept of judicial review.

True/False?

5 English and alternative legal systems 5

1 As the Quran forbids alcohol, it follows that drugs are also forbidden. This deduction is an example of:

A Ljma
B Qiyas
C Maslahah mursalah
D None of the above

2   If clear guidance cannot be obtained from the Quran, a judge may turn to the Sunnah for help with interpretation. What is the Sunnah?

    A   Writings and thoughts of major jurists
    B   Interpretations of the Quran by Imams
    C   A written record of everything the Prophet Muhammad said, did or implied
    D   A council of clerics

3   Muslim states that uphold Sharia law should not have a written constitution as the law gives people all the guidance they need in their lives.

    True/False?

4   Under Sharia law, a judge must be suitably qualified, known as a Muhtahid. In order to become a Muhtahid a person must (amongst other things):

    A   Be a good and practicing Muslim
    B   Hold a law degree in the country they practice
    C   Be just, reliable and trustworthy
    D   Be appointed by the state

    Select the incorrect answer(s).

5   Select the countries that operate a civil or codified legal system.

    A   Germany
    B   South Africa
    C   USA
    D   Australia
    E   France

6   In codified (civil) law systems, judges have which of the following roles:

    A   To draft new statutes
    B   To apply the letter of the law
    C   To ensure statutes are in line with the constitution
    D   To interpret international law

7   International conventions are .... agreements between nations that create .... between them.

    Fill in the missing words using the following; **military, obligations, trade, voluntary, private, rights.**

8   Conflict of laws can occur when countries trade with each other and their respective legal rules are not compatible.

    True/False?

9 Select the incorrect statement(s).

    A   Sharia law separates moral and legal obligations

    B   Statutes under common law do not need to be comprehensive

    C   Codified systems are based on underlying principles

    D   Judges under codified systems are bound by decisions in previous cases

10 There is debate within the Sharia system as to whether further development of the law is needed. This contrasts with Common law, which is constantly evolving.

    True/False?

6 Establishing contractual obligations 1

1 A Ltd has been induced to enter a contract with B Ltd by the latter's negligent misrepresentation.

    Which of the following is **incorrect**?

    A   A Ltd may sue B Ltd for damages in the tort of negligence.

    B   A Ltd may sue B Ltd for damages under the Misrepresentation Act 1967.

    C   A Ltd may sue B Ltd for damages in the tort of deceit.

    D   A Ltd may treat the contract with B Ltd as voidable.

2 Consider the following chain of events. Is there a contract?

    1 April   Amy sends a letter to Beth offering to sell her a bicycle for £100.

    3 April   Amy changes her mind and writes to Beth informing her that the offer is no longer open.

    4 April   Beth receives Amy's offer letter and writes back to accept.

    5 April   Beth receives Amy's second letter.

    7 April   Amy receives Beth's letter of acceptance which she returns, unread.

    A   No. Amy has revoked the offer by the time that Beth accepts it by writing to Beth. Beth cannot accept a revoked offer.

    B   Yes. Beth can accept the offer until she receives notice of the revocation.

    C   No. Amy has not read the acceptance, therefore she has not agreed to it.

    D   No. Beth has given no consideration.

3 One party has been induced to enter into a contract by a negligent misrepresentation of the other party. Which of the following is **incorrect**?

    A   If rescission is available, damages in lieu may be awarded at the court's discretion under the Misrepresentation Act 1967.

    B   Rescission cannot be ordered if it is impossible to return the parties to their pre-contract position.

    C   Despite being the victim of a misrepresentation, the misrepresentatee may affirm the contract.

    D   For this type of misrepresentation, damages may be obtained under the tort of negligence but not under the Misrepresentation Act 1967.

[handwritten: consideration is not adequate, but sufficient (do more than contractual obligation)]

4   Which of the following examples of performance amounts to good consideration?

(i)   The performance of an existing duty under general law
(ii)   The performance of an existing contract in return for a promise by a third party
(iii)   The performance of an act, followed by a promise to pay for that act

A   (i) only
B   (ii) only
C   (i) and (ii) only
D   (iii) only

[handwritten: past consideration: person performs service before promise but is promised later that he will be paid]

5   An act which has already been performed before an act or promise is given in return is not usually sufficient as consideration. But it will be where:

A   A person performs a service at another's request and is later promised payment
B   A person spends money on his own initiative and another party later agrees in writing to repay it
C   A debt has become statute-barred but the debtor verbally acknowledges its existence
D   A promissory note is given in settlement of an existing debt

6   Tim offered to sell a stereo system to Neil for £200 on 2 September saying that the offer would stay open for a week. Neil told his brother that he would like to accept Tim's offer and, unknown to Neil, his brother told Tim of this on 3 September. On 4 September Tim, with his lodger present, sold the stereo to Ingrid. The lodger informed Neil of this fact on the same day. On 5 September Neil delivered a letter of acceptance to Tim. Is Tim in breach of contract?

[handwritten margin: Revoke.]

A   No. Neil delayed beyond a reasonable time and so the offer had lapsed by the time Tim sold to Ingrid.

B   No. Neil was told by a reliable informant of Tim's effective revocation before Neil accepted the offer.

C   Yes. Tim agreed to keep the offer open and failed to do so.

D   Yes. Tim was reliably informed of Neil's acceptance on 3 September so his sale to Ingrid on 4 September is breach of contract.

7   Which of the following statements is **correct**?

(i)   The parties to a social or domestic arrangement are presumed to have intended the arrangement to be legally enforceable.

(ii)   The parties to a commercial transaction are presumed not to have intended the arrangement to be legally enforceable.

A   (i) only
B   (ii) only
C   Both (i) and (ii)
D   Neither (i) nor (ii)

8   Maud goes into a shop and sees a price label for £20 on an ironing board. She takes the board to the checkout but the till operator tells her that the label is misprinted and should read £30. Maud maintains that she only has to pay £20. How would you describe the price on the price label in terms of contract law?

A   An offer
B   A tender
C   An invitation to treat
D   An acceptance

9   Consideration:

(i)   Must be of adequate and sufficient value
(ii)   Must move from the promisee
(iii)   Must never be past
(iv)   Must be given in every binding agreement

A   (i) only
B   (ii) only
C   (ii), (iii) and (iv) only
D   (iii) and (iv) only

10   Alexander wrote to Brian and offered to sell him his set of antique cigarette cards for £300. Brian wrote back that he accepted the offer and would pay for them in two instalments of £150. Is there a contract?

A   Yes. There is offer, acceptance and consideration. The contract is valid.
B   No. Alexander's letter was not an offer but an invitation to treat.
C   No. Until Alexander receives Brian's letter, the acceptance is not valid.
D   No. Brian's letter has varied the terms and so is a counter-offer, rejecting Alexander's original offer.

7 Establishing contractual obligations 2

1   Which of the following is an offer?

A   An advertisement in the newsagent's window
B   An invitation to tender
C   An auction bid
D   An exhibition of goods for sale

2   A fraudulent misrepresentation renders a contract:

A   Valid
B   Void
C   Voidable
D   Illegal

3   If a creditor makes a promise, unsupported by consideration, to a debtor that the creditor will not insist on full discharge of a debt and the promise is made with the intention that the debtor should act on it and he does so, the creditor cannot retract his promise unless the debtor can be restored to his original position. This illustrates which of the following?

   A   Revocation
   B   Promissory estoppel
   C   Misrepresentation
   D   Past consideration

4   Miranda owes Emma £500 for her wedding dress. Emma, because she is in need of cash, agrees to accept £400 in full settlement of the debt, but she later claims the full amount. Will she succeed?

   A   No. Miranda's payment is full consideration for Emma's promise to waive her rights.

   B   No. She is estopped from retracting her promise.

   C   Yes. Her waiver was not entirely voluntary.

   D   Yes. She had no intention that Miranda should act on the waiver and so the doctrine of promissory estoppel does not apply.

5   Which of the following is **not** an essential element of a valid simple contract?

   A   The contract must be in writing.
   B   The parties must be in agreement.
   C   Each party must provide consideration.
   D   Each party must intend legal relations.

6   A Ltd has been induced to enter into a contract with B Ltd by the fraudulent misrepresentation of C Ltd, a third party.

   Which of the following is **correct**?

   A   A Ltd may sue C Ltd for damages in the tort of deceit.
   B   A Ltd may sue C Ltd for damages under the Misrepresentation Act 1967.
   C   A Ltd may recover damages from C Ltd for breach of contract.
   D   A Ltd may treat the contract with B Ltd as void.

7   Francis buys a table from Matthew, who believes it to be worthless. Francis knows that it is by Hepplewhite. Neither party discloses his belief to the other. Later Matthew discovers that Francis has sold the table for £750,000, to another party in good faith. What is his remedy?

   A   Rescind the contract and sue for damages under the Misrepresentation Act 1967 for negligent misrepresentation.

   B   Rescind the contract and sue for damages for innocent misrepresentation.

   C   Sue for damages under the tort of deceit.

   D   Matthew has no remedy.

15

[Handwritten at top of page:]
Agreement
Social/Domestic = NOT Intended
Commercial = Intended
Separation = Intended.

8   Which of the following statements is **incorrect**?

A   If an agreement is of a commercial nature, it is presumed that the parties intend legal relations.

B   If an agreement is of a commercial nature, the parties cannot argue that there was no intention to create legal relations.

C   Even if an agreement is of a commercial nature, it is open to the parties to show that legal relations were not intended.

D   Even if a commercial agreement is in writing, it is open to the parties to show that legal relations were not intended.

9   A Ltd wrote to B Ltd offering to sell the company specified items of plant and machinery and requiring acceptance of the offer by fax. Which of the following is **correct**?

A   The acceptance is complete as soon as the fax is sent by B Ltd.
B   The acceptance is complete as soon as A Ltd receives the fax.
C   The contract cannot be concluded by fax.
D   Acceptance by fax is subject to the 'post rules'.

10   In relation to misrepresentation, which of the following statements is **incorrect**?

A   As a general rule silence cannot amount to misrepresentation.
B   The misrepresentee cannot claim damages if he has affirmed the contract.
C   A person cannot rely on the misrepresentation if it did not induce him to contract.
D   A half-truth may amount to a misrepresentation.

8 Establishing contractual obligations 3

1   Which of the following are essential requirements of a contract?

(i)   Offer and acceptance
(ii)   Consideration
(iii) Written contractual terms
(iv)   Intention to create legal relations

A   (i), (ii), (iii) and (iv)
B   (i), (ii) and (iii)
C   (i), (ii) and (iv)
D   (i), (iii) and (iv)

2   Which ONE of the following cannot be carried out by a simple contract?

A   A contract for the sale of a motor car
B   A contract of employment
C   A contract for the sale of land
D   A contract for the provision of services

3   Samantha offered to sell her car to Patrick for £2,000. She said he could think about it until Monday. Patrick rang her on Saturday and left a message on her machine asking if she would agree to his paying in monthly instalments for six months. She rang back in the evening to say she would want the full cash sum. On Sunday, Patrick accepted the original offer. Meanwhile, Samantha had sold the car to Iain on Saturday night.

What is the legal position?

A   Patrick's telephone message amounted to a counter-offer which was a final rejection of the original offer.

B   Patrick's telephone message was a counter-offer but he still had an option on the car until Monday.

C   Patrick's telephone message was merely a request for information, but as he and Samantha did not yet have agreement, she was free to sell the car to someone else.

D   Patrick's telephone message was a request for information only, Samantha had not revoked the offer, so his acceptance on the original terms means they have a contract.

---

4   Bill's will states that his son, Ben, should have use of his house during Ben's life. The executors allowed Ben to occupy the house in accordance with Bill's wishes and for nominal rent of £1 per quarter.

The executors later decide it would be better to sell the house. They claim that Ben has no right to stay in the house because he has not provided any consideration against their promise that he can stay.

Which of the following statements summarises the **true** legal position?

A   The executors are right. The nominal rent is a past act and there is no consideration to allow Bill to stay now.

B   The executors are right. Bill has provided consideration in paying the nominal rent, but it is not the market rent and therefore he will have to leave.

C   The executors are wrong. Bill has provided sufficient consideration in paying the nominal rent and he will be allowed to stay on the strength of their promise.

D   The executors are wrong due to the wishes of the deceased which are expressed in the will.

---

5   Elizabeth decides to sell her string of pearls to Mary and writes to her on 24 February, offering her the string of pearls for £250. At the same time, Mary decides that she wants the pearls and writes to her on 24 February, offering to buy them for £250.

Before either of these letters are received, Mary sees a similar necklace in a shop for £200 and decides to buy that instead.

What is Mary's legal position?

A   She is contracted to buy Elizabeth's necklace as they have agreement.

B   She is not contracted to buy Elizabeth's necklace as there is no consideration.

C   She is not contracted to buy Elizabeth's necklace as her offer does not constitute acceptance of Elizabeth's offer of sale.

D   She will only be able to avoid contracting with Elizabeth if she speaks to her before Elizabeth receives her letter.

---

6   Laine is selling her house to Catherine. They are about to exchange contracts. All the searches have been completed, but then Laine finds out that a shopping centre is going to be built on the land to the side of the house. She has previously told Catherine that she did not know of any such development plans.

May Catherine claim for misrepresentation if the contracts are exchanged now?

A   No, because silence cannot be construed as misrepresentation.
B   Yes, because what Laine has told Catherine has become misleading.
C   No, because Catherine should have found that out on her own behalf.
D   Yes, because with contract for property, all known facts must be stated.

7   In the absence of express statements as to whether or not legal relations are intended:

A   The courts always assume that legal relations were not intended.
B   The courts assume that legal relations were not intended unless they were social arrangements.
C   The courts will assume that legal relations were intended unless the parties can prove otherwise.
D   The courts assume that legal relations were intended in commercial cases unless proved otherwise.

8   David made an offer by fax which he sent from Singapore. Katy received this fax in London, just prior to getting on a plane to New York. Katy was keen that the contract should be sealed so she faxed an acceptance to David from New York. As he had flown from Singapore to Sydney, she faxed him there.

Where was the contract made?

A   Singapore. David made the offer there.
B   London. Katy received the offer there.
C   New York. Katy faxed her acceptance there.
D   Sydney. David received the acceptance there.

9   Simon is keen to buy some second hand golf clubs. His friend, Dave, advises him to talk to Lee, who is trying to sell a set. Lee tells Simon that he will sell his set for £250. Simon is unsure, because the golf clubs are better and more expensive than he intended buying. He asks Lee if he can tell him in a couple of days. Lee agrees.

Two days later, Simon rings Dave to discuss whether or not to buy the golf clubs. Dave tells him that Lee has changed his mind about selling them. Simon rings Lee up straight away and agrees to buy the clubs for £250.

Is there a contract?

A   Yes, because Lee has promised to keep the offer open.
B   No, because Simon's request to keep the offer open for a couple of days was too vague to be binding.
C   No, because Dave has told Simon of Lee's intentions and the offer has been revoked.
D   Yes, because Lee needed to tell Simon himself that he wasn't going to sell the clubs any more.

10   The law of contract is of special importance in providing a legal framework within which businesses can operate.

Which one of the following statements is **correct**?

A   A contract need not necessarily be in writing.
B   The consideration provided by the two parties to a contract must be of equal value.
C   A contract comes under the remit of criminal law rather than civil law.
D   A contract can be entered into validly by all adult persons.

9 Establishing contractual obligations 4

1   Which **one** of the following statements about the law of contract is **correct**?

A   Providing an agreement is in writing, it will always form a valid contract.

B   Cases involving breach of contract are normally heard in the Crown Court.

C   An agreement between two parties to undertake a criminal act is not a legally-recognised contract.

D   An agreement between two businesses to allow late payment for goods or services is not an example of a contract.

2   Deb was induced to enter into a contract by the negligent misrepresentation of Dave. The contract was to buy three concert tickets.

Deb wants rescission of the contract. Which of the following is **not true**?

A   Deb must tell Dave that she wishes to rescind the contract.
B   If Deb has sold one of the tickets to an innocent third party she cannot rescind the contract.
C   Deb will only be granted rescission within a reasonable time from the date of the contract.
D   Deb is not entitled to rescission because Dave's misrepresentation was not fraudulent.

3   An agreement to carry out an act which the law requires anyway amounts to:

A   Sufficient consideration
B   Insufficient consideration
C   Past consideration
D   Proper consideration

4   What is executory consideration?

A   An act or forbearance _executed consideration_
B   A promise of an act or forbearance _executory consideration_
C   Consideration performed on the basis of a promise made _executed consideration_
D   Consideration provided by an act performed before the contract is made _past consideration_

QUESTIONS

5   The directors of East Brimwoch Football Club were concerned with an outbreak of violence in the stadium following the introduction of bar facilities in the main stand. The chairman was authorised to approach the police and they agreed to provide additional police and riot gear at the ground during matches. Two days after the first match under this arrangement, the club received an invoice for £5,000. (This is a reasonable charge for the number of policemen provided.) The directors refused to pay the bill, stating that it is the job of the police to prevent crime, wherever it occurs, including in their football stadium.

What is the legal position?

A   The directors are right. The police have a legal duty to keep the peace, whatever that takes.

B   The directors did not need to pay on the grounds that consideration for the contract provided by the police is past consideration, making the contract invalid.

C   Both the directors and the police have a point. The directors need only pay for the cost of the additional police presence.

D   The police are right. The actions of the club have led to a need for increased police presence and they must pay for it.

6   Karl is interested in buying Marcus's car. Marcus is in trouble with his creditors and so is keen to sell. In the course of correspondence, Marcus refuses Karl's offer of £3,000 but states that 'for a quick sale, I will accept £4,000. Please let me know immediately if you are not interested at this price.' Karl accepted this price verbally which Marcus acknowledged.

Later, Marcus, having come into some money, denies that he has made an offer, but that he was providing information about acceptable prices to Karl.

What is the legal position?   — verbal acceptance = valid contract as acknowledged by Mc

A   Marcus was only providing information to Karl about prices and this does not constitute an offer for the purposes of contract.

B   In the context, it was clear that Marcus was making an offer of sale for that price which Karl has accepted, so they have a valid contract.

C   In the context, it was clear that Marcus was making an offer of sale for that price, however, Karl's acceptance was only verbal and therefore not valid, so they have not got a contract.

D   Marcus has made an offer and Karl has accepted, so they have a contract, but Marcus can avoid the contract because Karl has not yet provided the consideration of £4,000.

7   Which of the following statements is correct?

(i)   In an agreement of a social or domestic nature it is presumed that the parties intend to create legal relations.

(ii)   In a commercial agreement it is presumed that the parties do not intend to create legal relations.

(iii)   In a commercial agreement it is presumed that the parties do intend to create legal relations.

(iv)   In an agreement of a social or domestic nature it is presumed that the parties do not intend to create legal relations.

BPP
PROFESSIONAL EDUCATION

A   (i) and (ii)
B   (i) and (iii)
C   (ii) and (iv)
D   (iii) and (iv)

8   Misrepresentation results in a contract being:

A   Void
B   Voidable
C   Invalid
D   Valid

9   Which one of the contracts below is a standard form contract?

A   An oral agreement between two parties who have negotiated terms regarding the standards of performance to be met by each party in the main contract.

B   An oral agreement to enter into relations on the basis of conditions and warranties as agreed following negotiations between the parties.

C   A document signed by both parties to a contract in which contractual conditions and warranties as negotiated between them are set down.

D   A document put forward for the customer's signature by a supplier of goods in which pre-printed contractual conditions and warranties are set out.

10 Jude goes into a shop and sees a price label for £200 on a dishwasher. She agrees to buy the dishwasher but the till operator tells her that the label is misprinted and should read £300. Jude maintains that she only has to pay £200. How would you describe the price on the price label in terms of contract law?

A   An acceptance
B   An invitation to treat
C   An offer
D   A tender

10 Performing the contract 1

1   Dee Ltd has broken one of the terms of its contract with E Ltd. If that term is a condition, which of the following is **correct**?

A   E Ltd is entitled to damages only.
B   E Ltd is entitled to sue for damages or to repudiate the contract.
C   E Ltd is only entitled to repudiate the contract.
D   E Ltd may repudiate the contract and sue for damages.

2   Which of the following statements about oral evidence of contract terms is **correct**?

A   If a contract is in writing and is complete, the courts will still admit oral evidence concerning the contract if it is equitable to do so.

B   Oral agreement that written consent should not take effect until a conditional precedent has been satisfied is not acceptable.

C   If there is no written evidence for an oral contract, the courts will take into account what is reasonably understood by the oral terms.

D   Oral evidence may be given as an addition to a written contract if it can be shown that the document was not intended to comprise all the contract terms.

3   Which of the following statements is **not** a correct part of the definition of consumer per the Unfair Contract Terms Act 1977?

A   A consumer neither makes the contract in the course of a business nor holds himself out as doing so.
B   The other party does make the contract in the course of a business.
C   The goods are any type of goods to be used for any purpose excluding business purposes.
D   The goods are of a type ordinarily supplied for private use or consumption.

4   By virtue of the Unfair Contract Terms Act 1977, an attempt by any person to exclude liability for a negligent misrepresentation is:

A   Void unless reasonable

B   Effective only in a non-consumer transaction

C   Void

D   Valid if the other party to the contract knows of the exclusion clause or has been given reasonable notice of it

5   Which of the following statements concerning contractual terms are **untrue**?

(i)   Terms are usually classified as either conditions or warranties, but some terms may be unclassifiable in this way.

(ii)   If a condition in a contract is not fulfilled the whole contract is said to be discharged by breach.

(iii)   If a warranty in a contract is not fulfilled the whole contract is said to be discharged by breach, but either party may elect to continue with his performance.

(iv)   Terms which are implied into a contract by law are never contractual conditions.

A   (i) and (ii) only
B   (iii) and (iv) only
C   (i), (ii) and (iii) only
D   All of them

6   The Unfair Terms in Consumer Contracts Regulations 1999 provide that any terms which create a 'significant imbalance' in the rights and obligations of the parties to a standard form contract are not binding on a consumer. 'Consumer' means:

   A   Any natural person acting for the purposes of a trade, business or profession
   B   Any natural person acting outside the purposes of any trade, business or profession
   C   Any natural person or company acting for the purposes of a trade, business or profession
   D   Any natural person or company acting outside the purposes of any trade, business or profession

7   Grace and Geoffrey are both opera singers. They have each contracted with Opera Organisers Ltd to attend rehearsals for a week and then appear in the two month long run of a new production. Due to illness, Grace did not attend the rehearsals or the opening night but recovered sufficiently to appear by the fourth night. Due to illness, Geoffrey was unable to attend for the first four days of rehearsals. Opera Organisers Ltd have booked substitutes for both Grace and Geoffrey for the entire run. What is the legal position?

   A   Both Grace and Geoffrey are in breach of a condition of their contract and both of their contracts with Opera Organisers are completely discharged.

   B   Grace is in breach of condition of her contract, but Geoffrey is in breach of warranty only and his contract is not discharged.

   C   Grace is in breach of warranty and her contract is not discharged, while Geoffrey is in breach of condition, so his contract is discharged.

   D   Neither Grace nor Geoffrey are in breach of condition. They are both in breach of warranty, so neither contract is discharged.

8   Dee Ltd has broken one of the terms of its contract with E Ltd. If that term is a warranty, which of the following is **correct**?

   A   E Ltd may repudiate the contract with Dee Ltd.
   B   E Ltd can avoid the contract and recover damages.
   C   E Ltd is entitled to sue for damages only.
   D   E Ltd is entitled to sue for damages or to repudiate the contract.

9   Adam wants to buy a house from Steve. Steve's neighbour is Simon. Steve has regularly had to ask Simon to moderate the noise coming from his house and has recently even involved the police on the grounds of noise pollution. While Adam was looking around the house, he asked Steve what the neighbours were like. Steve replied that he didn't see much of them.

   Adam buys the house and discovers when he moves in that Simon is a difficult and noisy neighbour. Adam proposes to sue Steve for misrepresentation.

   What is the legal position?

   A   Steve is not liable for misrepresentation as he gave a statement of opinion, not fact.

   B   Steve is liable for misrepresentation as he had a duty to give an answer to Adam's question which was complete enough not to give a misleading impression.

   C   Steve is liable for misrepresentation as the contract was one of extreme good faith.

   D   Steve had no duty to disclose what he knew, Adam should have been a more careful buyer.

10   In which of the following situations has an actionable misrepresentation **not** occurred?

A   Peter, who wants to sell an antique vase, tells Paul, incorrectly, that it is Wedgwood, knowing that Paul will pass the information on to John, whose wife collects Wedgwood. John buys the vase.

B   Thomas makes a gun, hiding a defect with a metal plug. Matthew buys the gun without inspecting it. It later explodes and injures Matthew.

C   Judas is selling his arable farm to Andrew. He states, when questioned, that it would support 2,000 sheep, although he has never used it for sheep farming. This proves to be untrue.

D   Noah is selling his vet's practice to Shep. At the start of negotiations, he stated that it was worth about £30,000 a year. He then fell ill and custom fell away. When Shep took over, it was worth about £5,000.

11 Performing the contract 2

1   Wincey purchases a nylon and polyester electric blanket from Sleeptight Ltd by mail order. The contract contains the following clauses purporting to exclude Sleeptight's liability.

UCTA (i) C 'We accept no liability for death or personal injury caused by this product except where our negligence is proved.'

UCTA (ii) C 'The limit of our liability for loss or damage caused by this product is that of the enclosed Customer Guarantee.'

UCTA (iii) C 'We accept no liability for breach of Section 14 of Sale of Goods Act 1979.'

(iv)   'The product supplied under this contract satisfies the description applied to it by the catalogue and no liability attaches to the company if this is not so.'

UCTA (v) BC 'Any defect in the company's title to sell the product is not to affect the validity of this contract.'

Which of these exclusion clauses will be void if Wincey is (1) a consumer and (2) a business customer?

	(1) Consumer	(2) Business customer
A	(i), (iii) and (v) only	(i) and (v) only
B	(iii), (iv) and (v) only	(v) only
C	(ii), (iii), (iv) and (v) only	(v) only
D	All of them	(i) and (v) only

2   Which of the following statements is **correct**?

(i)   Any contract may be made in any form.
(ii)   Oral contracts must always be evidenced in writing.
(iii) A deed for land transfer must always be in writing and signed.
(iv)   A transfer of shares must be in writing.

A   (i) and (ii)
B   (ii) and (iv)
C   (iii) and (iv)
D   (i) and (ii)

3   Sian is negotiating with a manufacturer to buy stock for her new shop 'Kind Bath'. She will be selling a range of toiletries and bathroom items. She has explicitly told her shampoo manufacturer during the course of discussions that she does not want to buy goods tested on animals or that have had ingredients tested on animals. The manufactured replied that the products were not tested on animals.

Sian sold some of the goods in her shop, advertising them as kind to animal products. An animal rights group pointed out that one of the ingredients in the shampoo range had been tested on animals. Sian took the rest of the product off her shelves and refused to pay the supplier.

What is Sian's legal position with regard to her contract with the supplier?

A   The fact that Sian did not want her stock to be tested on animals was discussed before the contract but not expressly incorporated into the contract. The contract is valid.

B   The supplier has misrepresented the issue of the animal testing, but Sian may not rescind the contract as she has sold some of the goods.

C   Sian's representation that she would not buy products tested on animals was intended to be a term of the contract. The supplier has breached the contract.

D   The contract has been breached under the implied terms as to description under the Sale of Goods Act 1979.

4   By virtue of the Unfair Contract Terms Act 1977, an attempt by any person to exclude or restrict his liability for damage to property caused by negligence is:

A   Void unless reasonable

B   Effective only in a non-consumer transaction

C   Void

D   Valid if the other party to the contract knows of the exclusion clause or has been given reasonable notice of it

5   Which of the following statements concerning contractual terms are **true**?

(i)   Terms are usually classified as either conditions or warranties, but some terms may be unclassifiable in this way.

(ii)   If a condition in a contract is not fulfilled the whole contract is said to be discharged by breach.

(iii)   If a warranty in a contract is not fulfilled the whole contract is said to be discharged by breach, but either party may elect to continue with his performance.

(iv)   Terms which are implied into a contract by law are always contractual conditions.

A   (i) and (ii) only
B   (iii) and (iv) only
C   (i), (ii) and (iv) only
D   All of them

Incomplete contract = determine price

6   Which of the following methods is **not** an effective way to determine the price in a contract in which the details are incomplete?

    A   A clause stating it to be 'on usual hire purchase terms' — *price not certain / known*

    B   ✓Price to be set at that ruling in the market on the day of delivery

    C   An arbitrator to set the price ✓

    D   ✓Price to be set by course of dealing between the parties

7   Michael cannot read. He buys a railway ticket on which is printed 'conditions – see back'. The back of the ticket stated that the ticket was subject to conditions printed in the timetables. These included an exclusion of liability for injury. During Michael's journey, a suitcase fell off the racks and injured him. What is the legal position?

    A   The ticket office contained no notice of the conditions of carriage and the railway could not rely on the notice given on the back of the ticket.

    B   The conditions are contained in the timetable. As such, they are adequately communicated and the railway can avoid liability.

    C   The railway cannot rely on Michael being able to read. The conditions should have been communicated to him verbally and the railway cannot avoid liability.

    D   The railway cannot rely on the notice disclaiming liability as the contract had been made previously and the disclaimer was made too late.

8   What is an exclusion clause?

    A   It is a contractual warranty that the terms of the contract will be performed.

    B   It is a clause excluding the rights of persons other than the contracting parties to sue for breach of contract.

    C   It is a clause which limits the contractual capacity of one of the parties.

    D   It is a contractual clause which limits or excludes entirely a person's obligation to perform a contract or his liability for breach of contract.

9   During negotiations before entering into a contract for the sale of a car Howard says to Hilda 'the car will be ready for collection on the day you require it'. This statement is described as:

    A   A representation

    B   A term

    C   A warranty

    D   An advertiser's puff

10   Which of the following factors is **not** identified by the Sale and Supply of Goods Act to be an aspect of the quality of goods?

    A   Fitness for all purposes

    B   Freedom from minor defects

    C   Durability (ie satisfactory quality for a reasonable period)

    D   Finish and appearance

12 Performing the contract 3

1   The Unfair Contract Terms Act 1977 provides that an attempt by any person to exclude or restrict his liability for death or personal injury resulting from negligence in any contract is:

    A   Void unless reasonable
    B   Effective only in a non-consumer transaction
    C   Void
    D   Valid if the other party to the contract knows of the exclusion clause or has been given reasonable notice of it

2   Harriet bought an expensive coat from 'Coats are us'. She has exceptionally sensitive skin and the coat gave her a painful rash. Harriet is claiming that the coat was not fit for the purpose under the Sale of Goods Act 1979. What is the legal position?

    A   There is only one obvious purpose for a coat and it has failed in that purpose. Harriet is correct.

    B   Harriet has relied on the skill and judgement of the shop assistants, who have provided her with a product that doesn't meet her needs. Harriet is right.

    C   The Sale of Goods Act does not apply to this transaction. Harriet is wrong.

    D   There was a peculiarity connected with this purchase which Harriet should have brought to the attention of the shop assistants. Harriet is wrong.

3   Which of the following statements is **not** correct in relation to the implied terms of the Sale of Goods Act concerning description?

    A   If a description is applied to the goods, it is a sale by description.
    B   There is an implied condition that the goods correspond to the description.
    C   All descriptive words used form part of the contract terms.
    D   Description is interpreted to include ingredients, age, date of shipment, packing and quantity.

4   Lenny is the managing director of Hoodwink Ltd, a computer games developer. One day he purchases a company car from Cut and Shut Motors Ltd. Under the terms of the contract, Cut and Shut Ltd excluded any liability for mechanical problems. The next day, the car's exhaust systems falls off. What is the legal position of Hoodwink Ltd?

    A   The contract is of a commercial nature and therefore the clause stands and Hoodwink has no right of redress.

    B   Hoodwink is classed as a consumer therefore, the clause is not allowed under the unfair terms in consumer contracts regulations.

    C   Hoodwink must mitigate the cost of repairs.

    D   The sale of goods act does not apply to motor vehicles therefore Hoodwink must pay for the repairs itself.

5   Anne was induced to enter into a contract to purchase goods by the negligent misrepresentation of Bob. Anne seeks rescission of the contract.

Which of the following is **incorrect**?

A   Rescission is a court order requiring a contract to be correctly carried out.
B   Anne will be granted rescission only if she applies within a reasonable time.
C   The remedy may be refused if Anne has acted inequitably herself.
D   Anne will lose the right to rescind if an innocent third party acquires rights to the goods.

6   Which of the following is **not** true under the fitness for purpose provisions of the Sale of Goods Act 1979?

A   A buyer must make known the particular purpose for which he wants the goods, unless the goods have only one obvious purpose.

B   Where there is a peculiarity about the intended purpose for goods, the buyer must make the seller aware of that peculiarity.

C   The buyer must be explicit in his description of the purpose for which he wants the goods.

D   To claim that the goods supplied are not fit for the intended purpose, it must be shown that the buyer relied on the seller's skill and judgement, even if only partially.

7   What is the effect of the '*contra proferentem*' rule?

A   A person who signs a written contract is deemed to have notice of and accepted the terms contained in it in the absence of misinformation as to their meeting.

B   A person who seeks to enforce an exclusion clause in a consumer contract must show that it is reasonable.

C   The working of an exclusion clause will generally, in the absence of absolute clarity, be construed against the party seeking to rely on it.

D   The court acts on the presumption that an exclusion clause was not intended to work against the main purpose of the contract.

8   A term may be implied into a contract:

(i)   By statute

(ii)   By trade practice unless an express term overrides it

(iii)   By the court to provide for events not contemplated by the parties

(iv)   By the court to give effect to a term which the parties had agreed upon but failed to express because it was obvious

(v)   By the court to override an express term which is contrary to normal custom

A   (ii) and (iii) only
B   (i), (ii) and (iv) only
C   (i), (iv) and (v) only
D   (i), (iii), (iv) and (v) only

9   Katie took her wedding dress to the dry cleaners to be cleaned. It was a silk dress, made with intricate beading and sequins. She was given a receipt which contained conditions, which she was told restricted the cleaner's liability, particularly with regard to the risk of damage to the beads and sequins on her dress. The conditions actually stated that the cleaners had absolutely no liability for damage to the dress. Katie signed the agreement assuming that all dry cleaners would want to protect themselves against damaging beads and sequins.

The dress was badly stained in the cleaning process.

What is Katie's legal position?

A   She signed the document restricting the cleaner's liability so she is bound by its terms.

B   The conditions have been adequately communicated and so are binding regardless of her signature.

C   She was misled by the cleaners as to the extent of the exclusion clause and so she is not bound by the terms.

D   She is not bound by the terms because they were not made available to her at the time of the contract.

10   If one party announces his intention not to honour his agreement before the performance was due, this is called:

A   Misrepresentation
B   Fundamental breach
C   Substantial performance
D   Anticipatory breach

13 Performing the contract 4

1   The effect of signing a document is:

(i)   The person signing is prima facie assumed to have read the document.
(ii)   The person signing the document is bound by all its terms, irrespective of what they provide.

Which is **correct**?   *This is an exception = unless one has been 'MR'*

A   (i) only
B   (ii) only
C   Both (i) and (ii)
D   Neither (i) nor (ii)

2   Henry agreed to sell his horse to Richard at a given price. When the negotiations were over and the contract formed, Henry told Richard that the horse was sound and 'free from vice'. The horse turned out to be vicious and Richard wants to bring an action against Henry.

Richard will fail in his action because Henry's promise that the horse was not vicious was:

A   A statement of opinion not fact   *–T*
B   Made after the original contract and was not supported by consideration   *– contract already agreed & seldos. toolcte!*
C   Not relied upon by Richard   *–T*
D   Merely a 'sales puff'   *–T*

QUESTIONS

(handwritten notes at top of page)
To waive debt
- pay debt to creditor
- 3rd party makes payment
- settle debt early
- payment in kind.

3   John owes Catherine £26.89. Kathleen, John's mum, agrees to pay Catherine £20 on John's behalf and Catherine accepts it 'in full settlement'. Two weeks later, Catherine requested the remaining £6.89 from John. Is she entitled to the money?

A   Yes, because part payment does not provide sufficient consideration for a promise to discharge a debt.

B   Yes, because a third party cannot absolve others of their liability under a contract.

C   No, because part payment by a third party is good consideration for a promise to discharge a debt.

D   No, because intervention by a relative was not intended to be a legal act.

4   A Ltd has broken one of the terms of its contract with B Ltd. If that term is a warranty, which of the following is **correct**?

A   B Ltd may repudiate the contract and claim damages.

B   B Ltd may repudiate the contract and apply for rescission.

C   B Ltd is entitled to damages only.

D   B Ltd is entitled to damages and rescission.

5   Which of the following statements is **correct**?

A   A breach of condition entitles an innocent party to repudiate a contract unless he has accepted the breach.

B   A breach of a condition entitles an innocent party to repudiate a contract whether or not the breach has been accepted.

C   A breach of a condition entitles an innocent party to recover damages only.

D   A breach of a condition or warranty entitles the innocent party to damages only.

6   In a contract for the sale of goods between a business and a consumer, any attempt to exclude the terms implied by the Sale of Goods Act 1979 is:

A   Void

B   Void unless reasonable

C   Voidable at the option of the consumer

D   Valid if the consumer is given written notice of the clause

7   Grace owes Rebecca £40, which must be paid by 1 January. Rebecca really needs some money to do some Christmas shopping so she tells Grace that if she pays her at the beginning of December, she only has to pay £25, 'in full satisfaction of the debt'. Rebecca doesn't get as much Christmas money as she was hoping for and starts to wish, on 26 December, that she had asked Grace for the full amount.

Can Rebecca claim the remaining £15 from Grace?

A   Yes. However, she will have to wait until 1 January as that is when Grace will be breaching the contract.

B   Yes. She can claim it from Grace and Grace must pay her by 1 January.

C   No. Rebecca is bound in honour not to claim her legal rights.

D   No. Grace provided consideration for part payment by paying early, therefore Rebecca has no rights under the old contract.

BPP
PROFESSIONAL EDUCATION

8   All the following statements relating to contract terms are **correct** except one. The exception is:

    A   Contract terms are usually classified as either conditions or warranties, but some terms may be unclassifiable in this way.

    B   A breach of warranty gives the injured party the right to rescission and to claim damages.

    C   A breach of condition gives the injured party the right to terminate the contract and claim damages.

    D   Some contract terms may be implied by custom, statute or the courts.

9   Jack and Jill visited Bognor Regis and booked into a hotel for the night. On arriving in their room they noticed that there were many conditions of contract pinned to the back of the door, including clauses limiting liability by the hotel for loss of valuables which were not placed in the hotel safe. Jack and Jill had never seen these conditions before. Which of the following is **true**?

    A   The hotel has adequately disclosed the exclusion clause and Jack and Jill are bound by the conditions.

    B   Jack and Jill have signed for their room at reception, so the conditions are binding on them.

    C   The hotel has given them a misleading explanation of the terms, so Jack and Jill are not bound by the terms, even though they have signed for them.

    D   Jack and Jill are not bound by the terms, because the contract was made before they reached the room, so the hotel cannot rely on the exclusion clause.

10   Which of the following is **not true**?

    A   An exclusion clause must be incorporated into a contract before the contract has finally been concluded.

    B   An exclusion clause may be invalidated by the Unfair Contract Terms Act 1977, in a case to which the Act applies.

    C   If a person signs a document containing an exclusion clause he is held to have agreed to it, even if he has not read the document, unless he has been misled about the term's legal effect.

    D   Under the *contra proferentem* rule, when deciding what an exclusion clause means, the courts interpret any ambiguity in the favour of the person who relies on the exclusion.

correct word / language should b against not relies.

14 Contractual breakdown 1

1   One of the following statements regarding anticipatory breach is **untrue**. Which one?

    A   Repudiatory breach automatically discharges the contract. ✗

    B   Genuine mistakes will not necessarily repudiate a contract. ✓

    C   Action for breach can be delayed until actual breach occurs. ✓

    D   Subsequent events can affect the party's right to action. *True because, contract may subsequently be frustrated.*

2   The general rule for a contract to be discharged by performance is that performance must be exact and precise. Which of the following is **not** an exception to that rule?

A   Where time is not of the essence
B   Where the promisee prevents performance
C   Where the contract is substantially performed
D   Where the contract is partially performed

3   Where there has been anticipatory breach of contract the injured party is entitled to sue:

A   After a reasonable time

B   Only from the moment the other party actually breaches a contractual condition

C   From the moment the other party indicates that he does not intend to be bound

D   From the moment the injured party has fulfilled his obligations but the other party indicates that he does not intend to be bound

4   In an action for breach of contract, the court will **not** award:

A   Unliquidated damages
B   Nominal damages
C   Liquidated damages
D   Exemplary damages *— awarded in tort*

5   Which of the following is a genuine cause of a contract being frustrated?

A   Personal disinclination to perform a contract of personal service *→ breach in contract*
B   Non-occurrence of an event which is <u>part</u> of the purpose of the contract *x → not main purpose*
C   Personal incapacity to perform a contract of personal service *✓*
D   Increase in the cost of meeting contractual terms *x → not cause of frustration*

6   Rosie and Jim were married and owned their marital home jointly. Jim left the home, to go and live with his secretary. The spouses met to discuss their situation and Jim agreed to pay Rosie £750 a month. She agreed to pay the mortgage payments and Jim agreed to transfer the house to Rosie's sole possession when the mortgage was paid off. Rosie requested Jim to put the agreement into writing and to sign it, which he did.

Rosie paid off the mortgage and Jim refused to transfer the house into her name.

What is the position?

A   Rosie has not provided consideration for the agreement as all the money used to pay off the mortgage has come from Jim both before and after he left the marital home.

B   Rosie and Jim are married so the courts will assume that there was no intention to create legal relations.

C   Rosie and Jim are separated so the courts will presume that legal relations were intended and Jim will have to transfer the property.

D   The courts will assume legal relations but the consideration is inadequate due to all the mortgage payments that Jim made prior to leaving the marital home.

7   Which of the following statements is **true**?

A   Damages are an equitable remedy and are primarily intended to restore the party who has suffered loss to the same position he would have been in if the contract had been performed.

B   Damages are a common law remedy and are primarily intended to restore the party who has suffered loss to the same position as he would have been in if the contract had been performed.

C   Damages are an equitable remedy whereby the court orders a person to perform a contract so that the other party to the contract does not suffer loss.

D   Damages are a common law remedy whereby the court orders a person to perform a contract so that the other party to the contract does not suffer loss.

8   Daniel owns a mill. The main crank shaft of the mill has broken and it has to be sent to London to be used by specialist manufacturers as a pattern for a new one. Daniel contracts with Lionel to transport the broken shaft to London.

Lionel neglects to take the shaft to London on his next delivery, and the shaft does not get repaired and returned to Daniel for two weeks, when it was supposed to have taken one week. During that time, the mill has been out of operation as it cannot run without its main crank shaft. Daniel claims loss of profits against Lionel.

Which of the following is **true**?   *The loss has t be reasoncbly foreseeable t the defendant for damages t be awarded.*

A   The claim must fail. Daniel's loss could not reasonably be foreseen by Lionel.

B   The claim will succeed for the second week. Lionel was contracted to deliver within a certain time and might reasonably have known that delay would inconvenience Daniel.

C   The claim must fail. Damages are not awarded for loss of profits, but only for expenses arising from the breach. Daniel has incurred no extra expenses.

D   The claim will succeed in part. Only nominal damages will be awarded as the claim is speculative and it is impossible to ascertain the loss.

9   Cee Ltd ordered goods from Dee Ltd to be delivered to F Ltd.

If the goods are not delivered,

A   F Ltd can sue Dee Ltd for breach of contract.

B   Cee Ltd can sue Dee Ltd for breach of contract and recover compensation for its own loss.

C   Cee Ltd may sue Dee Ltd for breach of contract and recover compensation for its own loss and the loss to F Ltd.

D   Cee Ltd can sue Dee Ltd for breach of contract only if it was acting as the agent of F Ltd.

10   Which of the following statements is **correct**?

    (i)   The limitation period for claims for breach of contract may be extended if a debt or other certain monetary amount is acknowledged or paid in part before the original period of limitation has expired.

    (ii)   The claim must be acknowledged as existing by the defendant. This does not have to be in writing.

    A   (i)
    B   (ii)
    C   Both (i) and (ii)
    D   Neither (i) nor (ii)

15 Contractual breakdown 2

1   Which of the following statements concerning limitation to actions for breach is **incorrect**?

    A   The right to sue for breach of contract is usually statute barred after six years from the date on which the cause of action accrued.

    B   The right to sue for breach of contract by deed is statute barred after twelve years from the date on which the cause of action accrued.

    C   If the defendant is of unsound mind at the time of the contract, the six year period begins to run when his disability ceases or he dies.

    D   If the information relevant to possible claims is deliberately concealed, the normal period of six years can be extended after the period of six years has started to run.

2   Which of the following is **not** an equitable right in contractual breakdown?

    A   Rescission
    B   Specific performance
    C   *Quantum Meruit*
    D   Injunction

3   Which of the following statements is **true**?

    (i)   The purpose of an injunction is to enforce a negative restraint in a contract.

    (ii)   The purpose of an injunction is to restrain acts which appear inconsistent with the contract's obligations.

    A   (i)
    B   (ii)
    C   Both (i) and (ii)
    D   Neither (i) nor (ii)

4　　Chill 'n' Freeze is a supplier of hotel mini-bars. One of its customers, Posh Hotels, is seeking damages due to faulty bars which leaked chemicals into hotel rooms.

Under the commercial contract, Chill 'n' Freeze excluded liability for indirect and consequential losses.

Posh Hotels want damages for the loss of profit they would have made if the mini-bars worked correctly.

What is Chill 'n' Freeze's legal position?

A　　No liability for loss of profit as the damage is consequential.
B　　The term is unfair under the unfair contract terms act, so Chill 'n' Freeze is liable for the loss of profit.
C　　Partial liability as Posh Hotels did not mitigate its loss.
D　　Liable for the loss of profit as it is directly attributable to the breach.

5　　Which of the following statements is **untrue**?

A　　The courts will award damages for mental distress if that is the main result of the breach.

B　　The general principle of damages is to compensate for actual financial loss.

C　　The amount of damages awarded is only that which puts the claimant in the position he would have been in but for the breach.

D　　Damages may only be awarded for losses arising naturally from the breach which arise in a manner the parties may reasonably be supposed to have contemplated.

6　　Which of the following is **not** a definition of the doctrine of frustration of contract?

A　　Parties should be discharged from their contract if altered circumstances render the contract fundamentally different in nature from what was originally agreed.

B　　Parties should be discharged if an event, for which neither party is responsible and which was not contemplated occurs, which renders the contract fundamentally different and which results in a situation to which the parties did not originally wish to be bound.

C　　Parties who contract that something should be done are discharged if performance becomes impossible.

D　　Parties who contract that something should be done are discharged if their assumption that certain conditions would continue proves to be false.

7　　What is the object of an award of basic damages for breach of contract?

A　　To ensure that the injured party receives payment for the acts performed.

B　　To ensure that the injured party is in the same position as he would have been in had the contract been performed.

C　　To ensure that the defaulting party does not profit from his breach.

D　　To ensure that the defaulting party is penalised so that the breach will not recur.

8   Rodney and Horatio have entered into a contract whereby Rodney is to provide a ship to load waste at Palermo within 30 days of the ship's arrival. The ship arrives at Palermo but because the waste is unsafe, Horatio does not load it. The ship remains at Palermo but after 28 days the Italian government passes a law banning the transportation of unsafe waste by sea. The contract has been discharged by:

A   Anticipatory breach
B   Fundamental breach
C   Impossibility
D   Frustration

9   Emma was contracted to deliver two cases of champagne and 20 cases of wine from France to England for John's daughter's wedding. Emma was going to take the wine on the ferry while John flew back to England to carry on preparations that he was needed for there. Emma drove to Calais, but found that the ferry crossings had been cancelled due to high storms. She did not deliver the wine and the wedding guests had to drink water.

Emma claims that the contract was frustrated due to the cancellation of the ferry services because of the weather. What is the **correct** position?

A   Emma is right. The contract has been frustrated due to the weather preventing her completing her task.

B   Emma is wrong. The contract has not been frustrated by the weather, but by her inability to perform a personal service.

C   Emma is wrong. The contract has not been frustrated by the weather, but by the intervention of a third party, the ferry company.

D   Emma is wrong. The contract has not been frustrated at all. She could have carried out the delivery by an alternative route, such as the Channel tunnel.

10   Part payment of the contract price may not be recovered in exchange for incomplete performance where:

A   One party has prevented complete performance.
B   The work has been substantially completed.
C   Part of the work agreed under a fixed sum contract has been completed.
D   Part of the work agreed under a contract payable by instalment has been completed.

16 Contractual breakdown 3

1   Which of the following statements is **true**?

(i)   Specific performance is an order of the court directing a person to perform an obligation.
(ii)   An order for specific performance will be made when the contract is for land.
(iii)   An order for specific performance will not be made in a contract for personal services.

A   (i) and (ii)
B   (i) and (iii)
C   (i), (ii) and (iii)
D   None of the above

BPP
PROFESSIONAL EDUCATION

2   What must an injured party do when a contract is discharged by fundamental breach?

A   He must either treat the contract as discharged or affirm it as still in force.

B   He must treat the contract as discharged at once.

C   He must continue with his own obligations if he wants to claim damages.

D   He must seek an injunction if he wants to claim damages.

3   Which of the following is **not** a common law remedy?

A   Damages

B   Action for the price

C   *Quantum meruit*

D   Specific performance

4   A restitutory award which aims to restore the claimant to the position he would have been in but for the contract is known as:

A   Mareva injunction

B   *Restitutio in integrum*

C   *Quantum meruit*

D   Doctrine of laches

5   Harriet and Mark had entered into an agreement for the supply of goods to be delivered and paid for by instalments. Mark failed to pay the first instalment when it was due. Harriet refused to make further deliveries unless Mark paid cash on delivery. Mark refused to accept delivery on those terms. The price of the goods rose and Mark sued for breach of contract.

Which of the following is **true**?

A   Harriet was entitled to repudiate when Mark failed to pay her the first instalment.

B   Mark should have mitigated his loss by accepting the offer of delivery on cash payment terms.

C   Damages will be based on the difference in the price of goods at the due date of delivery and the date of damages to account of the price rise.

D   The contract has been frustrated by the price rise.

6   Robina agreed to write a book on Medieval Knights and Jousting for the History Alive Junior Series. She was
    to receive £4,000 on completion of the book. She had completed all the research and written a third of the
    book when History Alive decided to abandon the series.

    What is Robina's legal position?

    A   Robina has not discharged the contract by complete and exact performance, she will not be entitled
        to payment for what she has done.

    B   Robina has only managed partial performance, she will only be entitled to payment for what she has
        done if History Alive accept partial performance.

    C   Robina has been prevented from completing performance by History Alive. She is entitled to sue for
        damages or bring a *quantum meruit* action for the work she has done.

    D   The contract has been frustrated by the abandonment of the series, Robina will not be entitled to
        payment for what she has done.

7   Vincent sells paintings by Pablo in his art shop. He has undertaken not to advertise the paintings at a lower
    price than Pablo has specified, only to sell the paintings to private collectors, and not to display any of
    Pablo's paintings without his permission. They have agreed that if Vincent breaks any of these conditions, he
    will have to pay Pablo £10,000.

    Vincent hangs a picture that Pablo gave Vincent's wife for Christmas the previous year above the counter in
    his shop. Pablo claims that Vincent does not have permission to display the picture and is demanding
    £10,000.

    A   Vincent owes Pablo £10,000 as liquidated damages.
    B   Vincent owes Pablo £10,000 under a penalty clause.
    C   Vincent owes Pablo nothing because the penalty clause is void.
    D   Vincent may choose to not pay Pablo because the penalty clause is voidable.

8   Liquidated damages are:

    A   Damages which have been paid out of a sum previously lodged with the court by the defendants

    B   A fixed or ascertainable sum agreed by the parties at the time of contracting payable in the event of a
        breach

    C   A sum of money payable under a contract in the event of a breach whose purpose is to deter a
        potential difficulty

    D   A measure of the value of contractual work done awarded to put the claimant in the position he would
        have been if the contract had never been performed

9   Which of the following is **not** a genuine cause of a contract being frustrated?

    A   Destruction of the subject matter
    B   Non-occurrence of an event which is part of the purpose of the contract
    C   Personal incapacity to perform a contract of personal service
    D   Supervening illegality

10   Which of the following would cause a contract to be frustrated?

   A   An act beyond the control of the parties to the contract making the contract impossible to perform
   B   A rise in the cost of raw materials making it impossible for one party to complete the contract at a profit
   C   A large increase in orders making it impossible to deliver all the goods ordered by the date specified
   D   An act by one of the parties to the contract making it impossible to perform

17 Contractual breakdown 4

1   A contract may be discharged on the grounds of personal incapacity to perform a contract of personal
   service where:

   (i)   An employee's ill-health prevents him from performing his duties.
   (ii)   An employee dies.
   (iii)   An employee is sent to prison for six months.
   (iv)   An employee who is a foreign national is called up for military service.
   (v)   An employee is a national of a country on whom the UK declares war.

   A   (ii) only
   B   (i), (ii) and (iv) only
   C   (ii), (iii) and (v) only
   D   (i), (ii), (iii) and (iv) only

2   In damages for breach of contract, damages representing expectation interest are:

   A   Money to restore the claimant to the position that he would have been in if he had not relied on the
       contract.

   B   Money to put the claimant in the position that he would have been in if the contract had been properly
       performed.

   C   Interest charged on the sum of damages agreed between the date of breach of contract and the date
       of payment.

   D   Interest charged to cover the effects of inflation since the breach.

3   Davina engages Rupert as interior decorator and designer to do up her flat in South Kensington. The
   contract is for a fixed sum of £7,500. Within the allotted time Rupert informs Davina that the work is
   completed. On inspection Davina finds that the doorbell does not chime and an aspidistra she requested has
   not been supplied. Must she pay Rupert?

   A   Yes: though she may retain the purchase price of the aspidistra and amount for repair of the chimes.

   B   Yes: the contract has been substantially performed and the full £7,500 must be paid.

   C   No: the failures in performance constitute anticipatory breach.

   D   No: performance must be complete, entire and exact so nothing is payable until the defects are put
       right.

4   Whin Mechanics Ltd agree to service a fleet of trucks for Rigg Enterprises Ltd for a total price of £20,000. Work is agreed to commence on 1 June and to be completed by 15 June. Owing to a strike and to problems with spare parts, the service of all the trucks is only completed on 30 June. Whin Mechanics Ltd admit to breach of contract but dispute the amount of damages claimed, being £10,000 for loss of half a month's business profits (as certified by the auditors) £20,000 for the loss of certified profits on a highly lucrative new contract which was offered to the company on 20 June but which could not be taken up.

How much will Whin Mechanics Ltd have to pay?

A   Nothing. The losses are too remote.

B   £10,000. Only normal business profits are recoverable.

C   £20,000. Whin should have anticipated the special contract.

D   £30,000. Normal business profits are recoverable and it is foreseeable that a severe delay will lose a customer profits which may become available.

5   Betty runs a farm where she breeds dogs. She contracted with Seth to build a walk in refrigerator where all the food for the dogs would be kept. Seth built the refrigerator wrongly and all the dog food Betty put in there went mouldy. Betty did not realise that the food had gone bad and fed it to the dogs. All the dogs suffered stomach problems for a few days. One dog, a rare breed, developed an acute case of food poisoning and died.

Betty is claiming damages for the value of the dead dog and also loss of profits from selling the dog when it was more mature. Will she succeed?

A   No. The death of one of Betty's dogs as a result of an error in the refrigerator could not have been within Seth's contemplation.

B   Yes. But Seth is liable for the value of the dead dog only. It is unclear what profits would have arisen from the sale of the dog.

C   Yes. But Seth is liable for the value of a standard dead dog only. He could not have known that a rare dog would die.

D   Yes. Seth is liable for serious consequences, as food poisoning is not too remote to have been within his contemplation and he was working for a dog breeder, who was likely to own valuable dogs.

6   In which one of the following circumstances will a decree for specific performance not be available?

A   In a contract for the sale of land
B   In a contract made by deed for land
C   In a contract of employment
D   In a contract to pay money to a third party

7   Belinda engaged Botch Job Bathrooms to install a bathroom on the first floor of her house. The price of the job was £7,500 and it included converting the old bathroom into a study. On completion of the job, she discovered that the plumbing in the old bathroom had not been correctly removed and that there was a leak in the wall behind her bookshelves. The new bathroom is fine. She was forced to bring someone in to correct the plumbing in her study at a cost of £500. She is refusing to pay Botch Job Bathrooms.

What is the legal position?

A   The contract has been completed and Belinda must pay Botch Job Bathrooms.

B   Belinda has prevented Botch Job Bathrooms from completing performance by getting another plumber in. Therefore she must pay the full sum.

C   The contract was performed in a seriously substandard fashion and Belinda does not have to pay for it.

D   The contract has been substantially performed and Belinda must pay Botch Job Bathrooms £7,500 less the cost of righting the problems, that is £7,000.

8   Which of the following is **not** a reasonable ground for frustration of a contract?

A   The destruction by lightning of a hall let out for a concert.

B   The onset of illness in the lead singer of a pop group.

C   An outbreak of war, causing a ship to be trapped in a port until the end of hostilities.

D   The closure due to bad weather of a mountain pass, causing traffic to take an alternative route, 300 miles longer.

9   Tee Ltd contracted with Vee Ltd to deliver goods to Vee Ltd to the value of £5,000. Vee Ltd accepted the goods but the amount due remains outstanding. Tee Ltd may:

A   Recover damages for breach of contract subject to its obligation to take reasonable steps to mitigate its loss

B   Apply for an order of specific performance to force Vee Ltd to pay

C   Sue for the price without any obligation to mitigate

D   Take back the goods that have been delivered to Vee Ltd

10   Sarah owes her friend, Sally-Anne, £100. Sally-Anne agrees to waive her right to the debt if Sarah, who is a dressmaker, makes her a dress to wear to a ball that she has been invited to at college. Sarah makes the dress and gives it to Sally-Anne. Unfortunately, the ball is cancelled and Sally-Anne has no need for the dress. She returns the dress to Sarah, assuming it can be sold in the shop, and asks for payment of the £100 instead.

What is the legal position?

A   Sally-Anne is entitled to £100 under the original agreement.

B   Sally-Anne is not entitled to £100 as she has waived her right to the money and accepted a dress in its place.

C   Sally-Anne is entitled to the £100 as the dress is not as valuable as the £100 so the second promise has insufficient consideration.

D   Sally-Anne is entitled to the £100 as she would have had to pay for the dress, as dressmaking is Sarah's business.

18 Employment 1

1   An employer always has an implied duty to:

    A   Provide facilities for smokers
    B   Give employees who leave a reference
    C   Provide work
    D   Behave reasonably and responsibly toward employees

2   As a general rule, in relation to a claim for unfair dismissal, which of the following statements are **incorrect**?

    (i)   Only employees below the normal retiring age may claim
    (ii)   There is no qualifying period
    (iii)   There is frequently no limit on the amount of compensation that a tribunal can award
    (iv)   Claims must be made within three months of the dismissal

    A   (i) only
    B   (ii) only
    C   (ii) and (iii) only
    D   (i) and (iv) only

3   An inspector has wide powers which may be used against an employer who contravenes health and safety requirements. Which of the following is **not** available to him?

    A   A criminal prosecution
    B   A prohibition notice
    C   An improvement notice
    D   A civil action for damages

4   Which of the following reasons is **not** valid for the dismissal of an employee?

    A   Dishonesty
    B   Wilful disobedience of a lawful order
    C   Membership of a trade union
    D   Misconduct

5   Mick has been employed by Deck Line Ltd for four years. He was aware that the company was experiencing trading difficulties but is still shocked to be sent home without notice when Deck Line Ltd is compulsorily wound up. He sues for wrongful dismissal but at the hearing the liquidator proves that he has discovered that Mick has embezzled £20,000 from the company. Will Mick succeed in his claim?

    A   Yes. He has been constructively dismissed.

    B   Yes. He has been wrongfully dismissed without notice and no regard should be paid to the embezzlement discovered later.

    C   No. The employment contract was frustrated by Deck Line Ltd's liquidation.

    D   No. Deck Line Ltd was justified in its dismissal of Mick.

6   Miranda works for Little Company. The Big Company plc buys Little Company. Under the TUPE regulations, Miranda has the right to:

A   Resign and claim unfair dismissal

B   Recover redundancy pay if she chooses to leave her employment

C   Carry forward her period of employment with Little Company as continuous employment

D   Demand an employment contract under exactly the same terms as with Little Company, regardless of any organisational reasons for the contrary

7   In which of the following situations has there been no dismissal?

A   An employer asks an employee to leave his premises and never to return.
B   An employer completely changes the nature of an employee's job, as a result of which, she resigns.
C   An employment contract is frustrated by reason of the employee being in prison.
D   A fixed term contract expires and is not renewed.

8   In which **one** of the following areas is an employee not protected by legislation?

A   Dismissal on grounds of competence
B   Dismissal on grounds of race
C   Dismissal on grounds of disability
D   Dismissal on grounds of sex

9   Claire's employment with Wye Ltd began 8 years ago. Her contract of employment states that she may be required to work at any of the company's offices in London, Birmingham or Manchester. Claire has for the entire 8 years worked at the company's London office. The company has now asked Claire to move to its Manchester office.

Which ONE of the following statements is **correct**?

A   Claire cannot be required to move to the Manchester office.

B   Claire's contract contains a mobility clause which permits her employer to require her to work at any of the company's offices.

C   The fact that Claire has always worked in the London office prohibits her employer from requiring her to move to any of the company's other offices.

D   If Claire is required to move to the Manchester office, she may make a claim for automatic unfair and wrongful dismissal.

10   H plc carries on its business using both employees and independent contractors. It is important for H plc to be able to distinguish between its employees and independent contractors for a number of reasons.

Which of the following is **incorrect**?

A   Employees have a right not to be unfairly dismissed but this does not apply to independent contractors.

B   H plc must deduct income tax and national insurance contributions from the wages paid to its employees, but not from the amount paid to independent contractors.

C   Both employees and independent contractors can enforce contractual rights against H plc.

D   Both employees and independent contractors would rank as preferential creditors in respect of unpaid wages, if H plc went into insolvent liquidation.

19 Employment 2

1   The employment tribunal has just established that Ken was unfairly dismissed. There has been a breakdown of confidence between Ken and his former employers. The tribunal is likely to rule for:

A   Reinstatement
B   Re-engagement
C   Compensation
D   A punitive additional award

2   Which of the following statements is **true**?

(i)   The most common remedy for wrongful dismissal is damages. The measure of damages is usually the sum that would have been earned if proper notice had been given.

(ii)   Where breach of contract leaves the employer as the injured party, he may dismiss the employee and withhold wages.

A   (i) only
B   (ii) only
C   Both (i) and (ii)
D   Neither (i) nor (ii)

3   Which of the following tests is not an accepted test applied by the courts to determine whether a person is an employee or an independent sub-contractor?

A   The control test
B   The documentation test
C   The integration test
D   The multiple (economic reality) test

4   Pretty Plastics Ltd is a factory that takes raw materials and produces a range of plastic sheeting.

One day, a large amount of oil flooded an area of the yard outside. Sawdust was laid down, but a small patch was left uncovered when the sawdust ran out. Employees were warned of the dangers. An employee, Josh, slipped and injured his back. Is Pretty Plastics liable for damages?

A   No, it took all reasonable steps to prevent the accident.
B   No, as Josh was negligent.
C   Yes, as employers have a duty to prevent accidents.
D   Yes, as the company should have foreseen the accident and prevented it.

5   An employee has been continuously employed for one and a half years. He is entitled to:

A   Three months' notice
B   A minimum of a week's notice
C   One week's notice for every year of his employment (ie one and a half weeks' notice)
D   A month's notice

6   Which of the following is **not** one of the reasons that the distinction between employees and the independent sub-contractors is important?

A   Employers must account to the Inland Revenue for taxes due under Schedule D on independent sub-contractors' pay.

B   There is significant employment legislation which confers benefit and protection on employees.

C   Independent contractors may have to charge VAT on services provided.

D   Employers are generally vicariously liable for the tortious acts of employees during the course of employment. Liability is severely restricted in the case of independent sub-contractors.

7   Which of the following statements is **correct**?

(i)   An employer always has a duty to provide work for his employees.
(ii)   An employer has a duty to give a reference if an employee leaves to take up another job.

A   (i) only
B   (ii) only
C   Both (i) and (ii)
D   Neither (i) nor (ii)

8   In which of the following situations is being male **not** considered a genuine occupational qualification?

A   A job abroad in a country whose laws and customs might make it difficult for a woman to perform her duties

B   A job in parts of the UK where custom might make it difficult for a woman to perform her duties

C   A job as the attendant in a male lavatory

D   A job as a Catholic priest

9   Which of the following is **not** a duty of the employer?

   A   To provide a rest break of at least twenty minutes every six hours
   B   To provide an itemised pay slip (to those working more than eight hour weeks)
   C   To provide references for the employee when the employee seeks other employment
   D   To take reasonable care of employees

10   Which of the following is **not** a genuine rule for calculating length of service?

   A   A week is a week in which the employee is employed for at least eight hours under a contract for
         employment for eight hours or more.

   B   Maternity leave is included in reckoning continuity and length of service.

   C   If an employee works for the required number of hours under separate contracts for an employer he
         may aggregate the hours.

   D   A week in which an employee is otherwise absent or on strike does not break the continuity of service
         but is excluded in reckoning his length of service.

20 Employment 3

1   Which of the following statements is **correct**?

   A   A director cannot also be an employee of the company.
   B   A shareholder cannot also be an employee of the company.
   C   A partner cannot also be an employee of the firm.
   D   A lender cannot also be an employee of the firm.

2   Which of the following are sources of terms of a contract of employment?

   (i)   Custom and practice
   (ii)   A collective agreement between the union and the employer

   A   (i) only
   B   (ii) only
   C   Both (i) and (ii)
   D   Neither (i) nor (ii)

3   An employee is always entitled to:

   A   Patent rights on any invention produced by the employee at the workplace
   B   Use confidential information after the employment has ceased
   C   Require his employer to give a reference if other work is being sought
   D   Disobey an order from his employer if it is unreasonable

4   Claims for both common law damages for wrongful dismissal and statutory compensation for unfair dismissal may be heard by

(i)   The courts *—wrongful (for courts, claims >£25k)*

(ii)   Employment tribunals *—unfair dismissal*

Which of the above is **correct**?

A   (i) only
B   (ii) only
C   Both (i) and (ii)
D   Neither (i) nor (ii)

5   An employer must allow an employee time off work:

A   For trade union duties
B   To attend an interview for another job
C   To attend a course of training
D   To attend the funeral of a close relative

6   Which of the following might **not** be termination of employment by a breach of contract? *not breach of contract*

A   Summary dismissal *—sacked on the spot/asap for gross misconduct*
B   Constructive dismissal *—employee is paid less/feels his contract has been breached/ill-treated*
C   Wrongful dismissal *—sacked w/out notice due to employee incapability, denied of notice period*
D   Inability on the employer's behalf to continue *—breach of contract*

7   Which of the following statements suggests that John is an independent contractor in relation to the work he carries out for Zed Ltd?

(i)   He is required to provide his own tools.
(ii)   He is required to carry out his work personally and is not free to send a substitute.
(iii) He is paid in full without any deduction of income tax.

A   (i) and (ii) only
B   (ii) and (iii) only
C   (i) and (iii) only
D   (i), (ii) and (iii)

8   Which of the following statements are **correct**?

(i)   Employees have the right not to be subjected to any detriment or dismissed for taking steps to protect themselves and others from a danger they believe to be serious and imminent.

(ii)   The right not to be dismissed in connection with health and safety issues is subject to the usual rule on twelve month's continuous service.

(iii) The Public Interest Disclosure Act 1998 can protect workers from being dismissed or penalised for bringing health and safety dangers to light

A   (i) and (ii)
B   (i) and (iii)
C   (ii) and (iii)
D   (i), (ii) and (iii)

9   Which ONE of the following is normally implied into a contract of employment?

    A   A duty to provide a reference

    B   A duty to provide work

    C   A duty to pay wages

    D   An employee's duty to disclose his own misconduct

10   Which of the following is **not** a potentially fair reason for dismissal?

    A   Membership of a trade union

    B   Striking (where no victimisation can be proven)

    C   Being a threat to national security

    D   Legal prohibition, such as a van driver losing his driving licence

21 Employment 4

1   Which of the following groups are not excluded from the statutory unfair dismissal code?

    A   Armed forces

    B   Person ordinarily employed outside Great Britain

    C   Ministers of religion

    D   Employees dismissed while taking unofficial strike action

2   Where must a claim for wrongful dismissal be brought?

    A   The Employment Tribunal only

    B   The County Court only

    C   The High Court only

    D   The County Court, the High Court or the Employment Tribunal

3   Which of the following is **not** a duty of the employee?

    A   Reasonable competence

    B   Obedience to instructions (unless required act is unlawful or will expose employee to personal danger) *– implied duties of employees*

    C   Absence of error in work undertaken *– can never expect of human, everyone makes a mistake!*

    D   Personal service *– implied duties of employees*

4   Blue Ribbon Railways operates train services in the South East of England. It receives notice that one of its customers is seeking damages following an attack made on them by a guard on a train.

    Is Blue Ribbon liable for the damages?

    A   Yes, because the employee was working at the time of the attack.

    B   Yes, employers are always liable for the crimes of their employees.

    C   No, there is insufficient link between the crime and what the guard is employed to do.

    D   No, employers are never liable for criminal acts of their employees.

5 An employer must give an employee a statement of prescribed particulars of his employment within two months of the beginning of his contract. Which of the following is **not** required to be part of that statement?

    A   The names of the employer and the employee

    B   The rules on health and safety in the workplace

    C   Length of termination notice required on either side

    D   Whether any service with a previous employer forms part of the employee's period of employment

[handwritten: → written particulars gives reference to where health & safety doc. can be found]

6 Vicki has been employed by Ringview Ltd for ten years. She earns a basic salary of £12,000 pa. She has earned discretionary bonuses of £1,000 pa in the last three years. Her contract states that she is entitled to one month's notice. Ringview makes all its staff redundant on one week's notice. How much will the court award her as compensation for her wrongful dismissal?

    A   £692

    B   £1,000

    C   £2,076

    D   £2,250

[handwritten: compensation - less 1 mths notice; G = 9/52 of 13,000 including her bonus every year = 2,249.99 ≥ 2,250 diff 174]

7 In which of the following situations is the employee **not** automatically entitled to time off work?

    A   To receive ante-natal care

    B   To attend job interviews, having resigned from his position   *[handwritten: – he would cu been entitled if he was made redundant.]*

    C   To attend trade union branch meetings, provided that it is a recognised, independent union and the employee is a member

    D   To attend job interviews, having been made redundant

8 Which of the following reasons justify dismissal as fair?

    (i)   An auditor employed by an auditing firm is struck off the Institute's list for malpractice   *[handwritten: gross misconduct]*

    (ii)   A person employed as finance director and claiming to be a qualified accountant only has a maths 'O' level in fact   *[handwritten: capability / qualification]*

    (iii)   A nuclear scientist, despite frequent warnings, persistently fails to secure his experiments, thereby causing danger to colleagues   *[handwritten: – failure to provide safe environment @ work.]*

    (iv)   A solicitor's contract with a firm of solicitors is not renewed because the partners plan to windup the firm   *[handwritten: Other substantial reasons eg non-renewal of a fixed term contract.]*

    A   (i) and (ii) only

    B   (iii) and (iv) only

    C   (i), (ii) and (iii) only

    D   (i), (ii), (iii) and (iv)

9   Kay Michael Ltd operates a chemical processing plant at which it employs Roger. Although statute recommends their use, safety goggles are only kept in a locker in the canteen and there are instructions to use them posted at head office. The foreman discourages their use since they slow down work and so decrease the amount of productivity bonus which he earns. When Roger requests a pair therefore he is persuaded that he does not need them. There is an accident and Roger is blinded, but he can prove that had he worn goggles he would have been uninjured. What is Kay Michael Ltd's position?

(i)   It is liable to Roger for breach of statutory duty

(ii) ✓ It is open to the company to raise the defence that it took reasonable care to ensure Roger's safety

(iii)   It can raise the defence of consent against Roger

(iv) ✓ It is liable to Roger at common law for failure to provide a safe system of work

A   (i) and (iii) only

B   (ii) and (iv) only

C   (i), (iii) and (iv) only

D   (i), (ii), (iii) and (iv)

10   Nick commences employment under a three-year contract with Adieu Ltd on 1.8.X6. On 30.6.X9 he is given notice that the contract is not to be renewed. Assuming that he has a case, what claims may he bring against Adieu Ltd?

A   Wrongful dismissal only

B   Unfair dismissal only

C   Redundancy only

D   Redundancy and unfair dismissal only

22 Company formation 1

1   Which of the following is **incorrect**?

A private company limited by shares:

A   Cannot offer its shares or debentures to the public

B   Cannot allow its shareholders to offer their shares direct to the public

C   Must have a minimum of two members, otherwise the sole member may become personally liable for the debts of the company

D   Cannot be registered with a name which is the same as that of an existing registered company

2   In relation to a company's articles of association, which of the following is **incorrect**?

A   The articles of association set down the internal regulations of a company.

B   Promoters may or may not submit their own form of articles when submitting the forms necessary to form a company limited by shares.

C   The articles of association form a contract between the members and the company and the members amongst themselves.

D   The articles of association may be changed by special resolution, subject to the right of the holders of 15% of the company's shares or debentures to object to the court.

BPP
PROFESSIONAL EDUCATION

3   If a public company does business or borrows before obtaining a certificate from the registrar under s 117 Companies Act 1985, the transaction is:

A   Invalid and the third party cannot recover any loss

B   Invalid but the third party may recover any loss from the directors

C   Valid and the directors are punishable by a fine

D   Valid but the third party can sue the directors for further damages

4   What type of resolution is required to alter a company's name?

A   Special resolution

B   Ordinary resolution

C   Ordinary resolution with special notice

D   Extraordinary resolution

5   A public company limited by shares must have:

A   At least two directors, and one shareholder

B   At least one director, one company secretary and two shareholders

C   At least two directors, one company secretary and two shareholders

D   At least one director, one company secretary and one shareholder

6   If a contract is entered into by promoters before the incorporation of a company, which of the following is **incorrect**?

A   The company may adopt the contract as soon as it receives its certificate of incorporation.

B   Subject to agreement to the contrary, the promoters may be held personally liable on the contract.

C   The company cannot enforce the contract prior to its incorporation.

D   The company cannot be held liable even if it has adopted the contract after receiving its certificate of incorporation.

7   Which of the following companies would **not** be permitted to omit the word limited or Ltd at the end of its name?

A   Art for All Limited, whose object it is to bring art exhibitions to the deprived inner cities

B   Nigel's Nails Limited, whose object is the establishment of a chain of nail bars throughout the UK

C   The Lawyers' Information Service Limited, whose object is to encourage the distribution of information to students about the legal profession

D   Science for Schools Limited, whose object is to raise funds to supply scientific instruments for schools

8   Which of the following documents need **not** be submitted to register a company limited by shares?

A   A memorandum of association

B   Articles of association

C   A statement of the first directors and secretary

D   A statutory declaration of compliance with the requirements of the Companies Acts

9   If a company acts outside its objects clause, which of the following is **correct**?

    A   The shareholders may ratify the act by ordinary resolution.

    B   The shareholders may ratify the act by special resolution.

    C   The shareholders may ratify the act by extraordinary resolution.

    D   The shareholders cannot ratify the act.

10   The articles of association of a company limited by shares form a contract between:

    A   The shareholders and the company in respect of all provisions in the articles

    B   The shareholders and the directors in respect of all provisions in the articles

    C   The company and the directors in respect of directors' rights only

    D   The company and the shareholders in respect of shareholder rights only

23 Company formation 2

1   Tom has transferred his business to Tom Ltd, a company limited by shares. Which of the following statements is **correct**?

    A   Tom Ltd is fully liable for all debts and liabilities of the business incurred after the date of transfer.

    B   Tom is fully liable for all debts and liabilities of the business incurred after the date of transfer.

    C   Tom and Tom Ltd are jointly liable for all debts and liabilities of the business incurred after the date of transfer.

    D   Tom Ltd and its shareholders are fully liable for all debts and liabilities incurred after the date of transfer.

2   Which of the following records may be kept at a place other than the registered office?

    A   The register of charges

    B   The register of members

    C   The register of directors and secretaries

    D   The register of written resolutions

3   Which of the following is **not** an example of an artificial legal person?

    A   A company limited by guarantee

    B   A private company with only one member

    C   A partner in a partnership

    D   The Archbishop of Canterbury in his official capacity

4   By what percentage of members must an application to re-register a limited company as unlimited be approved?

    A   Over 50%

    B   75%

    C   100%

    D   There is no fixed percentage; the decision is taken by the board of directors since they control the company

5 Sally and Petra run a business jointly. They each have £5,000 of capital in the business and decide to form a registered company in which they will be the sole shareholders. What type of company should they form if they wish to protect their other assets?

   A   A private company limited by shares
   B   A public company limited by shares
   C   A private company limited by guarantee
   D   An unlimited private company

6 XYZ Ltd has as its sole object the operation of the XYZ Cinema. Which of the following proposed alterations to its objects can be effected by resolution under the Companies Act?

   A   Any of the proposals listed
   B   To operate a restaurant within the cinema
   C   To sell the cinema
   D   To amalgamate with Realto Cinemas plc

7 Tigger plc has 500,000 £1 shares. These are divided into 400,000 equity voting shares and 100,000 non-voting preference shares. Fluffy Ted Ltd has just bought 14,000 equity shares in Tigger plc. Does Fluffy Ted Ltd have to notify its shareholding to Tigger plc?

   A   Yes, because Fluffy Ted Ltd has acquired 3% of the equity voting shares of Tigger.

   B   No, because Fluffy Ted Ltd has not acquired 5% of the equity voting shares of Tigger.

   C   No, because Fluffy Ted Ltd has not acquired 5% of the total share capital of Tigger.

   D   No, because Fluffy Ted Ltd is a private company, and only public companies have to disclose significant shareholdings in other companies.

8 How can a promoter ensure that the expenses he or she incurs in setting up a company will be recoverable?

   A   By making it clear in all transactions that he or she is acting as agent for the company

   B   By entering into a contract with the company after its incorporation for reimbursement of expenses by the company

   C   He has no automatic right but by drafting the articles of the company, he can provide for the reimbursement of expenses

   D   By the promoter declaring in all transactions that he or she is a trustee for the company

9 Which of the following rules does not apply to partnerships under the Partnership Act 1890?

   A   No partner is entitled to remuneration such as salary for acting in the partnership business.
   B   The partnership agreement may be varied with the consent of all the partners.
   C   Partners share profits in the ratio of the amounts of capital that they originally contributed to the firm.
   D   No interest is paid on capital.

10   Which of the following changes must always be made to an off-the-shelf company when it is purchased
      from a formation agent?

      A   Changing its register of members
      B   Changing its objects clause
      C   Changing its articles
      D   Changing its name

24 Company formation 3

1   A public limited company cannot commence business or borrow money until the nominal value of the
      company's allotted share capital is not less than:

      A   £12,500
      B   £25,000
      C   £40,000
      D   £50,000

2   The case of *Salomon v Salomon 1897* confirmed which important principle of company law?

      A   A company and its members are separate legal persons.

      B   A director cannot take a decision to employ himself and later make a claim against the company as an
             employee.

      C   When a company is wound up, directors who knowingly carried on the business with intent to
             defraud creditors may be made personally liable for the company's liabilities.

      D   The sale of a business to a company owned by the vendor of the business will be a legal nullity if the
             sale made no change in the business's commercial position.

3   Within what period of time after the year end must a company file its accounts with the Registrar?

      A   Three months for a public company and six months for a private company
      B   Ten months for a public company and seven months for a private company
      C   Seven months for a public company and ten months for a private company
      D   Ten months for a public company and twelve months for a private company

4   How can a company alter the objects clause in its memorandum?

      A   By ordinary resolution
      B   By special resolution
      C   By extraordinary resolution
      D   It cannot alter its objects clause

BPP)))
PROFESSIONAL EDUCATION

5   To what extent is a member of a company limited by guarantee personally liable to contribute towards the company's debts?

    A   He is liable to contribute towards all the company's debts at any time.

    B   He is liable to contribute towards all the company's debts on a winding up only.

    C   His liability to contribute is limited to the amount stated in the memorandum upon a winding up.

    D   His liability to contribute is limited to the amount stated in the memorandum at any time.

6   Five brothers own and are directors of a limited company that carries on the family business. They are thinking of changing it to an unlimited partnership for tax reasons. What features of the business would be affected by this change?

    A   The ability to sue in the business's name

    B   The ability to mortgage the business's assets

    C   The member's rights to examine the business's accounts

    D   The ability to create a floating charge over the business's assets

7   Joe and Ken have applied to have Weston Ltd registered as a private limited company limited by shares, but have failed to submit any articles of association. What effect will this have on their application?

    A   The Registrar will refuse to register the company.

    B   Table A articles will automatically apply to the company.

    C   The company will be provisionally registered and the articles will be determined at the first meeting of the shareholders.

    D   The company will be provisionally registered but may not trade until articles are submitted.

8   What is the significance of the s 3A general commercial company objects clause?

    A   It is virtually impossible for a company to enter into an *ultra vires* commercial contract.

    B   All contracts with third parties will be enforceable even if they are not in accordance with the usual objects of a general commercial company.

    C   The company cannot ratify any contracts that are not those of a general commercial company.

    D   Shareholders cannot prevent a company entering any contracts.

9   In Paul Ltd's articles there is a clause stating that Fred should act as solicitor to the company for life. A number of members are unhappy with Fred's performance and have sufficient votes to change the articles to remove him from office. Are they able to do this?

    A   Yes, and Fred has no recourse against the company.

    B   Yes, but Fred can sue the company for breach of contract.

    C   No, because the articles cannot be changed for this reason.

    D   No, because the articles cannot be changed to override the contract with Fred.

10 Which of the following is **not** a characteristic of a partnership?

   A   Partners can by mutual agreement withdraw capital if they wish.
   B   A partnership must be governed by a written partnership agreement.
   C   Partners jointly own partnership property.
   D   Partners are agents of the partnership.

25 Company formation 4

1 A private company limited by shares must be registered with:

   A   At least one member, who may also be the sole director and company secretary
   B   At least one member, who may also be the sole director but not the company secretary
   C   At least one member, who cannot also act as a director or company secretary
   D   At least two members, one of whom may act as a director and the other as company secretary

2 Paul, a promoter, is in the process of incorporating Vendor Ltd, and has ordered goods to be used by the company. He has signed the order form 'Paul, for and on behalf of Vendor Ltd'. Who is liable if the goods are not paid for?

   A   Vendor Ltd
   B   Paul
   C   Paul and Vendor Ltd jointly
   D   Neither Paul nor Vendor Ltd as there is no contract

3 Mr X owns shares in Y Ltd. This means that Mr X

   (i)   Is a part-owner of Y Ltd
   (ii)   Is a part-owner of Y Ltd's property

   Which of the above is/are **correct**?

   A   (i) only
   B   (ii) only
   C   Both (i) and (ii)
   D   Neither (i) nor (ii)

4 Which of the following is **not** a situation in which the court will 'lift the veil of incorporation'?

   A   Where the members or managers are using the veil to evade their legal obligations

   B   Where the directors are in breach of the regulations governing the giving of financial assistance for the purchase of the company's own shares

   C   Where the true nationality of the company is being concealed

   D   Where it is suspected that the company is controlled by enemy aliens during wartime

5   All the following statements relate to a company's memorandum of association.

Which one of the following statements is **correct**?

A   The memorandum of association sets out the internal regulations governing the conduct of the company.

B   The memorandum of association is registered with the registrar of companies after the registrar has issued a certificate of incorporation.

C   The memorandum of association is required for a public company, but not for a private company.

D   The memorandum of association must state the company's name and the objects for which the company is formed.

6   What is an *ultra vires* action?

A   An illegal act for which a company cannot be given capacity

B   An act beyond the directors' powers, for which the company has the capacity but the directors do not have the authority

C   An act beyond the company's capacity to contract as defined by its objects clause

D   An act which is beyond the established commercial activities of the company

7   If the provisions of the memorandum conflict with those of the articles:

A   The memorandum will prevail over the articles.

B   The articles will prevail over the memorandum.

C   The articles must be altered by a resolution passed in general meeting to agree with the memorandum.

D   The memorandum must be altered so as to agree with the articles by application to the court for a variation order.

8   Crawley Ltd, a newly created private company, agreed to buy a valuable antique for £10,000 from Charles, one of its promoters, before issuing a prospectus which does not disclose the transaction. The antique is only worth £7,500, but the company have already entered into a contract to sell it on to Broadfield Ltd for £12,500. What action can Crawley Ltd take against Charles?

A   Rescind the contract
B   Pay Charles the cost price of £7,500 only
C   Sue Charles for £2,500
D   Nothing

9 Which of the following authorised and issued share capitals would meet the requirements for a private limited company re-registering as a public limited company?

A   30,000 shares with a nominal value of £1 (75p paid)
B   40,000 shares with a nominal value of £1 (fully paid)
C   50,000 shares with a nominal value of £1 (35p paid)
D   80,000 shares with a nominal value of £1 (20p paid)

10 What is the minimum percentage of the nominal value of the company's issued share capital that a member must hold in order to initiate proceedings to have an alteration of the objects clause cancelled?

A   5%
B   10%
C   15%
D   20%

26 Company formation 5

1 Enson Ltd has registered its own articles of association without excluding Table A. What is the status of Table A?

A   Table A is not applicable, since different articles have been registered.
B   Table A is applicable throughout – the registered articles act as a mere supplement.
C   Table A is applicable as it is not modified or excluded by the company's own articles.
D   Table A is only applicable if provisions in the company's articles are unclear or contradictory.

2 Tunnel Ltd has passed a special resolution to alter its articles of association, to allow the compulsory transfer to the directors of the shares of any member competing with the company's business. A minority of the shareholders are in a competing business, and are seeking to have this alteration declared invalid, in view of the hardship to them as minority shareholders. What is the position?

A   The alteration is valid if it is passed bona fide for the best interests of the company as a whole.

B   The alteration is invalid, since it constitutes a fraud on the minority.

C   The alteration is valid, irrespective of the motives behind it, since a company has an inherent right to alter its articles.

D   The resolution is invalid, since it contravenes statutory rights given to all members.

3 Wilde Ltd was incorporated on 1 February 20X6. The company has not given notice to the Registrar of Companies of a specific accounting reference date. When will the company's first accounting reference period end?

A   31 January 20X7
B   28 February 20X7
C   31 December 20X6
D   31 March 20X7

3-5 corrections

5/6/7 mock questions
7-10 - Practise real exam -

(CONTRACTUAL OBLIGATIONS)	(COMPANY FORMATION)
6) 7, 5, 10 [b] [a] [d]	26) 1, 3, 4, 5, 6, 8, 9
7) 8 [b]	
8) 3 [d]	✓
9) 4, 6, ✓	

(PERFORMING THE CONTRACT)	(COMPANY ADMIN + MNGNT)
11) 1, 5, 6, 10	28) 3, 7, 8 [a] [c] [d]
12) 1, 2, 3, 4, 6, 9 ✓	29) 1, 2, 3, 4, 5, 6, 8
13) 1, 2, 6, 10	30) 1, 7, 8, 10 [d]
	31) 4, 5, 6, 7, 9, 10 [d] [c] [a] [b]
(CONTRACTUAL BREAKDOWN)	32) 4 ✓
14) 1, 4, 5, 8, 10	
15) 1, 3, 4, 5, 6, 10	(ETHICAL CONFLICT)
16) 1, 2, 3, 4, 7 ✓	39) 1 Ethics (42) 3, 4, 5, 8, 9, 10
17) 1, 3, 5, 9,	40) 1, 2, 3, 4, 5, 7
	41) 1, 4, 6, 8, 9, 10
(EMPLOYMENT)	
18) 2, 6	(CORPORATE GOVERNANCE)
19) 2, 5, 6, 7, 9, 10 ✓	43) 1, 3, 6, 7, 8, 9
20) 1, 4 6	44) 4, 5, 6, 9,
3, 4, 5, 6, 7, 9, 10	45) 1, 3, 5, 6, 7.

4   Which of the following is **not** a difference between a public and private company?

    A   A public company has seven months from the end of its accounting period to produce and file its annual accounts; a private company has ten months.

    B   A company limited by guarantee can only be a private company; it cannot be a public company.

    C   The Companies Act rule that ordinary shares allotted for cash must be first offered to members applies to public, not private, companies.

    D   Under the Companies Act, a member of a public company can appoint more than one proxy, but a member of a private company can only appoint one.

5   Which of the following details about the company secretary must be contained in the register of directors and secretaries?

    A   Nationality
    B   Residential address
    C   Current and former directorships
    D   Date of birth

6   Which of the following types of limited company may omit the words limited from its name?

    A   All private companies provided certain conditions are met
    B   All companies limited by guarantee
    C   All companies limited by guarantee provided certain conditions are met
    D   No limited company may omit the word limited from its name

7   What is the legal position if a company enters into an *ultra vires* contract with one of its directors?

    A   The contract is void.
    B   The contract is void unless undertaken in good faith by the director.
    C   The contract is voidable by the company, and may be ratified in general meeting.
    D   The contract is valid, and cannot be retracted by the company.

8   Which of the following does **not** always apply to optional additional clauses inserted in a company's memorandum?

    A   Clauses can be entrenched by providing in the memorandum that they should not be altered.
    B   If the memorandum specifies a special alteration procedure, that must be followed.
    C   No alteration of the memorandum can compel a member to subscribe for additional shares.
    D   If the clause relates to class rights, these can be altered by a special resolution.

9   In which of the following situations will an alteration to a company's articles always be void?

   (i)   An alteration that applies new conditions in an existing situation

   (ii)   An alteration that takes away rights that a member has already acquired by performing a contract

   (iii) An alteration compelling members to accept increased liability for shares

   (iv)   An alteration that prescribes that a majority larger than three quarters of votes cast is needed to alter the articles

   (v)   An alteration where the minority suffer special detriment and others escape loss

   A   (i), (ii) and (iii)
   B   (i), (ii) and (iv)
   C   (i), (iv) and (v)
   D   (ii), (iii) and (iv)

10   Which of the following statements relating to a company's powers is **correct**?

   A   Borrowing can be a power or an object.
   B   Misappropriation of the company's property can be ratified by a majority of members.
   C   The company may have implied powers in addition to those expressly included in the objects clause.
   D   A company does not have the power to enter a transaction that is of no benefit to it.

27 Company formation 6

1   Which of the following statements are true about a private limited company?

   (i)   A private limited company is a company which does not qualify under the Companies Act to be a public company.

   (ii)   A private limited company is an incorporated business.

   (iii) A private limited company is not required by law to file annual accounts at Companies House.

   (iv)   The shareholders of a private company cannot benefit from limited liability.

   A   (i) and (ii) only
   B   (ii) and (iii) only
   C   (i), (iii) and (iv) only
   D   (i), (ii) and (iii) only

2   How may a clause contained in the articles be made unalterable?

   A   By declaring it to be unalterable in the articles
   B   By inserting it in the memorandum instead of the articles and declaring it to be unalterable
   C   By making a separate contract by which the company undertakes not to alter it
   D   By sending a Form 9 to the Registrar of Companies stating that the clause is unalterable

3   Lynn runs a florist. The name of the business is Lynn (Flowers) Ltd. From this information you can infer

    A   Lynn (Flowers) Ltd is a private company.
    B   Lynn (Flowers) Ltd is a public company.
    C   Lynn is a sole trader.
    D   Lynn has unlimited liability for the business's debts.

4   An English company creates a charge over its property in Scotland. It must give notice to the registrar in:

    A   Cardiff only
    B   Edinburgh only
    C   London only
    D   Cardiff and Edinburgh only

5   Ton Ltd is a wholly-owned subsidiary of MBI plc. Fred supplied goods on credit to Ton Ltd, knowing that it was part of the prosperous MBI group. Ton Ltd ran into trading difficulties and is now insolvent. Fred's legal remedy for recovery of his unpaid debt lies against:

    A   MBI plc
    B   The directors of Ton Ltd
    C   The directors of MBI Ltd
    D   Ton Ltd

6   Alf and Bert decided to form a company. On 25 April 20X6 they sent the necessary documents to the Registrar. On 10 June 20X6 they received the certificate of incorporation dated 1 May 20X6. Subsequently they discovered that the company was registered on 1 June 20X6.

    What was the date of incorporation?

    A   1 March 20X6
    B   1 May 20X6
    C   10 May 20X6
    D   1 June 20X6

7   Under s 24 Companies Act 1985, what is the consequence of the number of members of a public company falling below two?

    A   The company must cease trading within 6 months.

    B   The remaining member becomes jointly and severally liable with the company for the company's debts after 6 months.

    C   The company must notify the Registrar, but otherwise can continue trading as normal.

    D   The remaining member automatically takes over personal liability for the company's debts incurred while he is the sole member.

8   Krystle was formerly employed by Dynasty Ltd. She has entered into a covenant not to compete with Dynasty Ltd. The covenant is reasonable and not in restraint of trade. Krystle has formed a company, Krystle (Services) Ltd, which has started to trade in competition with Dynasty Ltd. Will Dynasty Ltd be able to get an injunction to prevent Krystle (Services) Ltd from trading?

A   No, because Krystle (Services) Ltd has a separate legal identity

B   Yes, because the company has been formed as a device to mask Krystle's carrying on of the trade

C   No, because a company is not liable for the actions of its shareholders

D   Yes, because Krystle (Services) Ltd is engaging in fraudulent trading

9   The provisions of Table A apply automatically unless excluded or modified by the articles of association in the case of:

A   All private companies

B   Companies limited by shares only

C   Companies limited by guarantee only

D   All limited companies

10   Which of the following are statutory grounds lifting the veil of incorporation?

(i)   A public company failing to obtain a s 117 certificate

(ii)   Incorrect use of the company's name

(iii) The director of a company that has gone into liquidation becoming a director of a new company with an identical or very similar name to the liquidated company

(iv)   A public company carrying on business once the number of members has been reduced to one

A   (i) and (iii)

B   (ii) and (iv)

C   (i), (ii) and (iii)

D   (i), (iii) and (iv)

28 Company administration and management 1

1   Which of the following is **incorrect**?

A   The board of directors is the agent of a company.

B   If the board of directors exceeds its powers, the company cannot be held liable on a contract with a third party.

C   Individual directors cannot contract on behalf of the company unless authorised by the company.

D   The board of directors may delegate authority to a managing director who may contract on behalf of the company.

2   To dismiss a director under s 303 Companies Act 1985 requires:

    A   An ordinary resolution with 14 days' notice to the company
    B   A special resolution with 14 days' notice to the company
    C   An ordinary resolution with 28 days' notice to the company
    D   A special resolution with 28 days' notice to the company

3   To enable a company limited by shares to call an extraordinary general meeting by giving 'short notice'?

    A   Shareholders holding not less than 95% of all the company's shares must agree.
    B   Shareholders holding 95% of the shares represented at the meeting must agree.
    C   95% of all the shareholders must agree.
    D   95% of all the shareholders present at the meeting must agree.

4   Which of the following **cannot** be achieved by ordinary resolution?

    A   An increase of authorised capital in a company's memorandum of association
    B   The dismissal of a director
    C   An alteration of a company's articles of association to include pre-emption rights
    D   The dismissal of an auditor

5   In relation to the company secretary, which of the following is **correct**?

    A   A company secretary of a private or public company is not required to be appropriately qualified.
    B   A single member company need not appoint a person to be company secretary.
    C   A company secretary cannot bind the company in contract.
    D   A company secretary cannot bind the company in contract if acting outside his actual or apparent authority.

6   Which of the following **cannot** be carried out by written resolution?

    A   The alteration of the articles of association
    B   The appointment of a director
    C   The removal of an auditor
    D   The alteration of the memorandum of association

7   Which one of the following is **not** a situation in which a meeting may be validly held that is only attended by one person?

    A   A board meeting
    B   Where a meeting is held by order of the court
    C   Where the articles provide a quorum of one for a general meeting, and the company is not a single member company
    D   A class meeting where all the shares are held by one member

8   Members wishing to remove a director cannot insist on their resolution being included in the notice of the meeting unless they qualify by:

A   Having one fifth of the voting rights and being at least 100 in number with shares on which an average of at least £100 has been paid up

B   Having one tenth of the voting rights and being at least 100 in number with shares on which an average of at least £100 has been paid up

C   Having one twentieth of the voting rights and being at least 100 in number with shares on which an average of at least £100 has been paid up

D   Having one tenth of the voting rights and being at least 50 in number with shares on which an average of at least £100 has been paid up

9   Waugh Ltd, a manufacturing company, wants to make a loan of £16,000 to the wife of one of its directors for her personal use. This transaction is:

A   Prohibited by the Companies Act 1985
B   Prohibited by the Companies Act 1985 unless sanctioned by an ordinary resolution in general meeting
C   Prohibited by the Companies Act 1985 unless sanctioned by a special resolution in general meeting
D   Permitted under the Companies Act 1985

10   Minutes of the general meeting must be held at the registered office and can be inspected by:

A   Members and creditors free of charge
B   Members and creditors by paying a reasonable fee
C   Members free of charge
D   Members by paying a reasonable fee

29 Company administration and management 2

1   A company has 5 members who are also directors. Each holds 10 shares. Normally the shares carry 1 vote each, but the articles state that on a resolution for a director's removal, the director to be removed should have 5 votes per share. On a resolution for the removal of Pamela, a director, Pamela casts 50 votes against the resolution and the other members cast 40 votes for the resolution. Has Pamela validly defeated the resolution?

A   No. The articles are invalid insofar as they purport to confer extra votes.

B   Yes. The proceedings and articles are valid.

C   Yes. Whilst the articles are invalid, a special resolution is required and the necessary majority has not been obtained.

D   No. A director is not entitled to vote on a resolution for her own removal.

2   Sophia is a director of a company which has just failed to win a valuable contract. She persuades the company to release her from her service agreement on the grounds of ill-health. Now that she is no longer a director, she feels free to attempt to obtain the contract for herself, which she successfully does. Is she accountable for this profit when the company sues her?

    A   No, since the company chose to release her from her service agreement and therefore from her obligations to it.

    B   No, since she is no longer a director and therefore no longer owes any duty.

    C   No, since the company could not have obtained the contract anyway and therefore lost nothing.

    D   Yes, she is accountable in this situation.

3   After a change of directors, the company must give notice to the registrar within:

    A   7 days
    B   14 days
    C   21 days
    D   28 days

4   A company decides to print the names of its directors on its business stationery. The list should include:

    A   All executive directors only
    B   All executive and non-executive directors only
    C   All directors excluding shadow directors only
    D   All directors

5   The quorum for a board meeting is:

    A   Whatever figure the articles state or allow the directors to decide
    B   Two, in all cases
    C   One
    D   Three, to avoid potential deadlock

6   Which of the following regarding EGMs is **incorrect?**

    A   The directors have power under the articles to convene an EGM whenever they see fit.

    B   Where the members requisition the directors to call an EGM, a signed requisition must be deposited at the registered office by the requisitioners stating the objects of the meeting.

    C   Where the members requisition the directors to call an EGM, the notice must give at least 28 days notice.

    D   If there is no quorum at an EGM requisitioned by the members, the meeting is adjourned.

7   The directors of a company allot 100,000 unissued shares to a third party, in order to thwart a takeover bid. An EGM is called one month later, at which an ordinary resolution is passed, with the support of the votes of the newly-issued shares, ratifying the allotment. A group of minority shareholders challenge the validity of the ratification. What is the position?

A   The ratification is valid.

B   The ratification is invalid, but only because a special resolution is required, not an ordinary one.

C   The ratification is invalid but only because the holder of the new shares should have been excluded from voting.

D   The ratification is invalid, but only because the EGM was called outside the required period after the allotment.

8   Walsall Ltd was incorporated on 1 July 20X5. It held its first annual general meeting on 31 October 20X6. What is the latest date by which the next annual general meeting must be held?

A   31 October 20X7
B   31 December 20X7
C   31 January 20X8
D   30 April 20X8

9   When may the members of a company who requisition an extraordinary general meeting convene the meeting themselves?

A   When the directors fail to convene a meeting to take place within 21 days of the date of the deposit of the requisition

B   When the directors fail to convene a meeting to take place within 28 days of the date of the deposit of the requisition

C   When the directors take action to convene a meeting within 21 days but the date of the meeting is set at a date more than 3 months from the date of the deposit of the requisition

D   When the directors fail within 21 days from the date of the deposit of the requisition to convene a meeting

10   John, a member of a public limited company, appoints Steve as his proxy for a forthcoming meeting. At that meeting, Steve will have the right to vote:

A   Only on a poll
B   Only on a poll and address the meeting
C   On a show of hands
D   On a show of hands and address the meeting

30 Company administration and management 3

1   What is the quorum for a general meeting of a public limited company?

    A   Two persons being members or proxies for members

    B   Five persons being members or proxies for members

    C   Two persons being members

    D   Five persons being members

2   If on 1 March 20X8 the secretary of Nutley & Co Ltd, a company with Table A articles, called an extraordinary general meeting to be held on 15 March 20X8, by sending notice in the post to all members entitled to attend and vote at the meeting, then the meeting:

    A   Is void

    B   Is properly notified

    C   May proceed provided that a majority of members holding at least 95% of the issued shares carrying voting rights consent to short notice

    D   May proceed provided all members of the company consent to short notice

3   Trends Ltd has an issued share capital of £100 in ordinary shares of £1, each carrying one vote. Larry is a shareholder in the company. He has received notice of an extraordinary general meeting at which a resolution is proposed to alter the company's objects. Larry does not agree with the proposed alteration.

    How many votes must be cast against the resolution to ensure that Larry defeats the resolution at the meeting, assuming all members entitled to do so attend the meeting and vote?

    A   25 votes

    B   26 votes

    C   50 votes

    D   51 votes

4   John is a director of Flush plc. He has a service contract with Flush plc with a term that the contract shall last for ten years but can be terminated by Flush plc with six months notice if John is declared bankrupt or insane. The company in general meeting has never considered this contract. What is the legal status of the term of the contract?

    A   It is valid.

    B   It is void and replaced by a term that entitles the company to terminate the contract by giving six months unconditional notice.

    C   It is void and replaced by a term that entitles the company to terminate the contract at any time by giving reasonable notice.

    D   It is void and replaced by a term that entitles the company to terminate the contract at any time by giving such notice as the company in general meeting may determine.

5   An application to the court under s 459 Companies Act 1985 for a petition that a company's affairs have been conducted in an unfairly prejudicial manner can be made by:

A   The company

B   Members holding not less than 15% in number of the issued shares of the company

C   A creditor of the company

D   Any member of the company

6   Alf and Bert, who are directors and shareholders in Oakhill Ltd, have recently purchased from the company for £100,000 land which is worth £120,000. On what grounds will Cedric, a minority shareholder, be able to sue the directors in the company's name?

A   It is just and equitable to do so.

B   The directors have used their position to make a personal gain.

C   The transaction is *ultra vires* the directors.

D   The transaction constitutes a substantial property transaction under s 320 Companies Act 1985.

7   A sale to a company of property owned by one of its directors is disclosable in its accounts. What are the consequences of non-disclosure assuming the transaction has been properly disclosed elsewhere?

A   The sale of the property is voidable by the company.

B   The director will hold any proceeds on constructive trust for the company.

C   The auditors must refuse to approve the accounts and resign.

D   The auditors must include details of the transaction in their report to members.

8   Which of the following is **not** true in relation to retirement by rotation of directors under Table A?

A   Every year one third of directors should retire.

B   At the first AGM all the directors should retire.

C   All directors are subject to retirement by rotation.

D   The question of who is to retire may be decided by lot.

9   Which of the following is **not** an example of an elective resolution?

A   To dispense with the annual appointment of auditors

B   To dispense with the requirement to be audited

C   To dispense with the laying of accounts before a general meeting

D   To dispense with holding an AGM

10   Which of the following statements about written resolutions is **true**?

A   Written resolutions can be used for any purpose except the removal of an auditor.

B   Auditors have the right of objection to written resolutions.

C   Written resolutions cannot be used if the company's articles forbid it.

D   Written resolutions can only be used by private companies.

31 Company administration and management 4

1 In relation to directors of companies limited by shares, which of the following is **incorrect**?

A   The board is the agent of the company.

B   The board is the agent of the shareholders.

C   Individual directors cannot contract on behalf of the company unless power has been delegated to them.

D   The shareholders cannot interfere with the management of the company unless authorised by the articles of association or the law.

2 Special notice must be given of:

A   All elective resolutions

B   A resolution to increase a company's authorised capital

C   A resolution to remove a director

D   A resolution to appoint a director

3 What is the minimum period of notice for an AGM?

A   7 days

B   14 days

C   21 days

D   28 days

4 If a member seeks to prove that he is a 'partner' who has been excluded from participation in the management of a quasi-partnership, he must demonstrate:

A   Mis-management

B   Prejudice to himself as a member

C   Bad faith

D   Expulsion from membership

5 Which of the following statements about loans to directors is **untrue**?

A   All loans to directors must be disclosed in the company's accounts.

B   In the case of relevant companies, the rules applying to loans to directors apply also to persons connected with directors.

C   All companies can make loans of up to £5,000 to directors.

D   A holding company cannot make loans to directors of its subsidiaries.

6   Which of the following statements about the duties of directors is **correct**?

A   The directors have a duty to ensure that no individual shareholder suffers a financial loss as a result of purchasing the company's shares.

B   Recent changes in company law require the directors to exercise the same duties on behalf of stakeholders, such as suppliers and customers, as they exercise on behalf of shareholders.

C   Duties are generally greater for directors of public companies than for directors of private companies.

D   Directors have a duty to distribute a dividend to ordinary shareholders each year.

7   What length of notice is required and what majority of a company's members attending and voting in person or by proxy is needed to pass an ordinary resolution at an extraordinary general meeting?

A   14 days notice and over 50%

B   21 days notice and over 50%

C   14 days notice and 75%

D   21 days notice and 75%

8   A disqualification order against a director of a company on the ground that his conduct makes him unfit to be concerned in the management of a company may last for:

A   A minimum of 2 years and a maximum of 5 years

B   A minimum of 2 years and a maximum of 15 years

C   A minimum of 5 years with no maximum

D   A maximum of 15 years with no minimum

9   Under Table A, a director shall not vote or be counted in the quorum present at a board meeting on a resolution concerning a matter in which he has a material interest unless the resolution concerns:

A   The grant of a service contract to him

B   The allotment of shares to him

C   The transfer of shares to him

D   The purchase of property from him ·

10   Which of the following statements are **correct**?

(i)   A company can be wound up if there is deadlock in the management of its affairs.

(ii)   A company can be wound up if in a quasi-partnership situation, the understandings between members or directors that were the basis of association have been unfairly breached.

(iii)   A company can be wound up if the directors deliberately withhold information.

(iv)   The Department of Trade and Industry can appoint inspectors to investigate the ownership of a company.

(v)   The Department of Trade and Industry must appoint inspectors to investigate the affairs of a company if members holding at least one tenth of issued share capital apply to it to do so.

A   (i), (ii), (iv) and (v)

B   (i), (ii), (iii) and (iv)

C   (ii), (iii) and (v)

D   (i), (iv) and (v)

32 Company administration and management 5

1   If a director breaches his fiduciary duty, which of the following **never** applies?

     A   The director may have to account for a secret profit if he has made one.

     B   If the director holds more than 50% of the shares he can ratify his own breach of duty at an annual general meeting.

     C   The director can be automatically absolved from breach of duty by the articles.

     D   The director may be fined by the courts.

2   Arabella visits her brother, Henry, who is a director of a large public company. After dinner, he shows her the draft accounts for the company, mentions that he is delighted that profits have soared and that the share price is bound to rise dramatically when the accounts are published the following week. The next day Arabella persuades her friend Tom to contract to sell her £50,000 worth of his shares in the company. Has she committed an offence?

     A   Yes. The information is obtained from a person connected with the company, and she has dealt in order to obtain a profit. This is insider dealing.

     B   No. The shares were not dealt on a recognised regulated market.

     C   Yes. Although this was a private purchase, all public company share dealings are potentially subject to the Criminal Justice Act 1993.

     D   No. Arabella is not herself connected with the company, and could only be liable if she had deliberately obtained the information.

3   Which one of the following is a valid compensation payment which does not require the approval of the general meeting?

     A   Settlement of a contractual claim arising from the premature termination of a service agreement

     B   Voluntary payment of compensation by the company under s 312

     C   A payment made to directors in connection with the purchase of a company's business under s 313

     D   The excess payment made by a takeover bidder when purchasing a director's shares at a higher price than it paid to other shareholders, under s 315

4   Which of the following are statutory exceptions to the prohibition on directors' loans under s 330?

     (i)   A loan to a director which is also its holding company

     (ii)   A loan approved in general meeting to allow a director to perform his duties

     (iii)   A loan to a director not exceeding £10,000

     (iv)   A loan made by a subsidiary to a director of its holding company

     (v)   A loan from a money-lending company to one of its directors on the same terms as it would normally employ, not exceeding £100,000

     A   (i), (ii), (iii) and (iv) only
     B   (i), (ii) and (v) only
     C   (iii) and (iv) only
     D   (ii), (iii) and (v) only

5   If a meeting becomes inquorate during its proceedings, the 1985 version of Table A provides that:

     A   The meeting may continue so long as a quorum was present at its start.
     B   The meeting as a whole is a nullity.
     C   The chairman may choose to adjourn at his discretion.
     D   The chairman must automatically adjourn.

6   Small Ltd was incorporated on 1 August 20X6. What is the latest date on which it can hold its first annual general meeting?

     A   1 August 20X7
     B   1 November 20X7
     C   31 December 20X7
     D   1 February 20X8

7   Bear Ltd has an issued share capital of 10,000 ordinary shares of £1 each. The directors wish to propose an elective resolution in order to enable them to have the authority to issue shares over an indefinite period. What is the minimum number of votes that must be cast to enable the resolution to be passed?

     A   5,000
     B   5,001
     C   7,501
     D   10,000

8   Andrew, a director of Beth Ltd, wishes to obtain approval for the sale of his flat to the company for £70,000. Which of the following net asset levels is the lowest level that would force Andrew to seek approval of the contract from shareholders under s 320?

     A   £100,000
     B   £700,000
     C   £1,000,000 $\frac{10\%}{1\%} \times 70,000 = 7000 = 70,000$
     D   £1,400,000

9   Omega Limited has three directors, Alpha, Beta and Gamma. Alpha works for the company full-time. Beta and Gamma (who is an experienced accountant) are non-executive directors. At Alpha's request, Beta and Gamma sign blank cheques, which Alpha then uses to make loans on behalf of Omega Limited, which are then lost. Which of the directors will be liable to the company?

   A   All three of them as in their capacity as directors they have a duty of care

   B   Alpha only, as he is the only full-time director, the other two being non-executive

   C   Alpha and Gamma, as the latter is an accountant and should know that signing blank cheques is negligent

   D   None of them, as they have acted diligently and shown a reasonable degree of skill

10 Which of the following is **not** a possible defence to a charge under the insider dealing rules in the Criminal Justice Act 1993?

   A   The individual did not expect there to be a profit or avoidance of a loss.

   B   The individual had reasonable grounds to believe that the information would be disclosed widely.

   C   No dealing has taken place if an individual has encouraged someone else to deal or disclosed inside information.

   D   The individual would have done what he did even if he had not had the information, for example, where securities are sold to pay a pressing debt.

33 Corporate finance 1

1   HIJ Ltd has borrowed money from K Bank plc and has provided security by executing a fixed charge debenture in favour of the bank. A fixed charge is:

   A   A charge over specific company property which prevents the company from dealing freely with the property in the ordinary course of business

   B   A charge over a class of company assets which enables the company to deal freely with the assets in the ordinary course of business

   C   A charge over specific company property which enables the company to deal freely with the assets in the ordinary course of business

   D   A charge over company land enabling the company to deal freely with the land in the ordinary course of business

2   Companies limited by shares are subject to the 'maintenance of capital' rule. Which of the following statements regarding the rule is **incorrect**?

A   A company cannot simply return share capital to its shareholders.

B   Share capital must be set aside and used to pay creditors in the event of the company becoming insolvent.

C   Share capital should be used to further a company's lawful objects.

D   Share capital may be returned to the shareholders following an approved reduction of capital scheme.

3   If a company issues new ordinary shares for cash, the general rule is that:

A   The shares must be offered to the existing members rateably in the case of a public but not a private company.

B   The shares must be offered to the existing members rateably in the case of a private but not a public company.

C   The shares must be offered to the existing members rateably whether the company is public or private.

D   The shares need not be issued to the existing members rateably.

4   If the net assets of a public company are half or less of the amount of its called up share capital, the directors must call an extraordinary general meeting. Within what period from their becoming aware of the need to do so must they issue a notice convening the meeting?

A   7 days
B   21 days
C   28 days
D   3 months

5   To enable a company to reduce capital, the shareholders must sanction the reduction by:

A   Ordinary resolution with the usual notice
B   Special resolution with the usual notice
C   Ordinary resolution with special notice
D   Special resolution with special notice

6   In relation to company charges, which of the following is **correct**?

A   A private company cannot create fixed charges.
B   A public company cannot create floating charges.
C   Both private and public companies may create fixed and floating charges.
D   All business organisations can create fixed and floating charges.

7   The term 'authorised share capital' is best defined as:

   A   The total amount of share capital which the company is authorised to issue by the capital clause of its
        memorandum

   B   The total amount of share capital which the board of directors may from time to time decide to issue

   C   The total amount of shares which have been allotted to members

   D   The aggregate amount of shares which have been fully paid up

8   If the company wishes to increase its authorised share capital, what type of resolution should it use?

   A   Ordinary resolution
   B   Special resolution
   C   Extraordinary resolution
   D   Whatever type of resolution the articles prescribe

9   What is the minimum percentage of the issued shares (or class of share) that must be held by members
     who wish to apply to the court to object to a private company giving financial assistance for the acquisition
     of its own shares?

   A   5%
   B   10%
   C   15%
   D   30%

10   Which of the following amounts to a variation of class rights?

   A   The issue of shares of the same class to allottees who are not already members of that class

   B   The return of capital to the holders of preference shares

   C   The creation and issue of a new class of preference share with priority over an existing class of
        preference shares

   D   An alteration to the prescribed procedure for a variation of class rights

34 Corporate finance 2

1   A private company has an issued share capital (fully paid) of £90,000, £10,000 on its share premium
     account and a negative balance of £5,000 on its revaluation reserve. Its net assets are £112,500. What is the
     maximum amount that it can distribute as dividend?

   A   £12,500
   B   £17,500
   C   £22,500
   D   It cannot pay a dividend

2   A floating charge is created on 1 March 20X2 and crystallises on 1 October 20X2. A fixed charge over the same property is created on 1 September 20X2. Assuming both are registered within the prescribed time limits, which ranks first?

A   The fixed charge

B   The floating charge

C   On crystallisation of the floating charge to a fixed charge, both rank pari passu (as fixed charges)

D   The floating charge becomes a fixed charge on crystallisation, and at that point ranks before the original fixed charge

3   Which of the following statements is **correct**?

A   A public company can issue shares at a discount.

B   A public company's shares can never be partly paid up.

C   A public company can issue shares in return for an undertaking to do work or perform services.

D   A public company must obtain an independent valuation for non-cash consideration for its shares from its auditor.

4   It appears that Unsteady Ltd is about to go into liquidation owing its creditors considerable sums of money. Which of the following statements is **true**?

A   The directors will always be liable to recompense the company's creditors.

B   The directors may be liable to recompense the company's creditors.

C   The directors will never be liable to recompense the company's creditors.

D   The members will always be liable to recompense the company's creditors.

5   A company creates a charge in June in favour of its bank. The necessary documents are executed, but left undated and not registered by the bank's solicitor. In November he realises his mistake, writes a November date on the documents and registers them within the specified period from that date. A certificate of registration is issued. In December the company goes into voluntary liquidation. The liquidator challenges the validity of the charge on the grounds that it was not registered within the specified time after its creation. Is the charge valid and enforceable?

A   No. The charge was registered out of time.

B   No. The charge was registered fraudulently and the solicitor can be sued.

C   Yes. The certificate is valid and conclusive.

D   Yes, but only if the court orders rectification of the certificate.

6   Under the Companies Act 1985 a shareholder has a statutory right of pre-emption:

A   On the allotment of equity shares for cash by the company

B   On any allotment of shares by the company

C   On a transfer of shares by another member of the same company

D   On the transmission of shares on the death of another member of the same company

7   James Ltd wishes to reduce its issued share capital under S135 CA 85. Which of these requirements must the company meet in order to do so?

    (i)   Power to do so must be included in the Articles

    (ii)   The company must pass a special resolution

    (iii)   The company must obtain the confirmation of the court to proceed with the scheme

    A   (i) and (ii) only

    B   (ii) and (iii) only

    C   (i), (ii) and (iii)

    D   None of the requirements, as only public companies can reduce their share capital in this way.

8   A provision in a company's articles which authorises a transfer of shares orally is:

    A   Void

    B   Voidable

    C   Unenforceable

    D   Valid

9   The directors of Pen Ltd are proposing a purchase by the company of its own shares out of capital. They have made a statutory declaration and called an extraordinary general meeting of members. What kind of resolution is required to approve this proposal?

    A   Ordinary resolution

    B   Ordinary resolution with special notice

    C   Extraordinary resolution

    D   Special resolution

10 Where the net assets of a public company are half or less of its called-up share capital the directors have a statutory duty to convene an extraordinary general meeting of the company. The purpose of this meeting is to

    A   Pass a special resolution to initiate a members' voluntary winding-up

    B   Pass an extraordinary resolution to initiate a creditors' voluntary winding-up

    C   Pass a special resolution for the reduction of issued capital

    D   Consider the steps, if any, that should be taken to deal with the situation

35 Corporate finance 3

1   HIJ Ltd has borrowed money from K Bank plc and has provided security by executing a floating charge debenture in favour of the bank. A floating charge is:

    A   A charge over specific company property which prevents the company from dealing freely with the property in the ordinary course of business

    B   A charge over a class of company assets which enables the company to deal freely with the assets in the ordinary course of business

    C   A charge over specific company property which enables the company to deal freely with the assets in the ordinary course of business

    D   A charge over company land enabling the company to deal freely with the land in the ordinary course of business

2   Which of the following is the correct period within which company charges must be registered with the Registrar of Companies?

    A   7 days following the issue of the charge
    B   14 days following the issue of the charge
    C   21 days following the issue of the charge
    D   28 days following the issue of the charge

3   Which one of the following is **not** an exception to the general rule that a company may not purchase its own shares?

    A   Redemption of redeemable shares
    B   Purchase of shares under the s 135 reduction of capital procedures
    C   The forfeiture of shares for failure to pay sums due in respect of those shares
    D   Purchase of own shares if a shareholder has made a bid for 90% of the issue share capital

4   Which one of the following is an **incorrect** statement of the relationship between ordinary shares and debentures?

    A   Debentures do not normally confer voting rights, whilst ordinary shares do.
    B   The company's duty is to pay interest on debentures, and to pay dividends on ordinary shares.
    C   Interest paid on debentures is deducted from pre-tax profits, share dividends are paid from net profits.
    D   A debenture holder takes priority over a member in liquidation.

5   A preference may be set aside by the liquidator of a company if it was:

A   Made within two years prior to the commencement of the liquidation, regardless of whether the recipient is a connected person

B   Made within two years prior to the commencement of the liquidation, or six months if in favour of a connected person

C   Made within three years prior to the commencement of the liquidation, or twelve months if in favour of a connected person

D   Made within three years prior to the commencement of the liquidation, regardless of whether the recipient is a connected person

6   A private company has resolved by special resolution to disapply the statutory right of pre-emption under s 89. The resolution was combined with a grant of authority to the directors to allot shares under s 80. What is the maximum permitted duration of the resolution?

A   There is no limit to the duration of the resolution
B   3 months
C   1 year
D   5 years

7   After a purchase of its own shares by either a market or off-market method, the company must make a return to the registrar under s 169 within:

A   7 days
B   21 days
C   28 days
D   3 months

8   Which one of the following is **not** an undistributable reserve?

A   Share premium account
B   Capital redemption reserve
C   A surplus of accumulated unrealised profits over accumulated unrealised losses
D   Contingency reserve

9   If there has been a variation of class rights, a minority of holders of shares of the class (who have not consented or voted in favour of the variation) may apply to the court to have the variation cancelled. The objectors must:

    A   Hold not less than 15% of the issued shares of that class and apply to the court within 28 days of the giving of consent by the class

    B   Hold not less than 10% of the issued shares of that class and apply to the court within 28 days of the giving of consent by the class

    C   Hold not less than 15% of the issued shares of that class and apply to the court within 21 days of the giving of consent by the class

    D   Hold not less than 10% of the issued shares of that class and apply to the court within 2 calendar months of the giving of consent by the class

10   A register of debenture holders is required:

    A   By law in all cases
    B   By law in some cases
    C   By a contractual term (if any) of the debenture
    D   By order of the court

36 Corporate finance 4

1   A company proposes to issue debentures carrying an immediate right of conversion into ordinary shares which are to be issued at par. £100 debentures are to be issued at a 20% discount. Thus a debenture issued for £80 cash should be converted into 100 £1 shares immediately. Is the debenture issue valid?

    A   Yes. There is no objection to the issue of debentures at a discount.

    B   No. It is illegal to issue debentures at a discount.

    C   No. Although debentures may be issued at a discount, the instant conversion means this is merely a method of issuing shares at a lower consideration than their nominal value, which is illegal.

    D   Yes. There is no objection to the issue of either debentures or shares at a discount.

2   A registered company has a nominal capital of £600,000 divided into 600,000 shares of £1 each, of which £400,000 is issued and only £100,000 is paid up. What is the amount of the uncalled capital that may be called up at 14 days' notice?

    A   £200,000
    B   £300,000
    C   £400,000
    D   £500,000

3   If a company is wound up insolvent what is the effect of non-registration of a floating charge under the Companies Act 1985?

    A   The debt is void against the liquidator and the chargee receives nothing.

    B   The charge is voidable by the liquidator if the company was insolvent when the charge was created.

    C   The charge is void against the liquidator and the chargee proceeds as an ordinary creditor.

    D   The charge is void against subsequent secured creditors and the chargee loses priority accordingly.

4   A floating charge is created by a company nine months before it goes into liquidation. The charge is in favour of a bank to secure a loan of cash paid to the company after the creation of the charge. The charge is:

    A   Valid as a fixed charge

    B   Valid as a floating charge

    C   Voidable by the liquidator because it was made within 12 months of liquidation

    D   Voidable by the liquidator as a fraudulent preference

5   Under the Companies Act 1985, the status of an allotment of shares made by the directors without proper authority is:

    A   Void

    B   Voidable

    C   Valid

    D   Invalid

6   Profits available for distribution in a private company may be defined as:

    A   Accumulated realised profits less accumulated realised losses

    B   Accumulated realised profits less losses for the current year

    C   Accumulated realised profits

    D   Accumulated realised profits less accumulated realised and unrealised losses

7   What are the consequences for the shareholders of a public company if the directors make a distribution in excess of the amount permitted by the Companies Act?

    A   The total distribution is repayable to the company by all the shareholders.

    B   The excess amount over that permitted is repayable by all shareholders.

    C   The excess over the permitted amount is repayable by shareholders who knew or had reasonable grounds to believe that the distribution was in contravention of the Act.

    D   The amount repayable is the total amount that was paid to shareholders who knew, or had reasonable grounds to believe, the distribution to be in contravention of the Act.

8   Where there is a qualification in the audit report of a public company, what effect does this have on a proposed distribution which would otherwise be lawful?

A   The distribution may go ahead if the auditors report that the qualification is not material in this context.

B   The distribution may go ahead if the members agree in general meeting.

C   No distribution is permitted.

D   It has no effect.

9   Which of the following schemes involves a reduction of capital, requiring the confirmation of the court?

A   A repayment of preference shares and the re-dating of £100,000 debentures from 20X2 to 20X9

B   A reconstruction involving the transfer of assets from one company to another with a members' voluntary winding up of the old company

C   The reduction in nominal value of shares from 100 pence to 80 pence by the cancellation of a call not yet made

D   The provision of financial assistance by way of loan for the purchase of shares in the company

10   The directors of Cob Ltd are proposing a purchase by the company of its own shares out of capital. They have made a statutory declaration and called an extraordinary general meeting of members to approve their proposal.

The statutory declaration made by the directors must contain a statement that in their opinion the company will be able to carry on business as a going concern and will be able to pay its debts as they fall due in the next:

A   Six months

B   Year

C   Eighteen months

D   Two years

37 Ethics and business 1

1   Which statement describes the principle of objectivity?

A   By following this principle, an accountant minimises the risk of passing on incorrect information.

B   Following this principle requires an accountant to keep their mind clear of distractions.

C   Following this principle requires an accountant to stay technically up to date.

D   Following this principle requires scepticism and close attention to detail when reviewing information.

2   You have a duty to respect employer confidentiality even if you have an ethical dispute with them.

True/False?

3   An accountant who refuses to take on work as they do not have any experience in that area can be said to be arguing what?

    A   Integrity
    B   Professional behaviour
    C   Objectivity
    D   Professional competence

4   How can accountants demonstrate the professional quality of scepticism? Select all that apply.

    A   By keeping their mind free from distractions.
    B   By seeking supporting evidence before accepting information is accurate.
    C   By investigating why information was given to them.
    D   By maintaining their objectivity.
    E   By reviewing the work of a junior before accepting it as correct.

5   How can accountants demonstrate accountability?

    A   By questioning work given to them.
    B   By taking responsibility for a mistake.
    C   By ensuring their work is free from error.
    D   By replying to an email on behalf of a colleague.

6   Which of the following is an example of an accountant's social responsibility?

    A   To increase the profitability of the business they work for.
    B   To ensure the maximum corporation tax is paid by their employer.
    C   To use recycling facilities if provided by their employer.
    D   To provide accurate financial information to shareholders.

7   Which of the following are reasons why IFAC and CIMA have a 'Code of ethics for professional accountants'? Select all that apply.

    A   To increase the profitability of businesses.
    B   To enhance the employability of accountants.
    C   To help protect the public interest.
    D   To indicate the highest level of behaviour expected of accountants.
    E   To indicate the minimum level of behaviour expected of accountants.

8   CIMA believes that by implementing a code of ethics the employment prospects of its members will be enhanced.

    True/False?

9   Accountants should conduct themselves with courtesy towards others has their behaviour reflects both on .... and the ....

    Fill in the missing words using the following; **system, law, profession, themselves, others, colleagues.**

10   When should CIMA members and students be satisfied that they have sufficient technical and personal skills?

    A   When they have completed all examinations.

    B   When they have completed all examinations and practical experience requirements.

    C   When they are admitted to membership and have completed professional development courses relevant to their career.

    D   They should never be satisfied.

38 Ethics and business 2

1   Why is the principle of integrity important? Select all that apply.

    A   To prevent passing on misinformation.
    B   To prevent bias affecting your work.
    C   To enhance the credibility of your work.
    D   To protect the security of information.
    E   To prevent the influence of others affecting your work.

2   Which professional quality does the accountant display below?

While working on a project, an accountant puts all thoughts of other work and personal issues to one side.

Select from the following; **scepticism, accountability, independence, social responsibility**

3   CIMA has its own reasons for upholding high ethical standards through a code of ethics for its members. Firstly it has an overriding commitment to protect the .... Secondly, high ethical standards enhances the .... of CIMA members.

Fill in the missing words using the following; **law, public, standards, prospects, ethics, accounting, interest, work, employability**

4   Why has IFAC issued a code of ethics for accountants worldwide?

    A   It was requested to do so by the world bank.
    B   Worldwide corporate scandals have eroded all confidence in accountants.
    C   To enhance the quality and standards of services provided by accountants.
    D   International law has required a worldwide code of ethics.

5   By consistently producing unreliable work, an accountant may find:

    A   Their professional competence being challenged.

    B   Colleagues' confidence in their future work is reduced.

    C   Their prospects of promotion are reduced.

    D   They need further training.

    E   IFAC investigating the standard of their work.

    Select all that apply.

6   An accountant's quality of .... will help safeguard confidential information as they do not take undue risks that could result in the information being made public.

    Another feature of this quality is they ensure their work is complete and meets ....
....

    Fill in the missing words using the following; **standards, accountability, scepticism, professional, public, responsibility, legal, employers, requirements**

7   Why is it important for accountants to be courteous?

    A   To show that they are competent.

    B   To show 'independence in appearance'.

    C   To give a good impression of the profession to those they meet.

    D   Liability insurance requires exemplary behaviour at all times.

8   By committing to continual personal development and lifelong learning, a CIMA member supports their
....

    Fill in the missing words using the following; **competence, employment, standards, professional, legal, ethical**

9   .... is the concept that an individual continually remains open to new ideas, skills and knowledge.

    Fill in the missing words.

10   A governing body attempts to anticipate every possible ethical situation when developing a code of ethics.

    The above statement describes a **rules-based/framework-based** approach to ethics.

    Delete the incorrect term.

39 Ethics and business 3

1   Match the personal/professional qualities expected of an accountant with the fundamental principle they support.

    (a)   Respect
    (b)   Scepticism
    (c)   Responsibility
    (d)   Independence

    (i)   Integrity
    (ii)   Objectivity
    (iii)   Professional behaviour
    (iv)   Confidentiality

2   How can an accountant demonstrate independence?

    A   By double-checking their work.
    B   By avoiding situations that might cause an observer to doubt their objectivity.
    C   By questioning the work of others.
    D   By considering the needs of their colleagues at work.

3   An accountant can demonstrate scepticism by .... information given to them and seeking supporting .... before accepting it as correct.

    Fill in the missing words using the following; **work, reading, evidence, advice, questioning, correcting**

4   Several judgements and decisions made by an accountant have been found to be ill judged. The accountant takes full responsibility for this. Which professional quality are they demonstrating?

    A   Social responsibility
    B   Scepticism
    C   Independence
    D   Accountability

5   Ethical codes such as those developed by IFAC and CIMA should:

    A   Enhance the standards of their members
    B   Eliminate unethical behaviour by members
    C   Indicate the highest level of behaviour expected of members
    D   Always consist of fundamental principles

6   An accountant's quality of .... will save their employer resources as work is completed when required.

    Fill in the missing word using the following; **responsibility, accounting, independence, timeliness, objectivity**

7   An accountant who does not follow the concept of .... risks their knowledge becoming technically obsolete due to changes in the accounting environment. This puts their .... in jeopardy.

Fill in the missing words.

8   'This approach is best suited to deal with complex situations and evolving environments.'

This is an advantage of which approach to developing an ethical code of practice?

A   Rules-based
B   Framework-based

9   How does a framework-based approach to developing an ethical code differ from a rules-based approach?

A   It sets out specific guidance for each specific ethical dilemma.
B   It expects members to adhere to the letter of the law.
C   It expects members to embody certain principles.
D   The governing body anticipates all potential ethical problems.

10   One definition of ethics is 'the moral principles that guide behaviour'.

True/False?

40 Ethical conflict 1

The following data is to be used to answer questions 1 to 5 below

The following five situations each describe a breach of one of CIMA's fundamental principles.

State the most appropriate ethical principle that has been breached.

1   A colleague in the accounts department continually submitting substantially inflated expense claims.

2   A finance director accepting a luxury holiday from the supplier of loan capital to the business.

3   An accountant taking a very important report home to check over a bottle of wine.

4   The management accountant of a health club using a database of members to source potential new customers for a health club their father is about to set up.

5   The continued use of estimates for the basis of trade receivables and trade payables.

6   When a CIMA member faces an ethical conflict, who should they look to first to resolve it?

A   CIMA
B   The board of directors
C   Themselves
D   Relevant outside professional advisors

7 CIMA as a Chartered body has a duty to uphold the .... High ethical standards held by members serves to enhance their reputation and ....

Fill in the missing words using the following; **interest, legal, law, social, employability, public, standards, ethical**

---

8 What is the main source of encouragement for businesses to behave in a socially responsible way?

A Public pressure
B Stock exchange regulations
C Legal requirements
D Accounting standards

---

9 Which of the following are potential consequences to the accounting profession if members are allowed to behave unethically? Select all that apply.

A Professional bodies may lose their 'chartered' status.
B Increased regulation of the profession by external organisations.
C Increased employability of accountants.
D Improved reputation of the profession.

---

10 What should a CIMA member do if the only option available to resolve an ethical issue with their employer involves breach of confidentiality?

A Proceed with the solution
B Take legal advice before proceeding
C Do not proceed with the resolution
D Take advice from friends and family

41 Ethical conflict 2

1 You work in a small accounts team and have recently started studying for your CIMA qualification. Due to the department's size, you are required to perform a wide range of work. In one particularly busy time your company's corporation tax return has become due. You have been asked by the finance manager to complete the return, when you explain that you have very little tax knowledge you are told, 'just do it, if you're not sure how to, just follow last year's workings'.

State three of CIMA's fundamental principles that are at stake.

---

2 When attempting to resolve an ethical dilemma by themselves, CIMA members should use their organisation's internal procedures if available.

True/False?

---

3   Which of the following examples of unethical behaviour could an accountant face criminal prosecution for if committed?

    A   Sending an abusive email
    B   Supplying confidential information about a public listed company to a stock broker
    C   Supplying management accounts to directors that are inaccurate
    D   Allowing personal problems to interfere with the production of management accounts

4   Unethical behaviour by accountants undermines the profession's .... and has consequences to .... as a whole.

Fill in the missing words using the following; **society, legality, law, reputation, interest, responsibility**

5   Corporate governance rules are required because:

    A   Shareholders want to be able to sue directors.
    B   Stock markets do not trust financial statements.
    C   Management need encouragement to act in the best interests of all stakeholders.
    D   Companies do not always behave ethically.

6   Which of the following situations may create a conflict of interest? Select all that apply.

    A   Working part-time for two rival businesses.
    B   Owning shares in a company that competes with your employer.
    C   Being employed by a close relative.
    D   Being offered a valuable gift by a friend who is also a business contact.
    E   Being paid a performance related bonus, assessed by your manager.

7   Which of the following is not a benefit of ethical of accountants to society?

    A   Credible, accurate and reliable financial statements for investors.

    B   Government collecting the correct amount of corporation tax, (where accountants are used to calculate the charge).

    C   Assistance to the authorities for the detection and prevention of fraud.

    D   Ensuring companies are profitable.

8   What matters should CIMA members record while attempting to resolve an ethical issue? Select all that apply.

    A   Meetings that take place.
    B   Decisions that are taken.
    C   Informal discussions and phone calls.
    D   Email communications made.

9   In the UK, corporate governance rules are an example of:

    A   Legal regulation
    B   Non-legal regulation
    C   Statutory instruments
    D   Government policy

10   Which of the following is an example of socially responsible behaviour by a business?

    A   Ensuring the chairman and chief executive roles are not performed by the same person
    B   Ensuring employees receive health and safety training
    C   Ensuring employees have access to recycling facilities
    D   Ensuring staff are hired on the basis of ability regardless of age, sex, religion or any handicaps

42 Ethical conflict 3

1   It is possible for accountants to be sued for damages if they are found guilty of unethical behaviour.

    True/False?

2   CIMA students are expected to demonstrate the same level of professional standards as full members.

    True/False?

3   Put the following in order according to how tightly regulated they are. 1 for most regulated down to 4 for the least regulated.

    A   Ethics
    B   The law
    C   Corporate governance
    D   Business social responsibility

4   An accountant is employed by a manufacturing company, but has permission to take on private work in their spare time producing management accounts for their own clients.

    Which of the following situations may create a conflict of interest? Select all that apply.

    A   Taking on work from a company that is in direct competition with their employer
    B   The income from one private client exceeds the salary received from their main employer
    C   A private client asks the accountant to work for them full-time
    D   Having to turn down private work as they do not have sufficient spare time to do the work

5   A conflict of interest is evidence of wrongdoing.

    True/False?

6   Unlike a university degree holder, a member of the CIMA qualification can be stripped of their status should their behaviour be deemed unethical.

    True/False?

7   An accountant may need to resign from their position if all other attempts to resolve the ethical issue and to remove themselves from the situation have failed.

    True/False?

8   When considering a course of action to resolve an ethical issue, an accountant should consider the .... facts, CIMA's fundamental .... the .... issues and any .... procedures available to them.

    Fill in the missing words using the following; **ethical, standards, external, relevant, responsibilities, independent, principles, social, detailed, internal, financial, behavioural**

9   To achieve ethical behaviour, an individual or business must first meet its .... and .... obligations first.

    Fill in the missing words using the following; **ethical, responsible, legal, social, financial, non-legal, public**

10 Businesses can act legally without necessarily acting ethically.

    True/False?

43 Corporate governance 1

1   Corporate governance is the system by which organisations are .... and ....

    Fill in the missing words.

2   Which statement describes the interaction of corporate governance with business ethics?

    A   Corporate governance determines what is ethical for businesses.
    B   Business ethics does not affect how an organisation is governed.
    C   Business ethics can influence corporate governance.
    D   An organisation's governance must always be ethical.

3   Which of the following are reasons for the need to develop corporate governance rules? Select all that apply.

    A   Companies listing on more than one country's stock exchange
    B   The need to reduce pollution in the environment
    C   Stock market crashes in the 1990's
    D   Loss of confidence in financial statements and company management
    E   A number of high profile scandals and corporate collapses

4   Which two countries saw world famous corporate governance scandals during the 1970s, 1980s and
     1990s?

    A   USA and Russia

    B   USA and UK

    C   UK and Belgium

    D   China and India

5   Performance bonuses for directors should only adversely affect a company if:

    A   The bonuses are paid in cash

    B   The bonuses are in the form of shares

    C   Directors make short-term decisions to achieve them

    D   Directors have to improve a company's share price to achieve them

6   How have corporate governance rules affected an executive director's duty of skill and care?

    A   No change

    B   Increased the level of duty

    C   Reduced the level of duty

    D   Made the level of duty statutory

7   A possible indicator of poor corporate governance is the lack of an adequate internal control function such
     as an .... team.

     Fill in the missing words.

8   German companies are based on a two-tier board structure. Select the names of the two boards from the list
     below.

    A   Policy

    B   Supervisory

    C   Functional

    D   Executive

9   What structure does the 2003 Combined Code recommend for remuneration committees when reviewing
     executive directors' remuneration packages?

    A   Mainly executive directors

    B   Mainly non-executive directors

    C   Exclusively executive directors

    D   Exclusively non-executive directors

10   Match the name of the committee/report with the corporate governance issue it reported on.

    (a)   Turnbull Committee
    (b)   Smith Report
    (c)   Higgs Report

    (i)   Non-executive directors
    (ii)   Internal controls and risk management
    (iii)   Audit committees

44 Corporate governance 2

1   Which statement describes corporate governance?

    A   The system by which companies are directed and controlled.
    B   The duties placed on the board of directors by the stock exchange.
    C   Regulations by which shareholders can hold directors to account for their actions.
    D   The concept that directors must act in a socially responsible manner.

2   Which statement most accurately describes the interaction of corporate governance with company law?

    A   Company law influences corporate governance.
    B   Company law has no influence over corporate governance.
    C   Company law dictates corporate governance.
    D   Company law only influences corporate governance because directors can be sued for their actions.

3   Directors' behaviour has been largely affected by corporate governance rules which have increased their
.... and the portion of their remuneration which is related to their
....

Fill in the missing words using the following; **independence, attendance, accountability, ability, performance, status**

4   Which TWO of the following are not direct reasons for the development of corporate governance rules?

    A   The differential treatment of domestic and foreign investors.
    B   The internationalisation of accounting qualifications.
    C   The development of international accounting standards.
    D   The globalisation of share trading.

5   Which of the following is an example of how company law has influenced corporate governance?

    A   Companies split the role of chairman and chief executive.
    B   Companies set up an audit committee.
    C   Companies set directors' notice periods at one year or less.
    D   Companies have an annual general meeting.

6   A board of directors should monitor various aspects of the business. Which of the following are examples of what it should monitor? Select all that apply.

   A   The chief executive
   B   The risk and control systems
   C   The communication of its strategies through the organisation
   D   The human capital within the business
   E   The performance of its strategies

7   Lack of contact with shareholders may be a sign of poor corporate governance.

   True/False?

8   Which THREE of the following are names of committee reports that were included in the 2003 Combined Code?

   A   Higgs
   B   Smith
   C   Lords
   D   Jones
   E   Turnbull

9   How often does the 2003 Combined Code recommend directors review the internal controls of their company?

   A   Every year
   B   Every 2 years
   C   Every 3 years
   D   As often as the directors feel necessary

10   Name the main source of corporate governance regulation in the UK.

   A   The Companies Act
   B   Sarbanes-Oxley Act
   C   The 2003 Combined Code
   D   The Cadbury Report

45 Corporate governance 3

1   Which of the following are examples of corporate governance? Select all that apply.

   A   Internal controls to protect a company's assets
   B   The board of directors providing employees with a mission statement
   C   Stock exchange rules that dictate when shareholders may buy and sell shares
   D   An employee performance related pay scheme

2 One reason for the need to develop corporate governance rules is to prevent future corporate scandals and collapses. Which 2 of the following are names of companies involved in such scandals?

A Dot.media
B Enron
C Leisureworld
D Worldcom
E West Coast Communications

3 One driver of the development of corporate governance rules concerns financial reporting. In many cases .... in the management and .... of companies was eroded, so rules were required to restore it.

Fill in the missing words using the following; **reporting, ability, confidence, desirability, executive, objectivity, independence**

4 As a result of recent corporate governance rules, directors have found their duty of skill and care substantially **increased/decreased/unchanged.**

Delete the two incorrect words.

5 Name the three main types of board structure.

1) .... executive

2) .... executive

3) .... non-executive

6 .... directors are concerned with the day-to-day running of the company whereas .... directors have the role of bringing balance to the board's structure.

Fill in the missing words.

7 What structure does the 2003 Combined Code recommend for audit committees?

A Mainly non-executive directors.
B Mainly executive directors.
C The committee should be equally balanced between executive and non-executive directors.
D Exclusively non-executive directors, the majority should be independent.

8 Any combination by a company of the chairman and chief executive roles should be justified publicly.

True/False?

9 What requires listed companies to comply with the 2003 Combined Code?

A The Companies Act
B The London Stock Exchange
C The Higgs report
D The Financial Standards Authority

10   All UK listed companies must comply with the 2003 Combined Code, and non-listed companies should look to the code as 'best practice'.

True/False?

Answers

1 English and alternative legal systems 1

1	B	The balance of probabilities (D) applies in civil cases.
2	B	(i) actually means precedent not delegated legislation.
3	D	(ii) is not correct as the County Court only hears cases up to £50,000.
4	B	The other three all do have the force of legislation.
5	C	An act prohibited by law is a crime, which is prosecuted by the state. Tort is to do with the infringement of individual rights and is prosecuted by individuals.
6	C	The Court of Appeal is superior to all UK courts except the House of Lords. It is also bound by its own previous decisions.
7	D	Only criminal law is concerned with punishment.
8	A	A High Court judge sitting alone is only compelled to follow a previous decision if it is binding on him and if the material facts are similar. To do this he must follow the **ratio decidendi**, not the **obiter dicta** (hence (ii) is incorrect). He is only bound by it if it was made by a court of higher status than the High Court – (iv) is incorrect because it includes the decisions of a High Court which in fact are not always binding on the future decisions of a High Court.
9	B	Options A and C relate to civil law. 'Claimant' is a civil law term. In criminal law, the CPS (in this example) is known as the **prosecution**.
10	A	This is a consequence of the company's legal personality.

2 English and alternative legal systems 2

1	D	Employment issues are dealt with exclusively in tribunals.
2	D	Criminal law is concerned with punishment. Civil law aims to compensate, recover property or enforce legal obligations.
3	D	In Option A, not all precedents are binding (for example, if the material facts differ or the previous court had a lower status). In Option B, the House of Commons is the main original source of legislation. In Option C, the European Court of Human Rights is not an EC institution.
4	A	This literally means 'the reason for deciding'.
5	B	Option C is wrong because there is a rigid status structure for court following judicial precedent. Option D is wrong because decisions are only binding on the recipient.
6	B	This is the rule decided in *Hedley Byrne v Heller and Partners*.
7	B	An EC regulation is binding secondary legislation issued by the Council of Ministers and European Commission.
8	D	The three elements make a claim for negligence possible. Option three is not necessarily true, but if the plaintiff has contributed to his injuries, damages may be reduced.
9	C	What is not reasonably foreseeable cannot be included in a claim.
10	B	Answer A would not be enough care; answer D is too vague; answer C is too personalised.

3 English and alternative legal systems 3

1   A   Do not confuse the Crown with Parliament.

2   C   This is the rule arising from *Donoghue v Stevenson.*

3   C   The County Court has jurisdiction in contract up to £25,000. While it does have jurisdiction in tort, only claims in tort for up to £25,000 will be heard in the County Court. A claim for over £50,000 would be heard in the High Court. B is a matter for the Criminal Courts.

4   B   Regulations of the European Union are not a form of delegated legislation; they come into automatic effect when issued. Acts of Parliament can be described as primary legislation; they are not delegated.

5   C   The most important element is proximity between the parties involved but there must also have been some foreseeable damage. In *Anns v Merton London Borough Council* it was stated that the court must test whether there is sufficient proximity between the parties, such that the harm suffered was reasonably foreseeable.

6   D   *Obiter dicta* are never binding. Ratio decidendi (the statements of law behind decisions) can be binding in some certain instances.

7   D   (iii) and (iv) are developed from *Hedley Byrne v Heller & Partners,* (i) and (ii) develop earlier case law.

8   D   The others are all civil cases.

9   A   Parliament may delegate the power to make legislation to local authorities, who thereby are allowed to make by-laws, (i). If it is so provided in the enabling Act, delegated legislation may have to go through the 40-day 'laying before' procedure without a resolution against it before it comes into force, (iv). (ii) is incorrect since ministerial powers are exercised by statutory instrument. Orders in Council are an emergency, not a common, measure. (iii) is incorrect because unless its Act provides otherwise, much delegated legislation is never seen by Parliament.

10   D   Although an Act may rebut these presumptions by express words, they apply in the absence of any express provision to the contrary. (i) is incorrect since in fact the complete opposite is true – an Act applies to the whole of the UK unless it is specially expressed to exclude some part of it.

4 English and alternative legal systems 4

1   C   Taqlid is the theory that no more interpretation is needed, Urf is the theory that local custom may be subsumed into the law if not contrary to Sharia, and Istihsan is the concept of equity or fairness.

2   True   Istishab is the concept that something is permitted until shown to be forbidden.

3   **(a)(iii), (b)(i), (c)(ii)**

4   **Comprehensibility, certainty**. Civil law seeks to be comprehensive and to create certainty.

5   False   Statutes under such systems are drafted as general principles in simple language so they are more accessible.

6   C   The ICJ will only hear a case where both parties agree its decision is binding.

7   C   Binding norms are normal practice that have existed between nations for a long enough time to be seen as binding.

8   D   Judges under Sharia and codified systems can only apply the law. Judges under common law and codified systems can be involved in judicial review to ensure the law is in line with certain principles such as a constitution.

9   False   In common law systems, judge made law is often put into statute. For example, the Sale of Goods Act 1979.

10   False   Some Muslim states, such as Pakistan, that follow Sharia law have judicial reviews to ensure the enacted statutes conform to Sharia.

5 English and alternative legal systems 5

1   B   Ljma is a consensus of opinion and maslahah mursalah is a concept similar to Istihsan.

2   C   The Sunnah is a record of the sayings and actions of the Prophet Muhammad and is not a creation of jurists and Imams.

3   False   Iran and Pakistan are examples of countries with a written constitution that uphold Sharia law.

4   A and C   The role is a religious one. There is no requirement for holding a law degree, nor do the appointments have to be made by the state.

5   A, B, E   The others used to be governed by the UK and still operate a common law system.

6   B   Judges do not make the law under such systems and it is the state that interprets international law, not its courts.

7   **Voluntary, obligations.** Conventions are entered into voluntarily, but create legal obligations.

8   True   Conflict of law occurs when parties under different legal rules trade and find their rights or obligations with each other conflict. For example a buyer may be entitled to a refund for faulty goods under their country's legal rules, but the seller only has to provide a substitute product under their local rules.

9   A   Sharia law is explicitly based on the religion of Islam and governs all aspects of a believer's life, both moral and legal. Therefore A is a correct statement.

10   True   Some Muslims would adhere strictly to the theory of Taqlid (that no more interpretation is necessary). However, there are others who would claim there is a need to deal pragmatically with the results of new western influences in their countries.

6 Establishing contractual obligations 1

1 C The tort of deceit is only applicable to fraudulent misrepresentations.

2 B A revocation is not actioned until received, whereas an acceptance is actioned as soon as it is sent. (The postal rule.)

3 D Damages are available under the Misrepresentation Act 1967.

4 B (i) is not good consideration as it is no more than one would be expected to do in the circumstances. (iii) is past consideration.

5 A A request for service carries an implied duty to pay. The amount can be fixed later.

6 B Revocation of an offer may be communicated by a reliable informant (*Dickinson v Dodds*) but communication of acceptance of an offer may only be made by a person actually authorised to do so: *Powell v Lee.* Hence Neil's brother's purported acceptance for Neil is invalid (Option D), but the lodger's communication of revocation to Neil is valid since his presence at the deal makes him a reliable informant (Option B). Tim's promise to keep the offer open was not supported by a separate option agreement and so he was free to sell before such time as he received acceptance (Option C). Since the offer was expressed to be kept open for a week, there is no question that Neil failed to accept within a reasonable time so that the offer lapsed (Option A).

7 D The opposite is true.

8 C That a price label, or even a display of goods, is an invitation to the customer to make an offer which the shop may then choose to accept. It is an invitation to treat (Option C).

9 B Consideration need only be sufficient – it need not be adequate: *Thomas v Thomas*, (i). It can be past consideration in limited circumstances, such as to support a bill of exchange, (iii). It need not be given in a contract by deed, (iv). Performance of an existing obligation: *Stilk v Myrick.* Hence only (ii) is correct – as consideration is the price of a promise, it must be paid by the person who seeks to enforce it: *Tweddle v Atkinson.*

10 D Brian varied the terms of the offer when replying to Alexander.

7 Establishing contractual obligations 2

1 C The others are invitations to treat. Do not confuse the auction itself (it is an invitation to treat) with a bid made at auction. A bid made is an offer to buy the item that is being auctioned.

2 C The contract is valid unless set aside by the representee.

3 B Promissory estoppel requires:
   – A creditor making a promise to a debtor that they will not insist on full discharge of the debt.
   – The promise is unsupported by consideration.
   – There is no intention that the debtor will act on the promise, but they do.
   (Central London Property Trust v High Trees House 1947)

The creditor is estopped from retracting the promise unless the debtor can be restored to their original position.

4   C   A promise to waive an existing right given for no consideration is not binding, and Miranda's payment of less than is due is not consideration for Emma's promise: *Foakes v Beer* (Option A). Emma would only be estopped from retracting her waiver if she had made it with the intention that Miranda should place reliance on it and Miranda then did so (Option B). In fact she made the promise because she needed cash. The fact that her waiver was not entirely voluntary (Option C) is irrelevant since this is only an issue if promissory estoppel is claimed: *D & C Builders v Rees*. Hence, because she had received no consideration and she is not affected by promissory estoppel, Emma may claim the £100 balance (Option D).

5   A   Contracts may be oral or implied by conduct.

6   A   As C Ltd is not a party to the contract, A Ltd cannot sue C Ltd in the law of contract.

7   D   There has been no misrepresentation in this scenario.

8   B   The assumption is rebuttable, so the parties are free to try and prove that legal relations were not intended.

9   B   This is similar to the use of a telex in *Entores v Miles Far Eastern Corporation*. The offeree must make sure that his acceptance is understood when using any instantaneous method of communication.

10   B   Misrepresentation makes a contract voidable, but not void. The contract remains valid, and the representee may choose to affirm it.

8 Establishing contractual obligations 3

1   C   The three essential elements of contract are: offer and acceptance (ie agreement), consideration and intention to create legal relations. Some contracts require written terms, but by no means all.

2   C   Contracts for the sale of land must be completed by deed and are therefore specialty contracts.

3   D   Patrick's query is only a query as to whether other terms would be acceptable, that is, a request for information. Samantha responded to that request for information but her response is not a revocation of her original offer. As she has not revoked her offer, it is still open for Patrick to accept. This means that on Sunday, Patrick and Samantha have a contract.

4   C   Option B is wrong because consideration does not have to be adequate, but it does have to be sufficient. Option A is a red herring because the rent is sufficient consideration against the ongoing promise that Ben can stay. Option D is incorrect on its own. Consideration from Ben is required to enforce the promise: *Thomas v Thomas*.

5   C   Two offers do not constitute agreement, even if they say the same thing. Therefore Option A is wrong. Option D is nearly right. She must revoke her offer before Elizabeth **accepts** the offer, **not** before Elizabeth **receives** the letter. Option B is not right because the lack of agreement comes before the issue of consideration. If there had been agreement, consideration would have been in place (a necklace on one side and £250 on the other).

6   B   A representor must amend previous statements if what he has said has become misleading. This can be seen in *With v O'Flanagan*. It is an exception to the silence rule in Option A. Option C is irrelevant.

7   D   The presumption that commercial cases are legally binding is rebuttable if otherwise shown. Options A and B are wrong because the courts will presume commercial arrangements were intended to be legal. Option C is wrong because social or domestic arrangements are presumed not to have been intended to be legal.

8   D   Faxes are not subject to the postal rule. Per the rule in *Entores v Miles Far Eastern Corporation*, instantaneous methods of acceptance must be received.

9   C   Revocation can be communicated by a reliable third party (as in *Dickinson v Dodds*). In this case, Dave can be seen as a reliable third party, because he has been involved in the process. Option A is wrong because the offer has been revoked. Option B is irrelevant as Lee has a right to revoke his offer at any time. Option D is wrong because Dave is a reliable third party.

10   A   A contract may be in any form unless a certain form is prescribed. Option B is wrong because legal relations must have been intended by both parties. Option C is wrong because contract is part of civil law. Option D is wrong because some adults may not have contractual capacity if they do not understand the purpose of a contract at the time of contracting.

9 Establishing contractual obligations 4

1   C   An illegal act cannot form the basis for a valid contract.

2   D   Lapse of time may act as a bar to rescission, but recission is in theory available for all types of misrepresentation.

3   B   An act the law requires in any case is not sufficient consideration. It is not necessarily past (the question did not specify) and it is not proper or sufficient by virtue of being insufficient.

4   B   Options A and C are executed consideration. Option D is past consideration.

5   D   The facts in this scenario are similar to those in *Harris v Sheffield United FC Ltd.* The police are being asked to provide a service outside their regular duties due to the actions of the directors, installing bars inside the football stadium.

6   B   Option C is untrue, as verbal acceptance is valid if acknowledged. Option D is untrue as the £4,000 is consideration for the car.

7   D   It is presumed in social and domestic situations that legal relations are not intended and it is presumed in commercial situations that they are.

8   B   The misrepresentee may choose to affirm or repudiate the contract.

9   D   Standard form contracts are unlikely to be oral. Option C is wrong because the point of a standard contract is that it is set out by the stronger party, not negotiated by the parties.

10   B   Jude offers to buy and the till operator can accept or reject the offer.

10 Performing thc oontraot 1

1　D　Breach of a warranty entitles the injured party to claim damages only.

2　D　Oral evidence will not be admissible in the case of a complete written contract. Oral agreements about written conditional precedents are acceptable and in the absence of written evidence of a contract, the courts will endeavour to discover what was actually said, not what could be reasonably understood.

3　C　The goods must be for private use or consumption.

4　A　What is 'reasonable' will depend on the precise situation.

5　B　Breach of warranty does not cause the contract to be discharged. Terms implied by statute may be conditions.

6　B　A consumer must be a natural person, not acting for the purposes of trade.

7　B　*Poussard v Spiers; Bettini v Gye.*
　　　Failure to sing on an opening night breaks a condition of the contract. Missing rehearsals does not.

8　C　A warranty is a minor term in the contract. Breach of a minor term does not entitle the injured party to repudiate the contract. The injured party must continue with the contract, but may claim damages.

9　B　Generally in contract there is no rule that you must say what you know, but you must give a complete enough picture so as not to be misleading. Steve's answer may be true, but it is misleading because he hears his neighbour a lot, even if he doesn't see him, which makes him a bad neighbour. This is what Adam wanted to know. Similar to *Smith v Land and House Property Corporation.*

10　C　Judas has stated an opinion not a fact. This cannot be a misrepresentation. The facts in this case are similar to *Bisset v Wilkinson.*

11 Performing the contract 2

1　C　You should have spotted that (i) merely reiterates s 2(1) Unfair Contract Terms Act 1977 (UCTA) – an exclusion clause relating to death or personal injury is only void if it attempts to exclude liability arising from negligence. Where Wincey deals as a consumer, all the other clauses are void; a customer guarantee cannot limit liability for loss or damage (s 5 UCTA), the terms as to merchantable quality and fitness for purpose (s 14 Sale of Goods Act 1979 (SGA)) cannot be excluded and the product must comply with its description (s 13 SGA) by virtue of ss 6 and 7 UCTA. No supplier may exclude liability where he supplies goods to which he has no title (term implied by s 12 SGA): s 6(1) UCTA. But where Wincey does not deal as a consumer as defined by s 12 UCTA then only the exclusion clause as to title is void.

2　C　Option A is incorrect because some contracts (for example for land or shares) have a particular required form. Option B is also wrong. Oral contracts are generally acceptable as they are.

3　C　Sian's representation was intended to form part of the contract.

4　A　This is the rule in s 2 of the Act.

5   A   Most contractual terms in business agreements are identified as being either conditions or warranties, (i) – the importance of the distinction being that failure to fulfil the former, (ii) leads to the whole contract being at an end (discharged by breach), whilst breach of warranty leads only to a claim for damages, not to discharge, (iii). An unclassified term as mentioned in (i) is one which cannot be identified as either a condition or warranty until the effects of failure to fulfil it are known and assessed. (iv) is incorrect since statute often implies warranties as well as conditions (for example Sale of Goods Act 1979).

6   A   Although a legally binding contract must be complete in its terms it is possible to look outside its express terms in order to fix a price so long as the method fixed is not uncertain.

7   B   The facts in this case are very similar to *Thompson v LMS Railway* where it was held that the conditions of carriage were adequately communicated in the train timetables and the exclusion clause was valid.

8   D   Most exclusion clauses aim either to restrict liability in the event of breach of contract or to limit the person's obligation to perform some or all of what he took on.

9   A   A **representation** is a statement of fact made before a contract is entered into. It is usually incorporated as a contractual term (condition or warranty) but it could still be a representation even if a contract is not ultimately formed. A representation is made with the intention that the other party should place reliance on it. Howard's statement is one of simple fact. It is not an extravagant claim and so cannot be said to be 'advertiser's puff'.

10   A   The requirement of the Act is fitness for purpose, ie the purpose for which it is bought, not all purposes. The others are genuine requirements of the Act.

12 Performing the contract 3

1   C   Liability for death and personal injury due to negligence can never be excluded.

2   D   The Act provides that the purpose behind the purchase must be given to the seller. If it is obvious (as might be assumed with a coat) the reason does not have to be given. However, if there is a peculiarity associated with the purchase (and in this case, an allergy would count as a peculiarity), the buyer must intimate that to the seller.

3   C   While if a description is applied to the goods by the contract, it is a sale by description, it is not the case that all descriptive words used form part of the contract terms.

4   B   In the case of *R&B Customs Brokers Co Ltd v United Dominions Trust Ltd 1988* a company was held to be a consumer when purchasing a company car as car dealing was not its trade.

      Under UTCCR 1999 a consumer contract cannot exclude protection from the Sale of Goods Act. Therefore the exclusion clause is not allowed.

5   A   Rescission entails setting aside a contract as if it had never been made.

6   C   It is not the case that a buyer must be explicit. He may specify the particular purpose quite broadly, as in *Ashington Piggeries v Christopher Hill Ltd.*

7   C   Literally this phrase translated means 'against he who is relying'. Anything ambiguous in an exclusion clause is interpreted against the person who is seeking to rely on it. The rules stated in Options A and D are true but do not refer to contra proferentem. Option B is now wholly true since in many consumer contracts an exclusion clause is rendered void by UCTA 1977. In most standard term contracts the person imposing the exclusion clause must show reasonableness in order that a term restricting liability for breach or claiming entitlement to render substantially different or no performance should be binding (s 3 UCTA 1977).

8   B   Statute can imply a term either by overriding an express term (for example the Sale of Goods Act 1979) or by providing a term which applies unless overridden (for example the Partnership Act 1890). The latter method is also the way in which custom and trade practice imply terms. In order to give 'business efficacy' to an agreement which is only deficit because the parties have failed to provide expressly for something because it was so obvious, the court may also imply terms: *The Moorcock.* But the court will not imply a term to provide for events not anticipated at the time of agreement, (iii), to contradict an express term, (iv) nor to remedy a defective agreement.

9   C   The scenario is similar to *Curtis v Chemical Cleaning Co,* where the claimant was misled as to the extent of the exclusion clause. This is an exception to the rule that once a document is signed, the person who signed is bound by any exclusion clauses contained therein.

10   D   The fact that the party is informing the other in advance of the date of contract makes his actions 'anticipatory'.

13 Performing the contract 4

1   A   The answer is not Option C because although statement (ii) is generally correct, there are exceptions to this rule, for example, if the person has been misled about the contents of the document.

2   B   The other options could potentially all be true. It is important to look at the timing of actions in the question to establish that Option B is the correct answer.

3   C   Option A is generally true unless there is intervention by a third party. Option B is untrue. In Option D, the fact that Kathleen is John's relative is irrelevant to her contracting with Catherine, as she is not Catherine's relative.

4   C   Breach of a warranty does not destroy a contract as it is only a minor term. However, the injured party is entitled to damages.

5   A   Option C is wrong, because breach of a condition entitles the injured party to repudiate. Option D is wrong by the same reason.

6   A   Some exclusions are valid in non-consumer contracts.

7   D   By the rule in *Pinnel's* case, as Grace has paid the part payment earlier than the due date, she has provided Rebecca with consideration for the waiver of Rebecca's rights.

8   B   A breach of warranty gives rise to damages only.

9   D   The scenario is similar to *Olley v Marlborough Court.*

10　D　The **contra proferentem** rule means that the courts rule against the person seeking to rely. A literal translation of the Latin is 'against the one relying'.

14 Contractual breakdown 1

1　A　The other statements are all true. Option B was the decision in *Re Vaswani Motors (Sales and Services) Limited*. Option D is true because a contract may subsequently be frustrated.

2　D　This is not an exception in itself. The exception arises when the promise accepts partial performance.

3　C　Anticipatory breach or repudiation occurs when one party, expressly or by implication, indicates that he does not intend to be bound by an agreement. The injured party is entitled to sue immediately, though he may elect to allow the contract to continue until there is actual breach: *Hochster v De La Tour*. Because the right to sue is instantaneous, the injured party need not complete his obligations nor wait a reasonable time in order to effect his intentions.

4　D　Exemplary damages are awarded in tort.

5　C　Option A is wrong because disinclination to perform the contract would represent a breach. Option B is wrong because the event must be central to the purpose of the contract for non-occurrence to cause frustration. Option D is wrong because increased expense is not a cause of frustration.

6　C　Consideration need not be adequate. Option B is nearly right. The courts will presume in the first instance that legal relations were not intended between man and wife, but the presumption is rebuttable. In this case, the facts that Rosie and Jim are separated, the agreement is about property and is in writing would in all probability lead the court to presume legal relations were intended, as in *Merritt v Merritt*.

7　B　Damages are a common law remedy. Option D is incorrect because it actually describes an equitable order of specific performance.

8　A　The scenario in this question is similar to that in *Hadley v Baxendale*. The loss must have been reasonably foreseeable to the defendant for damages to be awarded.

9　B　The general rule of privity of contract states that only a person who is party to a contract has enforceable obligations under it. Hence, Options A and C are wrong because F is not a party to the contract and Option D is wrong because Dee is a party to the contract.

10　A　The debt must be acknowledged by the debtor in writing. This acknowledgement must be signed by the debtor.

15 Contractual breakdown 2

1　C　The limitation in Option C applies to the claimant not the defendant. The limitation period begins to run when the claimant's disability ceases or he dies.

2　C　*Quantum meruit* is a common law remedy.

3　A　An injunction will not be made merely to restrain acts inconsistent with the contract's obligation.

4	D	In *Hotel Services v Hilton International 2000*, loss of profit was considered direct in identical circumstances.
5	C	Damages generally seek to place the injured party in the position he would have been in had the contract been performed. Only sometimes are damages paid to cover expenses that have arisen as part of the breached contract.
6	D	Frustration occurs where the contract becomes fundamentally different from what was expected, or becomes impossible. It does not occur when assumptions are not proved correct.
7	B	Options C and D are wrong because the point of civil law is to compensate the injured party, not to punish the wrongdoer. The result in Option A would be achieved by an equitable remedy such as quantum meruit.
8	D	Horatio was within the terms of the contract in not loading the waste onto the ship within 28 days of arrival. Had he informed Rodney that he had no intention of ever loading the waste, there would have been anticipatory breach. However, as Rodney had not taken action against him, the frustrating event would have overridden the breach anyway. The contract is frustrated by supervening illegality.
9	D	A contract is not discharged by frustration if there is an alternative method of carrying out the contract, albeit a more expensive method. The facts in this scenario were similar to *Tsakiroglou & Co v Noblee and Thorl GmbH*.
10	C	Where the agreement states that a fixed sum is to be payable this will become due only when precise, exact and complete performance has been rendered. Failure in this respect will not entitle the person to part payment (Option C). Where one party prevents complete performance (Option A) the other may claim part payment by way of quantum meruit: *Planché v Colburn*. A divisible contract (where payment is to be made by instalments) requires that separate payment be made for each tranche or work (Option D). The doctrine of substantial performance (Option B) states that where work has been completed but a small number of deficiencies remain the contractor is entitled to payment less a deduction (or retention) to cover the cost of the outstanding work: *Hoenig v Isaacs*.

16 Contractual breakdown 3

1	C	An order for specific performance would not be made for a contract of personal service because the court would not be able to ensure that a person complied fully with the order.
2	A	In Option A, **fundamental breach** allows the injured party either to accept the other party's offer that the contract be discharged or reject it. In the latter case the contract remains in force, the injured party continues with his obligations and his remedy is to sue for damages for any loss caused by the other person's actions. Option C is incorrect because he may claim damages for breach as well as for loss following his continued performance. Option D is incorrect because either cause to claim damages is independent of an injunction.
3	D	Specific performance is an equitable remedy.
4	C	*Quantum meruit* literally means 'how much it is worth'.
5	B	Mark is entitled to sue for breach of contract due to the non-delivery. However, he will only recover limited damages as he should have accepted cash on delivery when he was offered it. The scenario in the question is similar to *Payzu Ltd v Saunders*.

6   C   Options A and B are not correct as Robina has been prevented from performing by History Alive. Option D is not right because the fact that one of the parties has cancelled the series is not a frustrating event, it is the other party breaching the contract.

7   C   Option A is not right, because the fact that the fixed sum of damages arranged covers several issues implies that it is a penalty clause rather than a genuine pre-estimate of loss. If the pre-arranged sum is judged to be a penalty clause, then the clause is void.

8   B   Option C is a description of a penalty clause. Option D is a description of damages to cover wasted expenditure. Option A was a red herring. In some instances parties lodge money with the court prior to court action. However, you should have recognised the description of liquidated damages in Option B.

9   B   To be a frustrating event, the event which is not occurring must have been the whole purpose of the contract.

10   A   Option D is wrong because if the problem is caused by one of the parties it cannot be frustration. Options B and C are wrong because increases in expense or difficulty do not amount to frustration either.

17 Contractual breakdown 4

1   D   Because frustration of a contract of personal service, such as an employment contract, occurs when the person is incapable of performance, this will clearly arise where the employee is too ill to work: *Condor v Barron Knights.* It will also be the case when he is dead, in prison or absent on military service (either in the UK or abroad). However, the contract of employment is not frustrated by the outbreak of war, (v). Instead it is rendered void since no person can continue to have contractual relations with an enemy alien.

2   B   This accounts for the expectations of the parties to the contract. Options C and D are red herrings. Option A describes reliance interest. You should have recognised the description in Option B.

3   A   Rupert has performed the contract substantially, he is entitled to payment, but Davina may withhold the costs of the minor corrections. The facts in this scenario are similar to *Hoenig v Isaacs.*

4   B   Under the rule in *Victoria Laundry (Windsor) v Newman Industries,* Whin Mechanics could not have known about the lucrative contract. Therefore they are not liable for the exceptional profits.

5   D   This is correct according to the rule in *H Parsons (Livestock) v Uttley Ingham.*

6   C   The courts will often use the remedy of specific performance in cases of land transfer. A contract to pay money to a third party could be enforced by specific performance. However, an order for specific performance is never used for contracts of employment as performance would be required over time and the courts could not be sure that performance would be maintained.

7   D   Botch Job have substantially performed the contract in that Belinda has a new bathroom on the first floor. However, Belinda may retain the cost of righting small defects in the job.

8   D   *Tsakiroglu & Co v Noble and Thorl Gmbh.* The other three are frustrating events: *Taylor v Caldwell* (A), *Condor v Barron Knights* (B) and *Avery v Bowden* (C).

9   C   An order for specific performance (B) is an equitable remedy, which would not be appropriate here. Tee Ltd can expect to reclaim the amount needed to put the company in the position it would have been in if the contract had been performed.

10   B   The rule in *Anon 1495* means that if alternative consideration is given in the form of goods, then waiver of a debt is valid. Option D is irrelevant. In Option C, the consideration of a dress may not be adequate, but it is sufficient. The bargain does not have to be good.

18 Employment 1

1   D   The duty to provide work is implied only in certain circumstances.

2   C   Generally there is a qualifying period of a year, and compensation is capped by the Employment Rights Act 1996.

3   D   The health and safety officer will not be bringing a claim personally, in civil law.

4   C   This should have been obvious. Dismissal for membership of a trade union is not allowed by statute.

5   D   Although summary dismissal on liquidation is a breach of contract which can be treated as **wrongful dismissal**, Deck Line Ltd's liquidator is allowed to justify his action by reliance on **evidence uncovered after the event** (which is not the situation with unfair dismissal). Hence Mick's dishonesty justifies Deck Line Ltd's action.

6   C   Options A and B are untrue. Option D is wrong because it is sometimes permissible for the new employer to vary the terms of employment if there are economic, technical or organisational reasons to do so.

7   C   Option A is clearly dismissal as the employer has expressly requested the employer to leave. Option B is constructive dismissal. In Option D, failure to renew a fixed term contract is also dismissal.

8   A   Protection is provided by Race Relations Act 1976, Disability Discrimination Act 1995 and Sex Discrimination Act 1975.

9   B   The mobility clause is a contractual term.

10   D   Only the employee would rank as a preferential creditor. The contractor would be an ordinary creditor.

19 Employment 2

1   C   Options A and B are unlikely due to the breakdown in confidence between the parties. D only would be awarded if Options A or B had been awarded and the employer had ignored the order.

2   C   The employer can withhold wages.

3   B   You should have recognised the other tests. Documentation may help to establish answers to the other tests.

4	A	The case is similar to *Latimer v AEC 1953*. It held where an employer has taken all reasonable steps to prevent an accident they should not be found liable.
5	B	An employee who has worked more than one month but less than two years is entitled to a minimum of a week's notice. When an employee has worked somewhere for two years, they are entitled to a week's notice for each full year of continuous employment.
6	A	This statement is untrue. Independent contractors must account to the Inland Revenue themselves for tax, having been paid gross. The others are all valid reasons.
7	D	The duty to provide work is only true in certain circumstances.
8	B	In the others being male is a genuine occupational qualification. In England, such custom is overridden by statute.
9	C	There is no duty to provide references, although most employers do so.
10	C	The others are genuine rules. An employee working under separate contracts for the same employer may not aggregate his hours, however.

20 Employment 3

1	C	All the people in Options A, B and D are entitled to be employees.
2	C	Terms may be implied by a collective agreement between the union and the employer if they satisfy three conditions: if they are a custom 'reasonable, certain and notorious' in the industry, known to the employee and a negotiated agreement.
3	D	The employee only has an implied duty of obedience to reasonable commands. The employer can be protected from the situations outlined in Options A and B. Option C is untrue because the employer has no duty to give references.
4	B	While claims for wrongful dismissal can be heard in the courts, claims for unfair dismissal must be heard by the tribunal. Thus, due to the wording of the question, Option B is the right answer.
5	A	Option B is only true if the employee has been made redundant.
6	A	Summary dismissal may not be a breach of contract, for example, if it was for misconduct. The others imply breach of contract. Constructive dismissal is when an employee feels their contract has been breached, wrongful dismissal is a breach of contract, and if the employer terminates through inability, it is still a breach of contract on his part.
7	C	Employers usually provide tools and equipment, and they are obliged to deduct income tax from an employee's wages.
8	B	Employees are entitled to protect themselves and others from health and safety risks and the Act seeks to protect them when doing so.
9	C	There is no specific duty to provide work.
10	A	Striking can be a fair reason for dismissal, as can being a threat to national security and legal prohibitions.

21 Employment 4

1   C   Members of the armed forces (A) are excluded from much legislation on grounds of national security; those employed outside Great Britain would not be subject to UK law and strike action can be a fair reason for dismissal.

2   D   In the past, wrongful dismissal was always heard in the courts. Now the jurisdiction of the employment tribunal has been extended to include wrongful dismissal.

3   C   The employee cannot be expected never to make mistakes. Only reasonable competence is required. Options B and D are also implied duties of the employee.

4   A   Employers can be vicariously liable for the acts of their employees if the act and the role are sufficiently close. *Fennelley v Connex South Eastern Ltd 2001* saw the employer liable in similar circumstances.

5   B   The written particulars must give reference to where the rules on health and safety can be found.

6   C   The compensation is 9/52 of pay, excluding any discretionary payments. She is entitled to the statutory minimum notice period regardless of what her contract says, which in this case is 10 weeks (one for each year of her employment), hence compensation for the nine she wasn't given.

7   B   He would have been entitled had he been made redundant.

8   D   These are all potentially fair reasons for dismissal.

9   B   Because the statue only recommends the wearing of goggles it does not of itself create a statutory duty and so on this point Kay Michael Ltd will not be liable to Roger, (i). It is open to Kay Michael Ltd to raise the defence of **reasonable care,** (ii) though it is unlikely to succeed given the location of the goggles and the notice, and the attitude of the foreman. An employer cannot raise the defence that the employee consented to a **dangerous working practice,** (iii): *Smith v Baker 1891.* Finally it is clear that the company is in breach of its common law duty as regards a **safe system of work,** (iv).

10   D   For the purposes of the Act, **dismissal** occurs when a fixed term contract is not renewed, even though such an eventuality is implicit in the fact that the agreement has a fixed term. Nick is therefore entitled to claim for **redundancy pay** and/or compensation for **unfair dismissal** if he can prove the requisite facts: ss 92 and 136 ERA 1996. However, non-renewal cannot give rise to a claim for wrongful dismissal, which is only possible when there has been summary dismissal or dismissal with less than the required period of notice.

22 Company formation 1

1   C   Since 1992 a private company may be formed and operate with only one member: s 1(3A).

2   D   The 15% applies to minority protection in cases of variation of class rights. S 7(1) states that articles prescribe regulations for the company (Option A); promoters can adopt Table A articles (Option B); and s 14 states that the articles form a contract which governs the company and its members (Option C).

3   C   S 117 (8) states that the transaction will be valid, s 117 (7) that the directors will be subject to a fine. The third party can only sue to the extent that loss has been suffered as a result of the company's failure to perform obligations arising and not for anything further (Option D).

4   A   A special resolution is required per S 28 (1)

5   C   S 282 states that a public company must have at least two directors; s 283 states that all companies must have a secretary; s 1 states that a public company must have at least two members.

6   A   A company cannot enforce a contract before it comes into existence (Option C), and cannot adopt a pre-incorporation contract (Option D). The promoters may be liable (Option B): s 36C(1).

7   B   Word 'limited' can be omitted if the company's objects are the promotion of art, commerce, science, education, religion, charity or any profession, and the profits are applied to promoting the objects.

8   B   A company need not submit its own articles; it can instead state that it is adopting Table A articles.

9   B   S 35(3). In any event the third party to the contract is also protected by S 35.

10   D   S 14. *Eley v Positive Government Security Assurance Co Ltd* illustrates that the statutory rules only apply to rights as a shareholder, and not rights of shareholders who are suing in another capacity.

23 Company formation 2

1   A   A company has a separate legal identity. *Salomon v Salomon Ltd*.

2   B   S 353 (1) states that the register of members may also be kept where it is made up, at another office of the company or at the office of a professional registrar.

3   C   A company limited by guarantee and a single member private company are legitimate artificial legal persons (Options A and B). The Archbishop of Canterbury is an artificial person known as a corporation sole (Option D).

4   C   S 49(8)(a). A special resolution (Option B) is required to convert an unlimited company to a limited company.

5   A   The capital available is £5,000 below the lower limit for a plc (Option B). They wish to protect their other assets, so should not form an unlimited company (Option D). They cannot be shareholders and give a guarantee (Option C).

6   A   Under s 4 (1) a company may alter its objects for any reason.

7   A   S 198 – 199 state that the key figure is 3% in any class of shares, and Fluffy Ted owns 3.5% of equity shares. The rules apply to any person acquiring shares in a plc; thus the fact that Fluffy Ted is a private company (Option D) is irrelevant. Only if Tigger was a private company would the interest be non-disclosable.

8   B   Answers A, C and D all relate to the period prior to incorporation, when the company does not exist; therefore he cannot act as agent or trustee, and the articles do not bind the company and third parties. However the Contracts (Rights of Third Parties) Act 1999 provides that a third party can be expressly identified in a contract by name even if the third party does not yet exist. This does not feature in the options here, so you must go for one of those that is available.

9   C   Profits are shared equally unless there is an agreement to the contrary.

10   A   The original members will be the formation agents, and when the company is purchased, the purchasers will want to become members themselves. None of the other changes is compulsory, though in practice all would generally occur.

24 Company formation 3

1   D   S 117. The company's paid up share capital must be at minimum £12,500 (Option A)

2   A   Option B is untrue; a director can do this (and has: *Lee v Lee's Air Farming*). Option C is a true statement, but is governed by s 213 Insolvency Act 1986, not Salomon's case. Option D is untrue – this is essentially what Mr Salomon had done, and the transaction was valid.

3   C   As specified by S 244(1)

4   B   A special resolution is required per S 4(1)

5   C   Liability is limited to the amount of the guarantee, and contribution is only required in the event of liquidation.

6   D   Although a partnership is not a separate legal entity, it can sue in its own name as a legal convenience (Option A). A partnership can grant a mortgage or fixed charge over a specific item of property (Option B).

7   B   Table A will apply per S 8(2)

8   A   Option B is true but is the subject of different provisions: s 35.

9   A   *Eley v Positive Government Security Life Assurance Co.*
The articles are a contract between a company and its members.

10   B   A partnership does not need to have a written agreement; it can be established by the actions of the partners.

25 Company formation 4

1   B   S 283 states that the sole director may not also be the company secretary. S 1(3A) allows a private company to be formed and operate with one member.

2   B   A company cannot be liable on a pre-incorporation contract as the company does not exist at the time the contract is made.

3   A   The company owns it own property.

4   B   The other options are illustrated by *Gilford Motor Co Ltd v Horne* (Option A) and *Daimler Co Ltd v Continental Tyre and Rubber Co Ltd* (Options C and D).

5   D   The articles set out internal regulations (Option A). The memorandum is registered before incorporation (Option B), by both public and private companies (Option C).

6   C   Literally: outside the powers.

7	A	This is because the Memo contains the constitution of the company, while the Articles contain its internal regulations.
8	B	If Crawley rescinds (Option A), then it won't have the antique which it is contractually bound to sell to Broadfield for a profit of £5,000 and Broadfield will sue it. It will lose £2,500 profit if it does nothing (Option D). Option C would be correct if Crawley had paid the money to Charles; as the company has not done so, the simplest solution is to pay Charles the cost price and leave him with no legal remedy.
9	C	S 101 (1) states that a public company can only allot a share only if a quarter of its nominal value is paid up, so Option D is incorrect. S 45 states that a public company must have a share capital of at least £50,000 nominal value so Options A and B are incorrect.
10	C	S 5(2). A member must hold a minimum of 15% of the company's issued share capital.

26 Company formation 5

1	C	S 8(2). Table A is applicable as it is not modified or excluded by the company's own articles.
2	A	The alteration is not a fraud on the minority (Option B). Shareholders voting on an alteration of the articles must vote in the best interests of the company: *Greenhalgh v Arderne Cinemas*, so Option C is incorrect. There is no infringement of statutory rights (Option D).
3	B	S 224(3) states that in the absence of notice, the first period will end on the anniversary of the month end following the date of incorporation.
4	C	S 89 applies to both types of company. Private companies can disapply the rule permanently, public companies for a period of five years, but both have to take action to do so.
5	B	S 290 (1). The other details have to be given in respect of directors.
6	C	S 30. The conditions are that the company's objects must be to promote commerce, art, science, education, religion, charity or any profession, the profits must be applied to furthering the objects with no dividends being paid to members and a statutory declaration must be made.
7	C	S 322A. The contract is voidable by the company and may be ratified in general meeting.
8	D	The approval of the relevant class of members must be obtained.
9	D	(ii), (iii), (iv) are correct. The alteration can apply new conditions to an existing situation (i), but cannot retrospectively take away rights acquired under a previous contract (ii). An alteration can never compel a member to accept extra liability (iii): s 16, nor can a company provide that a greater majority than 75% is needed to alter the articles (iv). The minority may be forced to suffer special detriment if the alteration is bona fide for the benefit of the company as a whole: *Greenhalgh v Arderne Cinemas*.
10	C	Borrowing can never be an independent object (Option A). Misappropriation (Option B) cannot legitimately be ratified, since it would constitute a fraud on the minority. A company can enter transactions which do not benefit it (Option D) if it has express powers to do so, for example giving pensions to former directors.

27 Company formation 6

1 A S 1(3) states that a private company is any company that is not a public company (i). S 1 talks about incorporated companies (ii). Under s 242 (1) all limited companies must file accounts (iii). A private limited company is so called because shareholders' liability is limited (iv).

2 B The articles can always be altered by special resolution (Option A), and a separate contract does not prevent the company from altering its articles (Option C). There is no such thing as a Form 9 (Option D).

3 A The business would have to be called Lynn plc if it was a public limited company (Option B). A sole trader cannot state that it is limited (Option C), and the company is stated as being limited, not unlimited (Option D).

4 A For English and Welsh companies, the registry is in Cardiff; for Scottish companies it is in Edinburgh. There is a search room in London, not a registry (Option C). Throughout its existence a company deals only with the registry that holds its file, and as the company is English, it gives notice to the Cardiff registry.

5 D *Adams v Cape Industries* emphasises that companies within groups should generally be treated as separate legal entities.

6 B The certificate of incorporation is conclusive evidence of the date and fact of incorporation.

7 B S 24. The remaining member becomes jointly and severally liable with the company for the company's debts after 6 months.

8 B *Gilford Motor Co v Horne*.

9 B The other options are incorrect as Table C and D articles apply to companies limited by guarantee.

10 C (iv) is incorrect; the veil is only lifted six months after the public company has become a single member company. (ii) is a possible reason for lifting the veil, even though the courts may grant relief for minor mistakes.

28 Company administration and management 1

1 B S 35(A)(1). Where directors exceed their powers, the company can be held liable on contracts with third parties.

2 C Special notice

3 A S 369 (3) and (4). Shareholders holding at least 95% of the company's shares must agree.

4 C A special resolution is required to alter the articles: s 9 (1).

5 D A public company secretary is required to have qualifications: s 286 (Option A). Every company is required to have a company secretary: s 283(1)(Option B). A company secretary can bind the company in some contracts, as specified in Option D: *Panorama Developments (Guildford) Ltd v Fidelis Furnishing Fabrics Ltd*, so Option C is wrong.

6	C	Special notice is required: s 379 (1).
7	C	The articles cannot override the principle that a meeting cannot consist of only one person, though the court can (Option B). A private company's board may only consist of a single director (Option A) and the shareholder class may only consist of a single member (Option D), so in both cases one would be a valid quorum.
8	C	S 376. Members must hold one twentieth of the voting rights and being at least 100 in number with shares on which an average of £100 has been paid.
9	D	There are no limits on loans to persons connected with directors of a private company. The loan would be prohibited (Option A) if Waugh was a public company.
10	C	S 838 (1). A fee may be charged (Option D) if the members request a copy of the minutes.

29 Company administration and management 2

1	B	*Bushell v Faith*
2	D	This is still counted as obtaining a personal advantage through being a director.
3	B	S 288(2)(a). Notice must be served within 14 days.
4	D	S 305(4)(a) specifically includes shadow directors.
5	A	In the absence of a quorum fixed by the articles or directors, it is however deemed to be two.
6	C	Option A is a provision in Table A. Option B reflects s 368 CA 85. Option D is a provision in Table A. The notice required is 21 days, not 28.
7	C	If directors use their powers irregularly to allot shares, the votes attached to the new shares may not be used in reaching a decision in general meeting to sanction it: *Howard Smith Ltd v Ampol Petroleum Ltd.*
8	B	S 366 states that AGMs subsequent to the first must be held no later than 15 months after the last one and at least once every calendar year. Although 31 January 20X8 is 15 months after the last date, holding the next AGM then will mean that there is no AGM at all in 20X7; therefore the last day a meeting can be held is 31 December 20X7. S 366 refers to holding a meeting once every calendar year, not once every 12 months, so Option A is incorrect. 18 months (the period for Option D) is the period allowed between incorporation and the first AGM, but not for subsequent AGMs.
9	D	S 368(4).The meeting need not take place within 21 days, so Option A is wrong. The meeting must take place within 28 days of the date of the notice convening the meeting, not within 28 days of the requisition (Option B). Option C is wrong; 3 months is relevant here in that if the directors fail to convene a meeting within 21 days and the members convene a meeting themselves, that meeting must be held within 3 months.
10	A	S 372(1) states that a proxy only has speaking rights at a meeting of a private company. S 372(2) states that a proxy can only vote on a poll unless the articles provide otherwise.

30 Company administration and management 3

1   A   S 370(4). Two members or proxies are required.

2   C   S 369(4) sets out the short notice requirements which need to be followed here because adequate notice has not been given. Although the notices have been posted 14 days before the EGM, the secretary has ignored the requirements of Table A which require clear days notice and allowance to be made for postal delays. Thus the notice is deemed to be received 48 hours later, on 3 March 20X8, the 14 day period to begin on 4 March and expire on 17 March. Thus the first date that the EGM can be held without recourse to the short notice procedure is 18 March. The consent of all members (Option D) is required for short notice of an AGM.

3   B   A special resolution is needed to change the objects clause, requiring 75 votes at least, not more than 75 votes. Thus 25 votes (Option A) will not be enough to defeat the resolution. 50 votes (Option C) would be needed to defeat an ordinary resolution (where the vote needed in favour is more than 50%.)

4   C   Under s 319, contracts of more than five years duration must be approved by the company in general meeting or are terminable on reasonable notice.

5   D   Any one member, regardless of their shareholding, can apply. A creditor can apply for liquidation; the company itself and a minority of members can apply for a DTI investigation.

6   B   *Daniels v Daniels*

7   D   The transaction is not voidable because there has been sufficient disclosure elsewhere. The auditors have a statutory duty under s 237(4) to remedy disclosure deficiencies and need not resign.

8   C   Article 84 states that managing directors and directors holding other executive office are not subject to retirement by rotation.

9   B   Most companies, depending on size, must still be audited. The elective resolution enables a company to dispense with the procedure of appointing an auditor every year; the auditor just continues in office from year to year with no requirement for reappointment.

10   D   Written resolutions cannot be used to remove a director, so Option A is incorrect. Auditors must be sent copies of written resolutions, but have no right of objection (Option B). Written resolutions can be used notwithstanding any provisions in the company's articles, so Option C is incorrect.

31 Company administration and management 4

1   B   Options A, C and D are correct.

2   C   S 303. The articles generally cover the appointment of directors.

3   C   S 369. 21 days notice is required.

4   B   *Ebrahimi v Westbourne Galleries*

5   D   A holding company can make loans to its subsidiaries' directors provided that they are not directors of, or connected to directors of, its holding company.

6   C   Directors do not have a responsibility to individual shareholders (A). B does not reflect changes in the **law**, but in codes of practice. D is incorrect as a dividend is only paid if there are funds available. C is correct as many areas of company law are more onerous for plcs.

7   A   21 days and 50% (Option B) are the figures for an ordinary resolution proposed at an annual general meeting. 14 days and 75% (Option C) are the figures for an extraordinary resolution proposed at an extraordinary general meeting, and 21 days and 75% (Option D) are the figures for an extraordinary resolution proposed at an annual general meeting, and a special resolution proposed at any meeting.

8   B   Under s 6 Company Directors Disqualification Act 1986 a director must be disqualified if he is unfit to be concerned in the management of a company.

9   B   Table A Article 94

10   B   (v) is incorrect because the decision to appoint inspectors is at the discretion of the DTI; there is no obligation on it to do so: s 431. Deadlock, breach of understandings of quasi-partners, and deliberate withholding of information are all just and equitable grounds for winding up a company. Under s 442-443, the DTI can appoint inspectors to investigate the ownership of a company (iv).

32 Company administration and management 5

1   C   S 310 renders void clauses in the articles or in a contract exempting directors from liability.

2   B   S 52(3) Criminal Justice Act 1993. The definition of insider dealing given in Option A is accurate as far as it goes but not complete. Option C is untrue, and the reason given in Option D is wrong; Arabella's lack of connection with the company is irrelevant, as she obtained the information from a person who is connected with it.

3   A   Such a claim is contractual in nature

4   B   (iii) is incorrect because the de minimis exemption is £5,000, not £10,000. (iv) is expressly prohibited by s 330(2) (a).

5   D   However the company need not adopt Table A on this point.

6   D   S 366(2) states that the first AGM must be held within 18 months of incorporation.

7   D   This is an elective resolution, which requires the consent of all the members entitled to attend and vote.

8   B   The rule is 10% of net assets, but if the transaction is worth more than £100,000 (Option A), it must always be disclosed. Hence net assets figures of above £1,000,000 (Option C) are not significant for the application of the rule.

9   A   *Dorchester Finance Co Ltd v Stebbing.*

10   C   The encouragement or disclosure are key here; whether any dealing takes place is not relevant.

33 Corporate finance 1

1	A	B is the definition of a floating charge.
2	B	A company can use the money it receives from share issues to trade and perhaps make losses and become insolvent.
3	C	S 89 sets out the general rule which applies unless otherwise sanctioned in general meeting.
4	C	S 142 (1). 28 days notice is required.
5	B	S 135(1). There is no such thing as a special resolution with special notice (Option D).
6	C	Option D is incorrect since unincorporated organisations cannot create floating charges as they have no separate legal existence.
7	A	Remember the concepts of authorised, issued (Option B), allotted (Option C) and paid up (Option D) capital are separate. Not all the authorised share capital need be issued to members.
8	D	Table A articles prescribe an ordinary resolution (Option A) but this is not compulsory.
9	B	S 157(2). 10% is the minimum percentage that must be held.
10	D	A variation alters the benefits or duties attached to a class of share. Only option D affects a class of shares in that way.

34 Corporate finance 2

1	B	112,500 − 90,000 − 10,000 + 5,000. Option A is the maximum amount that a public company could distribute. The share premium account is an undistributable reserve, so Option C is wrong.
2	A	Charges rank in the order of their creation, but fixed charges take precedence over floating charges unless the charges themselves state otherwise.
3	D	S 108(1). No company can issue shares at a discount: s 100 (1) (Option A). A public company's shares can at minimum be a quarter paid up: s 45(2)(b) (Option B). A public company is prohibited from accepting an undertaking to do work or perform services: s 99(2) (Option (C)).
4	B	The directors may be liable if found guilty of fraudulent or wrongful trading, or if the articles state that they have unlimited liability, but they are not automatically liable (Option A). Unsteady is a limited liability company, hence its members will only be liable for the amounts unpaid on their shares (Option D).
5	C	S 401(2)(b). Fraud is not the same thing as a mistake (Option B). The court cannot override the decision of the registrar (Option D), and the certificate is valid and conclusive evidence that the charge was registered properly within the appropriate time period (Option A).
6	A	S 89, though the articles may also give the rights listed in Options B to D.
7	C	All three requirements must be met. D is wrong as it is only private companies that can carry out the procedure.

8	A	It is void because it would be a means of avoiding the payment of stamp duty. It is also void because a transfer of shares is the type of contract that must be made in writing, as you have seen in contract law.
9	D	S 173(2). A special resolution is required.
10	D	S 142(1). The purpose is to consider the steps that should be taken to deal with the situation.

35 Corporate finance 3

1	B	A is the definition of a fixed charge.
2	C	S 395 (1). Registration must occur within 21 days.
3	D	Options A, B and C are exceptions.
4	B	The company has a duty to pay interest on the debentures based on the contract under which they were formed. There is, however, no necessity for the company to pay a dividend to ordinary shareholders; a decision not to do so is within the company's discretion. A debentureholder (whether or not secured by a charge over the company assets) is a creditor of the company (not a member) and therefore takes precedence in a liquidation (Option D).
5	B	S 239 Insolvency Act 1986
6	D	S 91(1). Private companies can disapply the rights permanently (Option A), but by provisions in their memorandum and articles, not by special resolution.
7	C	S 169 CA 85. A return must be made within 28 days.
8	D	Options A, B and C are defined as undistributable by s 264 CA 85, plus any other reserve which statute or the company's memo and arts state shall be undistributable.
9	C	S 127. 10% is the threshold for certain other rights of minority objection, for example to purchase of own shares out of capital.
10	C	Company law lays down certain rules regarding the register if it is kept, but does not require it to be kept.

36 Corporate finance 4

1	C	Debentures can be issued at a discount (Option B), but shares cannot be (Option D) and the instant conversion has been held to be an illegitimate method of bypassing the rules on consideration for shares.
2	B	Only the remaining issued capital may be called up, not all of the remaining nominal capital.
3	C	S 395 (1) states that the charge is void, not voidable (Option B), if not registered within 21 days of creation; the existence of subsequent secured creditors is irrelevant (Option D). The charge however is the security for the debt, not the debt itself which remains valid; thus it is not inevitable that the creditor will receive nothing (Option A).

4	B	S 245 Insolvency Act 1986 states that the charge is invalid if created within 12 months of the onset of insolvency except to the extent that fresh consideration is provided for them, as here with the loan. The fraudulent preference rules (Option D) only apply to actions within six months of liquidation that relate to unconnected persons.
5	C	S 80(10). Such allotment is valid.
6	A	S 263(3). Distributable profits are accumulated realised profits less accumulated realised losses.
7	C	S 277(1). Where shareholders had reasonable grounds to believe the distribution contravened the act, the excess amount is repayable.
8	A	S 271(3) and (4). The distribution can be made providing the qualification is not material.
9	C	The cancellation of calls is one of the three scenarios envisaged in s 135 for the reduction of capital.
10	B	S 173(3). A declaration of going concern must be made for the coming year.

37 Ethics and business 1

1	B	Objectivity requires intellectual honesty and keeping your mind free from bias. A and D both describe integrity and option C describes professional competence.
2	True	You should maintain confidentiality at all times unless you have a legal or professional duty to disclose.
3	D	An important principle of professional competence is not taking on work if you are not competent to do it.
4	B, C, E	Option A and D describe objectivity. The correct options demonstrate questioning and non-acceptance that work is correct on face value.
5	B	Accountability can be demonstrated by taking responsibility for your own actions.
6	D	Financial information is publicly available and citizens use it as a basis to invest their money. Therefore accountants have a duty to ensure it is as accurate as possible.
7	B, C, E	The code is not intended to improve the profitability of businesses and it sets out the minimum level of behaviour expected of accountants.
8	True	CIMA believes high standards contribute to the integrity of the qualification and the employability of its members.
9		**Themselves, profession.** Courtesy reflects favourably on the individual accountant and the accounting profession.
10	D	CIMA members are encouraged to adopt the concept of lifelong learning. That means they never stop learning and are always open to new ideas, decisions and skills.

38 Ethics and business 2

1   A and C   By applying integrity, accountants seek to minimise the risk of passing on incorrect information and this enhances the credibility of their work. B and E describe the benefits of objectivity and D confidentiality.

2   **Independence.** The accountant demonstrates 'an independent mind'.

3   **Public interest, employability.** CIMA as a chartered body has an overriding duty to uphold the public interest. The employability of members will be enhanced if they all uphold high ethical standards.

4   C   IFAC's mission is to enhance the quality of services and to develop high professional standards of accountants.

5   A, B, C, D   These are all potential consequences of producing unreliable work. E is incorrect as IFAC does not investigate an individual's work.

6   **Responsibility, professional standards.** Accountants should act in a responsible manner to protect confidential information. They are also responsible for ensuring their work meets professional standards.

7   C   Courtesy by accountants provides a good impression of the profession to those they meet professionally. Courtesy is not a prerequisite for competence or independence.

8   **Professional competence.** Accountants are required to stay technically up to date to be considered professionally competent.

9   **Lifelong learning**. Lifelong learning is the concept that an individual never stops learning.

10   Delete **Framework-based**. Under a rules-based approach, a governing body attempts to anticipate possible ethical situations and lays down a specific rule for members to follow.

39 Ethics and business 3

1   (a)(iii)   Disrespectful behaviour may constitute unprofessional behaviour.

     (b)(i)   By applying scepticism, accountants question the information they have produced or received and are less likely to pass on incorrect data.

     (c)(iv)   Responsible behaviour is required to respect the confidential nature of information.

     (d)(ii)   Objectivity requires an 'independent mind' and 'independence in appearance'.

2   B   The accountant maintains their 'independence of appearance'.

3   **Questioning, evidence.** Questioning information and seeking supporting evidence before accepting information as correct demonstrates scepticism.

4   D   Accountants are accountable for their own judgements and decisions.

5	A	Codes of practice seek to enhance the standards of behaviour of members. They cannot eliminate unethical behaviour entirely, but it indicates a minimum level of behaviour expected. Codes can be rules-based, not just principles-based.
6		**Timeliness.** Timeliness can save resources as colleagues can start work when they plan too.
7		**Lifelong learning, professional competence.** By following lifelong learning, an accountant aims to keep technically up to date which is required by the fundamental principle of professional competence.
8	B	An advantage of a framework-based approach to ethics is that it can deal with complex, evolving environments.
9	C	The other options describe the rules-based approach to developing a code.
10	True	Ethics can be viewed as the moral principles that guide behaviour.

40 Ethical conflict 1

1		**Professional behaviour.** The actions are certainly dishonest and may constitute fraud.
2		**Objectivity.** It could appear to a reasonable observer that the finance director received the holiday in return for accepting the loan.
3		**Professional competence and due care.** The accountant is unlikely to be able to exercise due care if he has consumed a bottle of wine.
4		**Confidentiality.** The database contains personal information about the members that should only be used by the health club concerned. Supplying the information to a third party breaches that confidentiality.
5		**Integrity.** The continued use of estimates risks inaccurate trade receivables and payables and therefore misleading accounts.
6	C	A CIMA member should always look to resolve the matter themselves before taking it further.
7		**Public, interest, employability.** As a chartered body, CIMA has a duty to uphold the public interest. It also believes high standards enhance members' employability.
8	A	Ultimately regulation through laws, listing rules and accounting standards may be required to enforce social responsibility, but the main driving force affecting company behaviour in this area is public pressure.
9	A and B	Professional bodies can lose their 'chartered' status if they are no longer seen to act in the public interest. The profession may be subject to external regulation or legal regulation by government if it cannot regulate itself adequately. C and D are both examples of the benefits of ethical accountants to the profession.
10	B	Legal advice should always be taken before breaching any duty of confidentiality to minimise any risk of legal action by the affected party. A and D both involve breaching confidentiality, and C would mean the accountant behaving unethically and at risk of disciplinary action by CIMA.

41 Ethical conflict 2

1   **Professional competence and due care, integrity, professional behaviour.** Lack of experience means you may not be competent. Just following last years workings may mean errors in this years calculation. The manager is breaching professional behaviour standards by insisting you breach your ethical code.

2   True   Members should make use of any procedures available to them in order to resolve an ethical problem.

3   B   Supply of such information is insider-dealing – a criminal offence.

4   **Reputation, society.** Unethical behaviour damages the reputation of accountants and has an implication for society.

5   C   Shareholders do not need corporate governance rules to be able to sue directors. There is no serious mistrust of financial statements by stock markets. Corporate governance rules were developed to help protect stakeholders from corporate collapses, to improve financial reporting and to facilitate the globalisation of investment, not to ensure all companies act ethically.

6   A, C, D   Owning shares in a company that competes with your employer does not create a conflict of interest, as you are not in a position to affect its results. The performance bonus would only cause a conflict if you were able to determine if you were eligible.

7   D   Although ethical accountants may in some cases help improve the profitability of companies, they cannot 'ensure' companies are profitable. Interfering with a company's results to make them profitable is unethical behaviour.

8   All   The accountant should keep a record of all communications, meetings and decisions as they may be important evidence that the member has done all they can to resolve the issue.

9   B   Corporate governance rules are requirements of the London Stock Exchange that have no basis in company law.

10   C   Splitting the chairman and chief executive role is recommended under corporate governance guidance, companies are legally required to provide health and safety training and not to discriminate against candidates because of the age, sex, religion or any handicaps.

42 Ethical conflict 3

1   True   If the unethical behaviour causes damage to a third party.

2   True   The CIMA code of conduct applies equally to students and full members.

3   1B – The law
        2C – Stock market regulations
        3A – Ethical codes of conduct
        4D – Public pressure, no regulation

4	A and B	Working for direct competitors will create a conflict as each would require the accountant to put their interests first. High fee income from one private client may cause the accountant to put their needs before those of their employer. A job offer is not a conflict of interest. Option D is an example of preventing a conflict of interest as the accountant is only taking on work they can do in the time they have available – no party is disadvantaged.
5	False	A conflict of interest describes a situation where an individual has competing professional or personal interests. It is virtually impossible for finance professionals to avoid conflicts entirely. It only becomes wrongdoing if the professional exploits the situation for his or her own benefit.
6	True	The ultimate sanction CIMA has over any unethical members is to remove them from the organisation. A degree holder will have their qualification for life.
7	True	If the matter is serious enough, resignation may be the only course of action left to avoid unethical behaviour.
8		**Relevant, principles, ethical, internal.** Accountants should consider the relevant facts, fundamental principles, ethical issues and internal procedures available.
9		**Legal, non-legal.** Ethical behaviour is the highest level of behaviour that is expected by society. To demonstrate it, an individual or business must first meet its legal and non-legal obligations.
10	True	Behaving legally means a business meets the minimum level of behaviour expected by society, this is not necessarily the same as acting ethically which is the highest level of behaviour expected by society.

43 Corporate governance 1

1		**Directed, controlled.** This definition is per CIMA's Official Terminology 2005, taken from the Cadbury report.
2	C	Ethics can influence directors' behaviour and therefore will affect corporate governance.
3	A, D, E	Options B and C had no bearing on the need to develop corporate governance rules.
4	B	The UK and USA saw a succession of famous corporate scandals such as Polly Peck, BCCI, Maxwell Communications.
5	C	The form of payment should not adversely affect a company provided the bonus scheme is correctly set up. By increasing their company's share price, the directors should have improved the financial position of the company, which is to the company's benefit.
6	A	The Combined Code has not affected the fundamental duty of skill and care of executive directors.
7		**Internal, audit.** Internal audit is an important part of a company's internal control.
8	B and D	The executive board is comprised entirely of managers and is concerned with the day-to-day running of the business. The executive board is monitored by the supervisory board consisting of workers' representatives, shareholders and its banks.
9	D	Executive directors should not be involved in the review of their own or other executive directors' remuneration.

10   **(a)(ii), (b)(iii), (c)(i).** Turnbull reported on internal controls, Higgs on non-executive directors and Smith on audit committees.

44 Corporate governance 2

1   A   The answer is the definition from CIMA's Official Terminology. Remember that governance is about how companies are run, not how directors are regulated.

2   A   Company law sets out a large framework of rules that determine the minimum level of behaviour expected from companies (of which the ability to sue directors is only one part). It does not dictate corporate governance as directors have a free choice of how to implement the rules, and they may even choose to exceed the standards required. Therefore it can only be said to influence corporate governance.

3   **Accountability, performance.** Directors have had to change their behaviour as they are now more accountable for their actions and because more of their remuneration is determined by performance.

4   B and C   The internationalisation of accounting qualifications has no bearing on the need for corporate governance rules. Development of international accounting standards may have helped facilitate the globalisation of share trading, but it is not a direct reason for the need to develop corporate governance rules.

5   D   The AGM is a company law requirement. The other options are 'best practice' under the Stock Exchange Combined Code that is not a legal requirement.

6   All   They are all roles that that board should perform.

7   True   Directors on long service contracts whose salary is not largely governed by their performance may lose touch with the interests and views of shareholders.

8   A, B, E   The Higgs, Smith and Turnbill committee reports were included in the 2003 Combined Code.

9   A   Directors should review internal controls annually and report to the shareholders that they have done so.

10   C   The 2003 Combined Code is the main source of corporate governance rules in the UK. Sarbanes-Oxley is the source of US regulations and the Cadbury Report is included as a part of the 2003 Combined Code.

45 Corporate governance 3

1   A, B, D   All describe methods that control and direct the company. Option C are external rules that apply to the shareholders of a company, and do not affect how the company is run.

2   B and D   Enron and Worldcom are the two most famous corporate scandals of recent years.

3   **Confidence, reporting.** Confidence was lost in the management and reporting of companies.

4		Delete **increased, decreased.** Directors have found their duty of care substantially unchanged.
5		**All, majority, majority.** Boards either consist of all executive directors or have a majority of executive or non-executive directors.
6		**Executive, non-executive.** Non-executive directors have no input into the day-to-day running of the business.
7	D	The audit committee should consist of non-executive directors, the majority being independent.
8	True	The Combined Code recommends the roles should be separated, if they are combined, the reasons why should be justified publicly.
9	B	The London Stock Exchange requires all companies listed on the exchange to comply with the 2003 Combined Code.
10	True	Non-listed companies are encouraged to follow the code where possible as an example of 'best practice'.

Mock assessments

CIMA
Paper C5 (Certificate)
Fundamentals of Ethics, Corporate Governance and Business Law

Mock Assessment 1

Question Paper	
Time allowed	**2 hours**
Answer ALL seventy-five questions	

DO NOT OPEN THIS PAPER UNTIL YOU ARE READY TO START UNDER EXAMINATION CONDITIONS

CIMA

Paper C5 (Certificate)

Fundamentals of Ethics,

Corporate Governance and

Business Law

Mock Assessment 1

Question Paper	
Time Allowed	2 hours

Answer ALL seventy-five questions

DO NOT OPEN THIS PAPER UNTIL YOU ARE READY TO START UNDER EXAMINATION CONDITIONS

Answer ALL questions

1   Exe Ltd was under contract to deliver goods by road to London for Wye Ltd for £2,000. After part of the journey was completed, the delivery vehicle broke down and Wye Ltd was forced to arrange for Zed Ltd to complete the delivery.

If there are no provisions in the contract to deal with this situation, which of the following is **correct**?

A   Exe Ltd is entitled to part of the delivery fee
B   Exe Ltd is entitled to nothing
C   Exe Ltd is entitled to a reasonable sum for the work done
D   Exe Ltd is entitled to the full £2,000

2   Which of the following must be included on a statement of written particulars of employment?

- [x] Names of employer and employee
- [x] Date on which employment began
- [ ] Name of former employer (if applicable)
- [x] Pay rate and intervals at which it is paid
- [ ] Right to future pay increments
- [x] Details of any pension
- [x] Hours of work
- [ ] Set holiday dates in the first year of employment
- [ ] Details of disciplinary methods
- [x] Job title

3   Which of the following minority rights are **correct**?

- [x] Right to apply to the court in respect of unfairly prejudicial conduct
- [x] Right to petition the DTI for winding up on the just and equitable ground
- [x] Right of 15% of holders of class right to apply to the court for a cancellation
- [x] Right of 200+ members to apply to the DTI to investigate the company's affairs
- [ ] Right of 20%+ of holders of shares to apply to the court to prevent a purchase of the company's own shares

4   Which of the following are correct differences between Sharia and Codified law systems?

(i)   Sharia law transcends national boundaries
(ii)   Judges under Sharia law cannot create law
(iii)   Codified law is written by man
(iv)   Countries under Sharia law do not have a written constitution

A (i), (ii) and (iii)
B (i) and (iii)
C (ii), (iii) and (iv)
D All of the above

---

5 Which **one** of the following remedies is **not** available for a breach of a contract to provide personal services?

A Damages
B A decree of specific performance
C An injunction
D An action for the price

---

6 What is corporate governance?

A Stock market regulations which govern how public companies are run
B Ethical guidelines for directors
C The system by which companies are directed and controlled
D Directors' legal obligations

---

7 Which of the following is an example of how company law has influenced a company's corporate governance?

A A company that splits the role of chairman and chief executive
B A company that sets up an audit committee
C A company that sets directors' notice periods at one year or less
D A company that has an annual general meeting

---

8 Which of the following require Parliament to give effect to them?

- [✓] Delegated legislation
- [✓] Statute
- [ ] Regulations
- [✓] Directives
- [ ] EC Decisions

---

9 In which of the following is there a presumption that legal relations are intended?

A A promise by a father to make a gift to his son
B A commercial transaction
C A domestic arrangement
D A social arrangement

---

10 Which of the following statements about issuing shares are **correct**?

☑ For plcs, authority to allot shares must be given until a specified date

☑ Ltd companies may give authority to allot shares indefinitely

☑ All companies must specify a maximum number of shares that may be allotted

☑ If the directors have wilfully allotted shares illegally, the allotment is valid

☐ A special resolution is required to give authority to allot shares

11 Which **one** of the following may requisition an extraordinary general meeting?

A Members holding not less than one-twentieth of the company's issued share capital which carries voting rights

B Members holding not less than one-tenth of the company's issued share capital which carries voting rights

C Members holding not less than one-tenth of the company's issued share capital which carries voting rights

D Members holding not less than one-half of the company's issued share capital which carries voting rights

12 Accountants have a public duty as well as a duty to their employer.

True/False?

13 ABC Ltd has contracted with DEF Ltd. If ABC Ltd acts in breach of a warranty, which of the following is **correct**?

(i) DEF Ltd may terminate the contract and sue for damages

(ii) DEF Ltd may sue for damages but may not terminate the contract

(iii) DEF Ltd may ignore the breach and continue with the contract

A (i) only

B (i) and (iii)

C (ii) and (iii)

D (i), (ii) and (iii)

14 Name the two types of board committee the 2003 Combined Code recommends companies should set up.

(1).......................................

(2).......................................

15 Which **one** of the following is **correct**?

A All English courts must apply European Law even if it contradicts English Law.

B If European and English Law conflict, English courts cannot apply either law.

C An English court must apply English Law unless it obtains the Government's permission to apply European Law.

D All English courts are obliged to apply English Law even if it contradicts European Law.

16 When obtaining professional advice to resolve an ethical conflict, special care must be taken to avoid breaching which fundamental ethical principle?

A   Integrity
B   Objectivity
C   Confidentiality
D   Professional behaviour

17 Under the Employment Act 2002, the maximum total period of statutory maternity leave that a woman may be entitled to is **six weeks/twenty six weeks/fifty two weeks** (delete as appropriate).

18 How can accountant develop their quality of respect? Select all that apply.

- [✓] By developing constructive relationships with others
- [✓] By recognising the rights of others
- [ ] By avoiding disagreements with others
- [ ] By not challenging the views of those more qualified than them
- [✓] By arguing their own opinion but accepting the views of others

19 Which of the following are consequences that a CIMA member may face if their unethical behaviour is found to constitute to professional misconduct? Select all that apply.

- [✓] Unlimited fine
- [✓] Admonishment
- [✓] Living with guilt afterwards
- [✓] Damage to their personal reputation through publication of the complaint to the newspapers, professional journals and the CIMA website
- [✓] Loss of their job

20 Which of the following is an example of how business ethics may influence corporate governance?

A   When a business chooses a supplier on the basis of cost
B   When a business chooses a supplier on the basis of product quality
C   When a business chooses a supplier on the basis of its employees' working conditions
D   When a business chooses a supplier on the basis of speed of delivery

21 Which of the following would strongly indicate that a person was an employee?

A   He uses his own tools
B   He is delegated work
C   He renders invoices to the company
D   He has a contract with the company

22   The repeated practice of certain principles can create an obligation to continue to do so in the future. This is a source of law under which system?

A   Common law
B   Codified systems
C   Sharia law
D   International law

23   Which of the following private company resolutions may be passed by elective resolution?

- [x] To confer authority to issue shares indefinitely
- [ ] To disapply pre-emption rights
- [x] To dispense with holding an AGM
- [x] To dispense with the annual re-appointment of auditors
- [ ] To amend the articles of association

The following information relates to questions 24 to 28.

The following scenarios may or may not present you with an ethical dilemma. Consider each of them and state the fundamental principles at stake. Write NO DILEMMA is there is no ethical dilemma.

24   You are working as an assistant management accountant in a large manufacturing company and your role involves costing new products. A long-time supplier has invited you and your colleagues out for lunch.

25   Your manager has passed you their work for you to double-check. You find a large number of errors but your manager insists it is fine and tells you to send it to the finance director.

26   Whilst working in your company's payroll department, an employee has asked you to post their salary details to a building society in support their mortgage application. You have been given the name and address of the person dealing with the application at the building society and the approval from the payroll manager to send out the details.

27   A colleague has recently gained promotion and you have taken over their work on the sales ledger. During the hand-over, the colleague gives you a list of customers that he calls 'trouble-makers'. He says, 'you won't get on with them, they are all rude and never pay on time'.

28   On a Friday night out in town you meet with a friend who works for a company that supplies materials to yours. Your friend's employer is facing closure, but earlier that day you learned that your company awarded them a new contract that will save it. The supplier will announce the news to its employees first thing on Monday morning, but your friend is obviously still very concerned that their job may be at risk. They know that their company tendered for the contract and they ask if you have heard anything.

29   Tee Ltd placed some computers in its shop window with a notice which read:

'Special offer, Internet-ready computers for sale at £400'

Which of the following is **correct**?

(i)   The notice amounts to an invitation to treat
(ii)   When Anne called in to the shop and offered £350 for one of the computers, she had made a counter offer
(iii)   Tee Ltd is obliged to sell a computer to anyone who can pay the price

A   (i) and (ii)
B   (i) only
C   (i), (ii) and (iii)
D   (ii) only

---

30   Charles recently purchased some goods at an auction sale

Which of the following is **correct**?

(i)   The contract was concluded by the fall of the Auctioneer's hammer
(ii)   The Auctioneer's call for bids was an invitation to treat

A   (i) only
B   (ii) only
C   Both (i) and (ii)
D   Neither (i) nor (ii)

---

31   An employer must provide an employee with a written statement of particulars of the employment

A   Within one month of the employment commencing
B   As soon after the commencement of employment as possible
C   Within two months of the employment commencing
D   Within a reasonable time of the employment commencing

The following information relates to questions 32 to 35

George Thompson has carried on business for a number of years as a self-employed retailer of office furniture. He has now decided to incorporate his business, and to register GT Limited to acquire the business.

---

32   **Complete this sentence.**

In order to register a private limited company, George will need to submit certain documents to the

.... (three

words) who will issue a certificate of incorporation if everything is in order.

33   Complete these sentences.

One of the documents which George will need to submit contains the company's name, the situation of the company's registered office, a statement that the liability of the members is limited, and the authorised share capital and its division into shares. This document is called the ....

.... (three words).

**34   The document referred to in question 33 also contains the ....

.... (two words) which sets out the business(es) which the company is authorised to carry on.

35   Complete this sentence.

If, at a later date, George wishes to increase the authorised share capital of the company, he may do so by passing an **ordinary/special/extraordinary** resolution (delete as appropriate).

36   Which ONE of the following statements is *incorrect?*

A   Payment by the debtor of less than the full amount of the debt will satisfy the whole debt at common law, if paid early at the request of the creditor.

B   Payment by a third party of less than the full amount of the debt will discharge the whole debt at common law.

C   Payment of less than the full amount of the debt will discharge the whole debt at common law, if agreed to by the creditor.

D   Payment of less than the full amount of the debt will discharge the whole debt at common law, if extra consideration is provided by the debtor.

37   Consider the following statements concerning how judges deal with cases.

(i)   Under common law, the judge will consider the facts, relevant statute law and any previous similar cases.

(ii)   Under codified systems, judges may only consider the facts and apply the letter of the law.

(iii)   Under Sharia law, a judge will apply the law to the facts presented, turning to the Sunnah for guidance on interpretation if necessary.

Which statements are correct?

A   (i) and (ii)
B   (i) and (iii)
C   (ii) and (iii)
D   (iii) only

38 An employee should ensure the health and safety at work of whom?

    A   Employees

    B   Independent contractors

    C   Visitors

    D   All of the above

39 What problems cannot be overcome by the adoption of continual personal development and lifelong learning by an accountant?

    (i)   Technical errors in their work

    (ii)   Poor time keeping

    (iii)   Ethical dilemmas

    (iv)   Lack of assertiveness

    A   (i) and (ii)

    B   (iii) only

    C   (iii) and (iv)

    D   All of the above

40 Which of the following indicate poor corporate governance? Select all that apply.

    [✓] Domination of the board by a single individual

    [✓] Board focus on short-term profitability

    [ ] The payment of bonuses to directors

    [✓] Contradictory information given to stakeholders

    [ ] An employee discovering errors in a report after following company checking procedures

41 Which of the following is **correct**?

    (i)   A public company cannot commence trading until it has received a certificate from the Registrar of Companies confirming that it has satisfied the minimum requirements as to authorised and issued share capital.

    (ii)   If a public company commences trading without a trading certificate, and fails to meet its obligations, the directors may be held jointly and severally liable for those obligations.

    (iii)   A private company may commence trading upon receipt of its certificate of incorporation

    A   (i) and (ii)

    B   (ii) and (iii)

    C   (i) and (iii)

    D   (i), (ii) and (iii)

42 A governing body sets out fundamental principles for its members to follow when developing a code of ethics.

The above statement describes a **rules-based/framework-based** approach to ethics.

Delete the incorrect term.

43 Which of the following is **incorrect**?

(i)   Legal title cannot pass on a contract induced by misrepresentation
(ii)   Misrepresentation renders a contract voidable
(iii)   A victim of negligent misrepresentation may seek rescission and damages

A   (i) only
B   (ii) only
C   (i) and (iii)
D   (ii) and (iii)

44 The Sunnah and the Quran are the primary sources of Sharia law.

True/False?

45 Under the terms of the Woolf reforms, claims with a value of over £ .... are allocated to the multi-track claims system.

46 Why has the globalisation of share trading contributed to the need for corporate governance rules?

A   Investors need to be able to compare financial statements produced under different accounting standards.

B   Investors need confidence in foreign management and reporting standards before they will trade outside their own country.

C   Investors in foreign countries cannot always attend the annual meeting.

D   Investors invest large amounts of capital and require it to be protected.

47 Which of the following courts is bound by a decision of the High Court (a judge sitting alone)?

☑ Magistrates Court	
☑ County Court	
☑ Crown Court	
☐ High Court (judge sitting alone)	
☐ High Court (judges sitting together)	
☐ Court of Appeal	
☐ House of Lords	
☐ European Court of Justice	

HL
↑
CoA
↑
HC *civil court*
↑
MC

48 What two ultimate actions can a CIMA member take when all attempts to resolve an ethical conflict have failed?

Select TWO from the following.

A   Request a transfer to a new department or role
B   Report the matter to CIMA
C   Resign
D   Report the matter to the board of directors

49 Which ONE of the following is *incorrect*?

A An employer is obliged to provide an employee with a reference

B An employer must allow health and safety representatives reasonable paid time off work to perform their functions

C An employer must provide an employee with a safe working environment

D All employees are entitled to paid leave

50 Which of the following statement is/are *correct*?

(i) If an agreement is stated to be 'binding in honour only', the parties have decided that the agreement should not have contractual force

(ii) If an agreement is not in writing, the parties are presumed to have intended that it should not be legally enforceable

A (i) only
B (ii) only
C Neither (i) nor (ii)
D Both (i) and (ii)

The following information relates to questions 51 to 56

Greg, Harry and Ian are the sole shareholders of GHI Ltd. The company has an authorised share capital of £100,000 divided into 100,000 ordinary £1 shares. Greg is the sole director of the company and Harry is the company secretary. At present, the issued share capital is held as follows:

Greg	51,000	shares
Harry	29,000	shares
Ian	20,000	shares
Total	100,000	shares

The company, which has been valued at £300,000, has decided on the following transactions.

- To raise £60,000 in cash by issuing shares to Fiona
- To borrow £40,000 from AB Bank plc

51 In order to facilitate the issue of new shares, the authorised capital must be increased by at least

.... ordinary £1 shares (write the number in figures).

52 In order to issue the shares, Greg must be authorised by the shareholders or by the

.... (three words).

53 Fiona will become a member of the company when she has been entered in the

.... (three words).

54 She must also be sent a .... (two words) within two months of allotment.

---

55 If AB Bank plc requires security in the form of a debenture containing a .... (one word) charge, then the company will not be able to deal freely with the assets charged in the ordinary course of business.

---

56 However, GHI Ltd will be able to deal freely with assets which are secured by a .... (one word) charge.

---

57 Which of the following statements is *correct*?

(i) An employer has an implied duty to behave reasonably and responsibly towards employees.
(ii) An employer has an implied duty to provide facilities for smokers

A (i) only
B (ii) only
C Neither (i) nor (ii)
D Both (i) and (ii)

58 Which of the following will influence on an individual's ethical beliefs? Select all that apply.

- [x] Their education
- [x] The culture they live in
- [x] The beliefs of their family
- [x] The rules of their work place
- [x] Their religious beliefs

59 An accountant who recognises that when their judgements and decisions are called into question they are ultimately responsible, is demonstrating which professional quality?

A Independence
B Accountability
C Social responsibility
D Scepticism

---

60 The right to sue for breach of a contract made by deed becomes statute-barred after .... years.

---

61 Identify the correct concept from the scenario below.

An accountant has a very tight deadline to ensure the published financial statements of their company are completed in time. They decide to work overtime to make sure the work is completed in enough detail to be as accurate as possible.

    A   Independence

    B   Social responsibility

    C   Scepticism

    D   Professional competence

62   Select the TWO types of decision that a board of directors would not become involved in.

    A   The purchase of a new computer network

    B   The allocation of parking spaces to employees

    C   The disposal of one company car

    D   The choice of bank loan to support the purchase of a new factory

    E   The size of the advertising budget

63   Which of the following are characteristics of limited liability?

    ☑   Perpetual succession

    ☑   Limited liability of the business organisation

    ☑   Strict rules concerning withdrawal of capital

    ☑   Assets owned by the business organisation

    ☑   Limited liability of members

64   Which is the correct statement regarding CIMA's Code of ethics?

    A   The code indicates the highest level of behaviour expected of accountants.

    B   The code indicates the minimum level of behaviour expected of accountants.

    C   Members do not have to follow the code as it is optional.

    D   The code will not have any influence on the employability of CIMA members.

65   Which ONE of the following statements is *correct?*

    A   If a person signs a contract, he/she is bound by all its terms

    B   A contract which has not been signed is not binding on any of the parties

    C   A person who signs a contract is deemed to have read it

    D   A person who has not read a contract cannot be bound by it

66   In respect of misrepresentation, which of the following are **correct**?

    ☐   The person entering the contract must have been aware of its existence

    ☐   The statement can have been made to the public at large

    ☑   It is sufficient that the misrepresentor knows that the statement would be passed on to the other party

    ☑   Silence is not generally misrepresentation

    ☐   However, what has been said must be complete enough not to mislead

BPP
PROFESSIONAL EDUCATION

67 The Memorandum of Dee Ltd, a property development company, states that the company has power to borrow in furtherance of its objects and that the directors have authority to borrow up to £200,000. The board has resolved to purchase a piece of land for £300,000. The Midwest Bank plc has agreed to make a loan of £250,000 to Dee Ltd to acquire the land.

Which **one** of the following is **correct**?

A The loan is void as Dee Ltd has acted *ultra vires*

B As the directors have exceeded their authority, the bank cannot enforce the loan against Dee Ltd

C As the directors have resolved to obtain the loan, the transaction is lawful

D The loan is *ultra vires* the directors who will be personally liable for any loss caused to the company unless their actions are ratified by the shareholders

68 CIMA has its own reasons for upholding high ethical standards. Select the correct reason(s).

- [x] To eliminate unethical behaviour by its members.
- [x] To help protect the public interest.
- [x] To enhance the integrity of the CIMA qualification.
- [x] UK Company law requires high ethical standards from accounting bodies.
- [ ] The 2003 Combined Code recommended listed companies should only employ accountants who are members of highly ethical bodies.

69 What is the maximum recommended length for director service contracts according to the 2003 Combined Code?

A One year
B Two years
C Three years
D Five years

70 Which of the following statements is/are *correct*?

(i) A contractual term which attempts to exclude liability for damage to property caused by negligence is void unless reasonable

(ii) A contractual term which attempts to exclude liability for death or personal injury is void

A (i) only
B (ii) only
C Neither (i) nor (ii)
D Both (i) and (ii)

71 Four of the following statements are unique to either common law, Sharia law, codified legal systems or international law. Match the correct statement to the correct legal system. Two statements are not unique and should be ignored.

(a) The law seeks comprehensibility and certainty
(b) Interpretation of the law is not a matter for courts
(c) Judges may only apply the law
(d) Judges are involved in judicial review
(e) The law permits something until it is shown to be forbidden
(f) Judges can be bound by the decisions of other courts

(i) Common law
(ii) Sharia law
(iii) Codified legal systems
(iv) International law

72 Which of the following statements is/are *correct*?

(i) A contract of employment must be in writing
(ii) An employer must provide written particulars of the employment for the employee

A (i) only
B (ii) only
C Both (i) and (ii)
D Neither (i) nor (ii)

73 An accountant demonstrates the need to meet deadlines as failure to do so can waste their employer's money and other resources. Which personal quality does this statement describe?

....

74 What best practice does the 2003 Combined Code recommend regarding the roles of chairman and chief executive?

A The chairman must previously have been the chief executive
B The chairman and chief executive roles should ideally not be performed by one individual
C The chairman should not have previously been chief executive
D The chairman and chief executive roles should be combined if possible

75 A Ltd placed the following advertisement in a local newspaper:

'We are able to offer for sale a number of portable colour television sets at the specially reduced price of £5.90. Order now while stocks last.'

The advertisement contained a mistake in that the television sets should have been priced at £59.00. B Ltd immediately placed an order for 100 television sets.

Which of the following statements is correct?

A B Ltd has accepted an offer and is contractually entitled to the 100 television sets.
B A Ltd can refuse to supply B Ltd as the advertisement is not an offer, but an invitation to treat.
C A Ltd can only refuse to sell the television sets to B Ltd if it has sold all its stock.
D As B Ltd has not yet paid for the television sets, the company has no contractual right to them.

Answers

DO NOT TURN THIS PAGE UNTIL YOU HAVE
COMPLETED MOCK ASSESSMENT 1

1   B   Exo Ltd ic ontitlod to nothing ac the contract has not been completely performed

2   ☑ Names of employer and employee
      ☑ Date on which employment began
      ☐ Name of former employer (if applicable
      ☑ Pay rate and intervals at which it is paid
      ☐ Right to future pay increments
      ☑ Details of any pension
      ☑ Hours of work
      ☐ Set holiday dates in the first year of employment
      ☐ Details of disciplinary methods
      ☑ Job title

3   ☑ Right to apply to the court in respect of unfairly prejudicial conduct
      ☐ Right to petition the DTI for winding up on the just and equitable ground
      ☑ Right of 15% of holders of class right to apply to the court for a cancellation
      ☑ Right of 200+ members to apply to the DTI to investigate the company's affairs
      ☐ Right of 20%+ of holders of shares to apply to the court to prevent a purchase of the company's own shares

     The right to petition for winding up is a right to petition **the court**, not the DTI. Holders of 10% of shares may apply to the court to prevent a company purchasing its own shares.

4   B   Sharia law is based on the religion of Islam and it transcends national boundaries, whereas countries adopting a codified system have laws specific to them. Muslims believe that the Quran is directly sourced from God (Allah) whereas codified law is man made. Judges in codified systems cannot create law. Iran and Pakistan are examples of countries under Sharia law that have a constitution.

5   B   Specific performance will never be granted in a contract for personal services.

6   C   Corporate governance is the system by which organisations are directed and controlled.

7   D   Under the Companies Act, companies must have an AGM. The other options are recommendations of the 2003 Combined Code which is not company law.

8
- ☐ Delegated legislation
- ☑ Statute
- ☐ Regulations
- ☑ Directives
- ☐ EC Decisions

9   B   *Rose and Frank and Co v Cromption:* legal relations are presumed in commercial transactions.

10
- ☑ For plcs, authority to allot shares must be given until a specified date
- ☑ Ltd companies may give authority to allot shares indefinitely
- ☑ All companies must specify a maximum number of shares that may be allotted
- ☑ If the directors have wilfully allotted shares illegally, the allotment is valid
- ☐ A special resolution is required to give authority to allot shares

Only an ordinary resolution is required for allotment.

11   B   S 368 CA 85. Members holding not less than one-tenth of the company's issued share capital which carries voting rights can requisition an EGM.

12   True   Accountants have a public duty to provide benefit to society as a whole.

13   C   You should know the different effects of warranties and conditions in breach.

14   **Audit, remuneration.** The code recommends companies should set up audit and remuneration committees.

15   A   European Law is regarded as the supreme source of law in all member states.

16   C   While obtaining professional advice you must respect your employer's right to confidentiality unless you have a legal or professional duty to do otherwise.

17   Fifty two weeks in total

18
- ☑ By developing constructive relationships with others
- ☑ By recognising the rights of others
- ☐ By avoiding disagreements with others
- ☐ By not challenging the views of those more qualified than them
- ☑ By arguing their own opinion but accepting the views of others

Accountants should not avoid disagreements nor should they refuse to challenge the views of those more qualified than them. They should however respect that people have different opinions and should not bring disagreements down to a personal level.

19 ☑ Unlimited fine

☑ Admonishment

☑ Living with guilt afterwards

☑ Damage to their personal reputation through publication of the complaint to the newspapers, professional journals and the CIMA website

☑ Loss of their job

They are all possible consequences.

20 C The other options are commercial reasons.

21 B D could be a contract for services or a contract of employment, A and C both indicate the person is an independent contractor.

22 D The statement describes international customary law.

23 ☑ To confer authority to issue shares indefinitely

☐ To disapply pre-emption rights

☑ To dispense with holding an AGM

☑ To dispense with the annual re-appointment of auditors

☐ To amend the articles of association

You should learn the five ways in which a private limited company may use an elective resolution.

24 **No dilemma.** There is no issue of objectivity since the meal is not valuable, has been offered to others, and appears just to be a general goodwill gesture between a supplier and a long-time customer.

25 **Integrity.** Sending inaccurate information to the finance director makes you party to misinformation.

26 **No dilemma.** There is no issue of confidentiality as the employee and the HR manager have given their permission to send out the details. There is little risk that the information may get into the wrong person's hands as you have the name and address of the person dealing with the application.

27 **Objectivity.** There is a risk that the colleague's statement will prejudice your treatment of the customers in future. You should form your own opinion of them.

28 **Confidentiality.** Even though the friend will find out the good news first thing on Monday, you should still respect confidentiality and not tell them.

29 B (ii) is incorrect, as such an advertisement would be construed to be invitation to treat, so her statement would be an offer.

30 C The bids are offers and the fall of the hammer accepts the highest offer.

31 C Unless he has already provided a written contract of employment.

32 Registrar of Companies

33 Memorandum of Association

34		Objects clause

35   **Delete special/extraordinary**.

36   C   All the other statements are true. If the debtor provides no kind of other consideration for a payment of less than the total, the debt is not discharged.

37   D   Under common law, judges cannot refer to 'any' similar case – the case must have created a precedent. Under codified systems, judges are not limited to the facts and legislation. They are permitted to refer to other previous cases although they are not bound by them.

38   D   The employer is responsible for 'persons at work' and 'persons other than persons at work'.

39   D   Personal development and lifelong learning can help an accountant resolve most problems they come across personally and professionally.

40

- [✓] Domination of the board by a single individual
- [✓] Board focus on short-term profitability
- [ ] The payment of bonuses to directors
- [✓] Contradictory information given stakeholders
- [ ] An employee discovering errors in a report after following company checking procedures

The payment of bonuses to directors is mentioned in the Combined Code as a method to improve corporate governance. Errors being discovered after following company procedure is an example of strong corporate governance control procedures put in place by the directors that have worked.

41   D   All the statements are correct.

42   **Delete rules-based.** Under a framework-based approach, a governing body describes fundamental principles for its members to follow. There is no attempt to prescribe detailed rules for every situation.

43   A   It is a general rule of misrepresentation that such a contract is voidable, not void.

44   True   The Quran is Allah's divine revelation to his Prophet, Muhammad. The Sunnah is 'the beaten track', what has come to be the acceptable course of conduct.

45   £15,000

46   B   The globalisation of stock markets could not work unless investors worldwide have confidence in the management of a company and its financial reports.

47

- [✓] Magistrates Court
- [✓] County Court
- [✓] Crown Court
- [ ] High Court (judge sitting alone)
- [ ] High Court (judges sitting together)
- [ ] Court of Appeal
- [ ] House of Lords
- [ ] European Court of Justice

48   A and C   Requesting a transfer or resignation are the only two options a member can take to remove themselves from an ethical conflict when everything else has failed. The other options would have been tried an earlier stage.

49   A   There is no requirement to provide references.

50   A   A contract may be made orally and no such presumption is made.

51   60,000

52   Articles of Association

53   Register of members

54   Share certificate

55   Fixed charge

56   Floating charge

57   A   There is no implied duty to provide facilities for smokers. However, the employer must behave reasonably and responsibly towards employees.

58

- [✓] Their education
- [✓] The culture they live in
- [✓] The beliefs of their family
- [ ] The specific rules of their work place
- [✓] Their religious beliefs

Work place rules will not necessarily influence an individual's ethical beliefs.

59   B   Accountants are accountable for their own judgements and decisions.

60   **12 years** (six years in the case of a simple contract)

61   B   Financial statements are used by the public to make investment decisions, the accountant recognises their social responsibility by taking the extra time to ensure their accuracy.

62 B and C They are not major policy or strategy decisions.

63   ☑ Perpetual succession
            ☐ Limited liability of the business organisation
            ☑ Strict rules concerning withdrawal of capital
            ☑ Assets owned by the business organisation
            ☑ Limited liability of members

The liability of the organisation itself is, of course, unlimited.

64 B The code sets out the minimum level of behaviour expected of CIMA members, following the code is not optional and is expected to enhance the employability of members as they have high standards set for them.

65 C A is incorrect because if the person signing has been mislead about the extent of the terms, they may not be bound (*Curtis v Chemical Cleaning Co*).

66   ☑ The person entering the contract must have been aware of its existence
            ☑ The statement can have been made to the public at large
            ☑ It is sufficient that the misrepresentor knows that the statement would be passed on to the other party
            ☑ Silence is not generally misrepresentation
            ☑ However, what has been said must be complete enough not to mislead

All the statements are correct.

67 D Due to s35, the bank cannot be prejudiced against due to the *ultra vires* actions of the directors.

68   ☐ To eliminate unethical behaviour by its members.
            ☑ To help protect the public interest.
            ☑ To enhance the integrity of the CIMA qualification.
            ☐ UK Company law requires high ethical standards from accounting bodies.
            ☐ The 2003 Combined Code recommended listed companies should only employ accountants who are members of highly ethical bodies.

High standards cannot eliminate unethical behaviour entirely. UK company law and the 2003 Combined Code make no such requirements.

69 A Services contracts should not exceed one year in length.

70 D Liability for death or personal injury due to negligence can never be excluded. Exclusion of liability for damage to property is permissible if reasonable in contracts.

71   (a) (iii) They are core principles of codified systems.

(b) (iv) Interpretation of international law is a matter for the state only.

(c) Not unique. Judges under Sharia law and Codified systems may only apply the law.

(d) Not unique. Judges under Common law, Sharia law and Codified systems can all become involved in judicial review.

(e) (ii) Sharia law permits behaviour until shown to be forbidden.

(f) (i) Precedent is unique to common law systems.

72   B   A contract may be oral, but some written particulars must be provided within 2 months of the employee starting work.

73   **Timeliness.** Submitting work late can cost employers money and waste resources as others rely on the work being completed on time.

74   B   The code requires a clear division of power so that one person does not have unfettered powers of decision.

75   B   A newspaper advertisement is an invitation to treat (*Partridge v Crittenden*).

CIMA

Paper C5 (Certificate)

Fundamentals of Ethics, Corporate Governance and Business Law

Mock Assessment 2

JUMOKE MALUMI

Question Paper	
Time allowed JUMOKE MALUMI	2 hours
Answer ALL seventy-five questions	

DO NOT OPEN THIS PAPER UNTIL YOU ARE READY TO START UNDER EXAMINATION CONDITIONS

Answer ALL questions

1 Which of the following registers must be kept at the registered office of a company?

☐ Register of members

☐ Register of directors and secretaries

☐ Register of charges

☐ Minutes of general meetings

☐ Register of substantial interests in shares

2 Tee Ltd has contracted to use Vee Ltd's 'Grand Hotel' for a business conference. Which of the following would be regarded as a valid reason for Vee Ltd for the unavailability of the hotel on the agreed date under the law of frustration?

(i) The hotel was closed due to flood damage.

(ii) The hotel was double booked.

(iii) The hotel manager had arranged to have the hotel redecorated. The decorators had failed to complete the work by the agreed date.

A (i) only
B (iii) only
C (ii) and (iii) only
D (i), (ii) and (iii)

3 In modern times, the concept of Riba commonly affects which aspect of a Muslim's life?

A Charitable donations they make
B The food they eat
C Prayer times
D Property purchases

4 Which part of a case decided by the courts is binding on lower courts dealing with the same material facts?

A Obiter dicta
B The decision of the judge
C The ratio decidendi
D All the above

5 A director may be removed from office under section 303 of the Companies Act 1985 by:

A Ordinary resolution with the usual notice
B Extraordinary resolution with the usual notice
C Ordinary resolution with special notice
D Extraordinary resolution with special notice

6   Select the correct action(s) that an accountant should follow in order to meet the fundamental principle of professional competence and due care.

☐   An accountant should spend enough time on a job to look into all matters in sufficient detail.

☐   An accountant should always accept work given to them by their employer.

☐   An accountant should attend all training and technical update courses available to them even if not relevant to their job.

☐   An accountant should (if relevant) use websites containing technical information to stay up-to-date.

7   Match the feature of poor corporate governance with the problem it can create.

(a)   Domination of the board by a single individual
(b)   Lack of employee supervision
(c)   Emphasis on short-term profitability
(d)   Misleading accounts and information

(i)   Concealment of problems or errors
(ii)   Manipulation of accounts
(iii)   Trading losses
(iv)   Poor corporate decision making

8   A Ltd contracted to deliver a quantity of goods to B Ltd for £5,000. The goods were delivered and A Ltd submitted an invoice to B Ltd for the amount due which contained a number of new terms.

Which of the following is **incorrect?**

A   The invoice is a contractual document and B Ltd is bound by the terms on the invoice

B   B Ltd is only bound by the terms if it was given notice of them at or before the time of the contract

C   B Ltd is bound by the terms if there is a sufficient course of dealings between A Ltd and B Ltd so that B Ltd is assumed to know of the terms

D   If B Ltd is unaware of the terms, it can only be bound by them if it agrees to be so

9   When deciding upon a course of action to resolve an ethical conflict with an employer, an accountant must make sure the resolution:

A   Is acceptable to the employer
B   Is consistent with CIMA's fundamental principles
C   Ensures the ethical conflict can never happen again
D   Has been endorsed by CIMA

10   Which of the following has not been given the statutory minimum notice period?

☐   Anne, who worked for 10 years and was given 12 weeks' notice

☐   Barry, who worked for 1 week and was summarily dismissed

☐   Catherine, who worked for 5 years and was given a month's notice

☐   David, who has worked for 18 months and was given a week's notice

☐   Emily, who worked for 6 months and was given 3 days' notice

☐   Fred, who worked for 20 years and was given 12 weeks' notice

11   The 2003 Combined Code makes recommendations regarding directors pay and service contracts. It suggests that service contracts should be of a period not more than ....
.... and a significant portion of a director's remuneration should be related to
....

Fill in the missing words using the following; **years, ability, one, two ,three, year, performance, skills, demand**

12   Which of the following are **correct**?

(i)   A company is owned by its shareholders and managed by its directors

(ii)   A company is entitled to own property in its own name

(iii)   If business is carried on through a company limited by shares, the shareholders can never incur personal liability over and above the amount due on their shares even if the veil of incorporation is lifted

A   (i) only
B   (i) and (ii) only
C   (i) and (iii) only
D   (i), (ii) and (iii)

13   Madhab are secondary sources of Sharia law, how many are there?

A   3
B   5
C   7
D   9

14   Which of the following is **correct**?

(i)   A contract of guarantee is unenforceable unless it is evidenced in writing.
(ii)   A contract to sell land must be in writing.
(iii)   A contract of employment must be in writing.

A   (i) and (ii)
B   (i) and (iii)
C   (ii) and (iii)
D   (i), (ii) and (iii)

15 An accountant who double-checks all the calculations in their reports can be said to be protecting their:

A   Objectivity
B   Professional competence
C   Integrity
D   Confidentiality

16 Which of the following are decisions that would be made by a board of directors? Select all that apply.

☐   The takeover of a rival company

☐   The purchase of a new company headquarters

☐   The appointment of a new auditor

☐   The appointment of a new management accountant

☐   The choice of office cleaner for the company's head office

17 Which ONE of the following is the highest court in England?

A   The Court of Appeal
B   The House of Lords
C   The High Court
D   The Crown Court

18 Which of the following is **correct**?

(i)   Auditors who provide negligent advice may be held liable for breach of contract by the company which appointed them.

(ii)   Auditors who provide negligent advice to the company which appointed them may be held liable for breach of contract by the company and its shareholders.

(iii)   Auditors who provide advice to a particular person and who know what the advice will be used for may be held liable to that person in the tort of negligence if the advice proves to be incorrect and was carelessly prepared.

A   (i) only
B   (i) and (ii)
C   (i) and (iii)
D   (ii) and (iii)

19 Under civil or codified legal systems, judges are not permitted to refer to the decisions of other judges.

True/False?

BPP
PROFESSIONAL EDUCATION

20   Brian has been employed by Wye Ltd for 10 years. His contract of employment states that if either Wye Ltd or Brian wishes to terminate the contract, each party must give the statutory minimum period of notice.

Which **one** of the following is **correct**?

A   Both Brian and Wye Ltd are entitled to 10 weeks' notice
B   Brian is entitled to 10 weeks' notice but Wye Ltd is entitled to only 1 week's notice
C   Brian is entitled to 1 month's notice and Wye Ltd is entitled to 10 weeks' notice
D   Both Brian and Wye Ltd are entitled to 1 week's notice

The following information relates to questions 21 to 24

Lucy, Mike, Neil and Owen are the only directors and shareholders in LMNO Ltd, each holding 25% of the company's issued share capital. The company carries on business as a wholesaler of books. The board has unanimously decided that a number of amendments need to be made to the constitution and administration of the company. The Articles of Association are to be amended and the company is to dispense with the need to hold an AGM.

21   **Complete this sentence.**

In order to alter the Articles of Association, the shareholders need to pass a/an .... (one word) resolution.

22   The resolution must be filed at Companies House within .... days of the date the resolution was passed. (Write the number in figures.)

23   To remove the need to hold an AGM, an **ordinary/special/elective** resolution must be passed. (Delete as appropriate.)

24   This type of resolution must be agreed to by .... % of the shareholders. (Write the number in figures.)

25   Which ONE of the following remedies for breach of contract can always be awarded by the court if there has been a breach of contract?

A   An injunction   *equitable remedy*
B   Damages
C   Specific performance   *equitable remedy*
D   Recission

26   Which professional quality does the accountant display?

Choose from the following words; **independence, competence, accountability, respect, scepticism**

An accountant avoids all situations that they believe could cause a reasonable observer to doubt their objectivity.

....

27 Who is responsible for the corporate governance of an organisation?

    A   The board of directors

    B   The audit committee

    C   The shareholders

    D   The stock exchange

28 Why is it important for an accountant's work to be reliable?

    A   As colleagues may incorporate it into their own work

    B   Because it is a matter of professional competence

    C   As reliable work is always submitted on time

    D   To ensure the person who receives the work does not have to check it

29 Which of the following would strongly indicate that a person was an employee?

    A   He uses his own tools

    B   He is delegated work

    C   He renders invoices to the company

    D   He has a contract with the company

The following information relates to questions 30 to 34

The following five situations each describe a breach of one of CIMA's fundamental principles. State the correct principle that has been breached.

30 A qualified accountant who refuses to update their knowledge.

31 Your supervisor never checks your work, as she knows it is always perfect.

32 You receive an abusive email at work addressed to the entire accounts department from a former work colleague.

33 A public shareholder contacts their company's finance director complaining about the results contained in the management accounts.

34 A management accountant decides to change the depreciation method used in the accounts without notifying anyone.

35 Which ONE of the following statements is *incorrect*?

    A   It is automatically unfair to dismiss an employee for trade union activity

    B   It is automatically unfair to dismiss an employee who becomes pregnant

    C   It is automatically unfair to dismiss an employee who enforces a statutory right

    D   It is automatically unfair to dismiss an employee who refuses to obey a reasonable instruction

36 Consider the English Common law concept of *obiter dicta*. Which of the following Sharia law terms is a direct comparison?

    A   Qiyas

    B   Urf

    C   Istishab

    D   None of the above

37 **Complete this sentence.**

Unethical behaviour by an accountant has consequences on the .... , the accountancy .... and .... as a whole.

The following information relates to questions 38 to 43

Edward, who is a self-employed builder, has experienced the following difficulties.

    (i)   He contracted to build a conservatory for Fiona at a cost of £15,000. On completion of the job, however, Fiona refused to pay the amount due, despite the fact that she had no complaints as to the quality of the workmanship. Instead, Fiona sent a letter to Edward stating that she had decided that the price was too high and that she was enclosing a cheque for £10,000 'in full and final settlement of the account'. At first, Edward agreed to accept the amount and cashed the cheque. Later, however, he changed his mind and decided to commence legal action against Fiona to recover the balance.

    (ii)   He contracted to carry out some building work for George for £8,000. After approximately half the work had been completed, Tom, who had worked for Edward for only 8 months, negligently caused some damage to George's property. As a result, George refused to allow Edward to complete the work despite the fact that Tom was instantly dismissed.

    (iii)   In March 20X3, he contracted to build an extension for Harry commencing in December 20X3. In April 20X3, Henry advised Edward that he had sold the house and no longer required the extension to be built.

38 At common law, Edward **can/cannot** sue Fiona to recover the balance due of £5,000. (Delete as appropriate.)

39 Edward **will/will not** be liable for the damage caused by Tom to George's property. (Delete as appropriate.)

40 **Complete this sentence.**

Tom will have a claim against Edward for .... (one word) dismissal.

41 Tom will not have a claim against Edward for .... (one word) dismissal.

42 By cancelling the contract before it was due to be carried out, Henry has acted in .... (one word) breach of contract.

43 Edward **will/will not** have to wait until after December 20X3 before he can sue for breach of contract. (Delete as appropriate.)

44 Which of the following statements are correct? Select all that apply.

☐ The UN General Assembly only deals with 'threats to peace' and its decisions are legally binding

☐ The UN Security Council deals with 'threats to peace' and its decisions are not legally binding

☐ The UN General Assembly deals with violations of the UN Charter and its decisions are not legally binding

☐ The UN Security Council's decisions are legally binding

45 Which of the following would be described as 'directly applicable'?

A Regulations
B Directives
C European Court of Justice
D Custom

46 Which of the following resolutions may be used to increase a company's authorised capital?

(i) Ordinary resolution
(ii) Written resolution

A (i) only
B (ii) only
C Both (i) and (ii)
D Neither (i) nor (ii)

47 Which of the following is **correct**?

(i) A wrongful dismissal cannot also be an unfair dismissal.
(ii) An unfair dismissal can also be a wrongful dismissal.
(iii) An unfair dismissal must also be a wrongful dismissal

A (i) only
B (ii) only
C (ii) and (iii)
D (iii) only

Tho following information relates to question 48 to 57

Zed plc has decided to carry out the following:

(i)　To appoint Michelle as the company's managing director.

(ii)　To borrow £5 million from Exe Bank plc secured by a fixed charge over the company's land and a floating charge over the company's stock.

(iii)　To acquire Frank's business by issuing to him 200,000 ordinary £1 shares in Zed plc.

(iv)　To purchase a number of its own shares on the Stock Exchange.

48　**Complete the sentence by deleting the wrong answers.**

Michelle may be appointed managing director by **the other directors/the shareholders/the auditor**.

49　**Complete the sentence by deleting the wrong answers.**

The appointment of all the other directors must be approved by the **managing director/shareholders/auditor**.

50　**Complete the sentence.**

The fixed and floating charges must be registered with the Registrar of Companies within .... days. (Write the number of days in figures.)

51　Complete the sentence by writing one word.

If they are not registered, they will be .... against the liquidator, administrator or any creditor of the company.

52　**Delete as appropriate.**

The 200,000 ordinary £1 shares to be issued by Zed plc **must/need not** be offered to Zed plc's existing shareholders first.

53　**Delete as appropriate.**

Before Frank's business can be acquired by Zed plc, it **must/need not** be valued by the auditor.

In questions 54 and 55 delete the wrong answers as appropriate.

54　As this is an/a **off market/market** purchase,

55　it must be authorised by **ordinary/special/extraordinary** resolution.

56　A public limited company must offer some of its shares for sale on a recognised Stock Exchange

True/False (delete as appropriate)

57 When a company alters its Articles of Association, it must file a copy of the altered articles within
.... days of the resolution being passed. (Write the number of days in figures.)

58 Which of the following is **incorrect**?

(i) A liquidated damages clause will be void if it amounts to a penalty clause.

(ii) A liquidated damages clause will apply where it is a genuine attempt to pre-estimate the loss caused by a breach of contract.

(iii) A liquidated damages clause cannot be valid if it is for an amount in excess of the actual loss caused by the breach of contract.

A (i) and (ii)
B (ii) only
C (i), (ii) and (iii)
D (iii) only

59 According to the 2003 Combined Code, as a minimum how often should board members stand for re-election?

A Every year
B Every two years
C Every three years
D Every five years

60 An accountant develops constructive relationships with their colleagues, and values the rights and opinions that they have.

Which personal virtue do they display?

Select from the following words; **responsibility, timeliness, respect, reliability, courtesy**

....

61 Which ONE of the following statements is *correct*?

A An employer is obliged to provide a careful and honest reference
B An employer is obliged to provide a safe system of work
C An employer is obliged to provide employees with smoking facilities during authorised breaks at work
D An employer with fewer than 20 employees is obliged to provide an itemised written pay statement

62 What benefits can continued personal development bring to an accountant?

A Improved communication skills
B Improved accounting standards knowledge
C Improved technical skills
D Improved business awareness

63   Which of the following are matters an accountant should consider when deciding how to resolve an ethical conflict with their employer? Select all that apply.

☐   Whether they have recently applied for promotion

☐   CIMA's ethical guidelines

☐   Any internal grievance procedures available to them

☐   The opinions of other CIMA members regarding the specific situation

☐   The consequences of potential resolutions

64   What does the 2003 Combined Code require listed companies to include in a compliance statement in the accounts? Select all that apply.

☐   How the principles of the code were applied

☐   The findings of the audit committee

☐   How applying the code has affected the income statement

☐   Whether or not the company complied with the code throughout the accounting period

☐   Reasons for any non-compliance with the code

65   Why is it important for a CIMA member to follow the concept of lifelong learning?

A   To develop their assertiveness skills
B   As the accounting environment is constantly evolving
C   As they are legally required to do so
D   To make sure they are more skilled than accountants from other accountancy bodies

66   Which of the following must be included on a statement of written particulars of employment?

☑   Names of employer and employee

☑   Date on which employment began

☐   Name of former employer (if applicable

☑   Pay rate and intervals at which it is paid

☐   Right to future pay increments

☑   Details of any pension

☑   Hours of work

☐   Set holiday dates in the first year of employment

☐   Details of disciplinary methods

☑   Job title

67 How does a rules-based approach to developing an ethical code differ from a framework-based approach?

   A   It sets out fundamental principles for members to follow.
   B   It attempts to anticipate every possible ethical dilemma.
   C   It offers general guidelines for specific circumstances.
   D   Members are expected to comply with the spirit of the code rather than the letter of the law.

---

68 What board structure is recommended by the 2003 Combined Code?

   A   The board should mainly consist of executive directors.
   B   The board should mainly consist of non-executive directors.
   C   The board should be structured so no individual or small group is dominant.
   D   The board should consist of executive and non-executive directors in equal numbers.

---

69 What are ethics?

   A   A set of moral principles that guide behaviour
   B   Religious rules that determine an individual's actions
   C   The principle that all individuals should work together for a common goal
   D   Professional guidance that guide behaviour

---

70 Which **one** of the following is **correct**?

   A   A contract is frustrated when something happens after it has been entered into which renders the contract more difficult to perform

   B   A contract is frustrated when a party expressly agrees to manufacture and supply goods and then discovers that they will be far more expensive to produce than he thought at the time of the contract

   C   A contract is frustrated when something happens after it has been entered into which renders the contract impossible to perform

   D   A contract is frustrated if it is impossible to perform at the time that it is made

---

71 An accountant questions information given to them and seeks other supporting evidence before accepting it.

Which professional quality do they display?

Select from the following words; **accountability, independence, scepticism, social responsibility**

....

72 What benefits do non-executive directors bring to a board? Select all that apply.

☐ They bring in experience and knowledge into the business that the executive directors may not possess.

☐ They will support the chairman by pushing through his ideas when other directors challenge them.

☐ They can appreciate the wider perspective when the executive directors become involved in complex, operational issues.

☐ They ensure the executive directors cannot defraud the company.

☐ They provide the executive directors someone to confide in regarding any concerns they have with other board members.

73 CIMA as a chartered institute has what overriding duty?

A To provide a source of management accountants to UK and worldwide businesses
B To ensure its examinations are demanding for students
C To protect the public interest
D To improve the quality of management accounts

74 An advert in a newsagent's window read: 'Hoover 2012. £50 ono. Tel: 0208 888 2124'. Karl rang the number and, having enquired about the Hoover said, 'I'll give you £25 for it.' Karl's statement is

A A request for information
B An invitation to treat
C An offer
D An acceptance

75 XYZ plc has issued shares on terms that they will be bought back by the company 12 months after the date of issue. What are these shares called?

A Ordinary shares
B Bonus shares
C Preference shares
D Redeemable shares

Answers

**DO NOT TURN THIS PAGE UNTIL YOU HAVE
COMPLETED MOCK ASSESSMENT 2**

1
☐ Register of members
☑ Register of directors and secretaries
☑ Register of charges
☑ Minutes of general meetings
☐ Register of substantial interests in shares

2   A   Frustration only arises where there has been some outside event, for which neither party is responsible, which makes performance impossible.

3   D   Riba is an unlawful gain that can be translated into interest paid or received. This can prevent the use of mortgages to purchase property.

4   C   Literally 'the reason for the judge's decision.' The actual decision will be specific to the facts of the case and *obiter dicta* are other comments, not legally binding.

5   C   One of the few instances where an ordinary resolution with special notice is required.

6
☑ An accountant should spend enough time on a job to look into all matters in sufficient detail.
☐ An accountant should always accept work given to them by their employer.
☐ An accountant should attend all training and technical update courses available to them even if not relevant to their job.
☑ An accountant should (if relevant) use websites containing technical information to stay up-to-date.

Accountants should not accept work from their employers if they are not competent or if they cannot exercise due care. Accountants are only required to stay technically up-to-date in areas relevant to their current role.

7
(a)(iv)
(b)(iii)
(c)(ii)
(d)(i)

8   B   The invoice is a post contractual document, so it cannot introduce new terms without the agreement of B Ltd.

9   B   The most suitable resolution to a conflict may not be acceptable to an employer, especially if the employer is behaving unethically to begin with. No resolution can ensure the conflict never arises again. CIMA is able to give advice to members, not to endorse their actions.

10

☐ Anne, who worked for 10 years and was given 12 weeks' notice

☐ Barry, who worked for 1 week and was summarily dismissed

☐ Catherine, who worked for 5 years and was given a month's notice

☐ David, who has worked for 18 months and was given a week's notice

☑ Emily, who worked for 6 months and was given 3 days' notice

☐ Fred, who worked for 20 years and was given 12 weeks' notice

The statutory minimum notice period is only relevant to people who have worked for one month or more, so Barry does not qualify. Emily should have been given a weeks' notice. 12 week's notice is the minimum for those who have worked over 12 years, so Fred's notice is sufficient.

11   **One year, performance.** Directors' contracts should not be longer than one year and performance related pay is recommended to encourage better performance.

12   B   Shareholders may incur additional personal liability when the corporate veil is set aside, depending on the circumstances.

13   B   There are 5 Madhab. These are schools of thought formed in the years immediately following the death of the Prophet. They are Shia, Hanafi, Maliki, Hanbali and Shafii.

14   A   There is no requirement for an employment contract to be in writing.

15   C   Integrity is the principle of honesty and not being party to the supply of false or misleading information.

16

☑ The takeover of a rival company

☑ The purchase of a new company headquarters

☑ The appointment of a new auditor

☐ The appointment of a new management accountant

☐ The choice of office cleaner for the company's head office

A board of directors will only become involved in major policy and strategic decisions, or where the decisions involve substantial financial commitments. The choice of a new management accountant or office cleaner is unlikely to fall into this area.

17   B   The House of Lords is the final point of appeal in the UK system, although there is still recourse to European courts.

18   C   Auditors do not have a responsibility to the shareholders.

19   False   Judges are allowed to refer to other decisions, but they can only be persuasive and do not create precedent as they do under common law.

20   B   Brian is entitled to one week for each year of his employment. The minimum period for an employee to give is one week.

21   Special resolution

22   15 days

23		**Delete Ordinary/Special**
24		100% of members entitled to attend and vote
25	B	Damages are always available as a remedy for breach of contract.
26		**Independence.** The accountant demonstrates 'independence in appearance'.
27	A	As stewards of a company, responsibility for governance lies with the directors
28	A	A colleague must be able to rely on an accountant's work meeting professional standards; this does not mean that it does not need to be checked. Work submitted ahead of a deadline may be unreliable. Professional competence means an accountant has the necessary skills and experience to perform a job, which is different from the work itself being reliable.
29	B	D could be a contract for services or a contract of employment, A and C both indicate the person is an independent contractor.
30		**Professional competence and due care.** Accountants have a duty to remain technically up-to-date.
31		**Objectivity.** Your supervisor has allowed your previous good work to influence her opinion of your future work.
32		**Professional behaviour.** The action of the former work colleague is abusive and might discredit the profession.
33		**Confidentiality.** Management accounts are for a company's internal use, someone has leaked the results to a member of the public.
34		**Integrity.** Changing the method of depreciation without notifying anyone may mislead users into thinking the results are better or worse than they otherwise would have been.
35	D	It could be found to be unfair dismissal (or wrongful dismissal) but it is not one of the automatically unfair grounds for dismissal.
36	D	*Obiter dicta* are reasons or comments made by a judge in a particular case that may have a persuasive influence on future judges through the concept of precedent. Sharia law has no concept of precedent so there is no direct comparison.
37		**Individual, profession, society.** The consequences of unethical behaviour have wider implications than just the individual concerned.
38		Edward **can** sue Fiona to recover the balance. She has provided no consideration for his agreement to accept less than the full amount. *Foakes v Beer*.
39		Edward **will** be liable. Tom is the employee of Edward and is acting in the course of his employment.
40		**Wrongful dismissal.** His summary dismissal on the grounds of negligence is not a justifiable reason. Therefore the dismissal is wrongful rather than unfair.
41		**Unfair dismissal**
42		**Anticipatory** (repudiatory) breach of contract
43		Edward **will not** have to wait until December 20X3 before he can sue for breach of contract

44	☐	The UN General Assembly only deals with 'threats to peace' and its decisions are legally binding
	☑	The UN Security Council deals with 'threats to peace' and its decisions are not legally binding
	☑	The UN General Assembly deals with violations of the UN Charter and its decisions are not legally binding
	☑	The UN Security Council's decisions are legally binding

The General Assembly deals with violations of the UN Charter, its decisions are not legally binding. The Security Council deals with 'threats to peace' and its decisions are legally binding.

45	A	Directives require national legislation to enact them. The term 'directly applicable' would not be used in connection with the ECJ or custom.
46	C	However, (ii) can only be used by a private company.
47	B	A dismissal can be wrongful and unfair at the same time. However, an unfair dismissal doesn't have to be wrongful – the correct notice period may have been given, for example.
48		Michelle may be appointed by the other directors
49		The appointment must be approved by the **shareholders**
50		21 days
51		Void
52		The shares **need not** be offered. Pre-emption rights apply in the case of equity shares issued for cash. In this instance, the shares are to be issued in return for Frank's business.
53		It **must be** valued by the auditor. Any non-cash consideration in an allotment of shares must be independently valued: s 103 CA85. This must happen within the six months prior to the allotment.
54		This is a **market purchase** as the shares are to be purchased on the Stock Exchange.
55		It must be authorised by an **ordinary resolution**.
56	False	A public company **may** offer some of its shares for sale to the public. It is only compulsory if it is quoted on the Stock Exchange.
57		15 days
58	D	The other two statements are correct.
59	C	Board members should be re-elected at least every three years.
60		**Respect.** Developing relationships and valuing the views and rights of others demonstrates respect.
61	B	There is no requirement to provide references (although if one is provided, it must be honest and careful).
62	A	Personal development improves qualities such as communication skills which have to come from with the individual.

63   ☐ Whether they have recently applied for promotion

     ☑ CIMA's ethical guidelines

     ☑ Any internal grievance procedures available to them

     ☐ The opinions of other CIMA members regarding the specific situation

     ☑ The consequences of potential resolutions

The risk of missing out on promotion should not affect an accountant's decision on how to resolve an issue. By discussing their specific situation with others, an accountant will breach their duty of confidentiality and this should be avoided.

64   ☑ How the principles of the code were applied

     ☐ The findings of the audit committee

     ☐ How the code has affected the income statement

     ☑ Whether or not the company complied with the code throughout the accounting period

     ☑ Reasons for any non-compliance with the code

65   B   Lifelong learning ensures an accountant keeps up to date with technical and other skills that are developed and change over time.

66   ☑ Names of employer and employee

     ☑ Date on which employment began

     ☐ Name of former employer (if applicable)

     ☑ Pay rate and intervals at which it is paid

     ☐ Right to future pay increments

     ☑ Details of any pension

     ☑ Hours of work

     ☐ Set holiday dates in the first year of employment

     ☐ Details of disciplinary methods

     ☑ Job title

67   B   The other options describe the framework-based approach to developing a code.

68   C   The board should be balanced to prevent domination by an individual or group. No numbers or proportions are specified.

69   A   Ethics are individual's moral principles that guide their behaviour

70   C   In Option D, the doctrine of frustration does not protect someone from having made a (really) bad bargain.

71   **Scepticism.** Questioning work and seeking evidence demonstrates professional scepticism.

72   ☑ They bring in experience and knowledge into the business that the executive directors may not possess.

         ☐ They will support the chairman by pushing through his ideas when other directors challenge them.

         ☑ They can appreciate the wider perspective when the executive directors become involved in complex, operational issues.

         ☐ They ensure the executive directors cannot defraud the company.

         ☑ They provide the executive directors someone to confide in regarding any concerns they have with other board members.

Non-executive directors are there to provide a strong, independent element on the board, not as 'henchmen' to enable the chairman to get his own way. Although the presence of non-executive directors may help deter fraud, they will never eliminate it.

73   C   Chartered institutes have an overriding duty to protect the public interest.

74   C   An advert is an invitation to treat. Karl is making an offer of £25, which, if it is accepted by the advertiser, will comprise agreement.

75   D   They are issued with a view to being repurchased.

Review Form & Free Prize Draw

Paper C5 Fundamentals of Ethics, Corporate Governance and Business Law

All original review forms from the entire BPP range, completed with genuine comments, will be entered into one of two draws on 31 July 2006 and 31 January 2007. The names on the first four forms picked out on each occasion will be sent a cheque for £50.

Name: _____ Address: _____

_____

_____

How have you used this Kit?
(Tick one box only)

☐ Home study (book only)

☐ On a course: college _____

☐ With 'correspondence' package

☐ Other _____

Why did you decide to purchase this Kit? *(Tick one box only)*

☐ Have used BPP Texts in the past

☐ Recommendation by friend/colleague

☐ Recommendation by a lecturer at college

☐ Saw information on BPP website

☐ Saw advertising

☐ Other _____

During the past six months do you recall seeing/receiving any of the following?
(Tick as many boxes as are relevant)

☐ Our advertisement in *Financial Management*

☐ Our advertisement in *Pass*

☐ Our advertisement in *PQ*

☐ Our brochure with a letter through the post

☐ Our website www.bpp.com

Which (if any) aspects of our advertising do you find useful?
(Tick as many boxes as are relevant)

☐ Prices and publication dates of new editions

☐ Information on Text content

☐ Facility to order books off-the-page

☐ None of the above

Which BPP products have you used?

Text	☐	Success CD	☐	Learn Online	☐
Kit	☑	i-Learn	☐	Home Study Package	☐
Passcard	☐	i-Pass	☐	Home Study PLUS	☐
MCQ cards	☐				

Your ratings, comments and suggestions would be appreciated on the following areas.

	Very useful	Useful	Not useful
Effective revision	☐	☐	☐
Exam guidance	☐	☐	☐
Multiole choice questions	☐	☐	☐
Objective test questions	☐	☐	☐
Content answers	☐	☐	☐
Mock assessments	☐	☐	☐
Mock assessment answers	☐	☐	☐

	Excellent	Good	Adequate	Poor
Overall opinion of this Kit	☐	☐	☐	☐

Do you intend to continue using BPP products?   Yes ☐   No ☐

The BPP author of this edition can be e-mailed at: Stephenosbourne@bpp.com

Please return this form to: Nick Weller, CIMA Range Manager, BPP Professional Education, FREEPOST, London, W12 8BR

Review Form & Free Prize Draw (continued)

TELL US WHAT YOU THINK

Please note any further comments and suggestions/errors below

Free Prize Draw Rules

1   Closing date for 31 January 2007 draw is 31 December 2006. Closing date for 31 July 2007 draw is 30 June 2007.

2   Restricted to entries with UK and Eire addresses only. BPP employees, their families and business associates are excluded.

3   No purchase necessary. Entry forms are available upon request from BPP Professional Education. No more than one entry per title, per person. Draw restricted to persons aged 16 and over.

4   Winners will be notified by post and receive their cheques not later than 6 weeks after the relevant draw date.

5   The decision of the promoter in all matters is final and binding. No correspondence will be entered into.